RECONSTRUCTING VALUE
LEADERSHIP SKILLS FOR A SUSTAINABLE WORLD

Elizabeth C. Kurucz, Barry A. Colbert, and David Wheeler

Reconstructing Value prepares contemporary business leaders for the increasingly important task of developing a sustainability vision and translating it across levels in an organization. The book is based on insights gained over the past decade from research involving hundreds of practitioners, front line managers to senior executives, who have been working to integrate sustainability within their organizations. It illustrates how building capacity for managing the complex issues of sustainability requires key process skills that leaders need to develop.

This book equips readers to respond to the risks and opportunities presented by global sustainability issues and reinvent new ways of doing business that will enhance organizational effectiveness while also building a more sustainable world. Each chapter includes process questions to guide reflective practice and to build the requisite leadership capabilities for turning a sustainability vision into a value-added organizational strategy. *Reconstructing Value* helps readers to build integrative thinking skills – such as how to engage critical, complexity, strategic and design thinking capabilities to enable organizational change – that can assist them with becoming successful sustainability champions within their organizations.

(Business & Sustainability Series)

ELIZABETH C. KURUCZ is an assistant professor of Organizational Behaviour and Sustainable Commerce in the Department of Business, College of Management and Economics at the University of Guelph.

BARRY A. COLBERT is an associate professor of Policy and Strategic Management in the School of Business and Economics at Wilfrid Laurier University.

DAVID WHEELER is President of Cape Breton University.

RECONSTRUCTING VALUE

LEADERSHIP SKILLS FOR A SUSTAINABLE WORLD

Elizabeth C. Kurucz
Barry A. Colbert
David Wheeler

UNIVERSITY OF TORONTO PRESS
Toronto Buffalo London

© University of Toronto Press 2013
Rotman-UTP Publishing
University of Toronto Press
Toronto Buffalo London
www.utppublishing.com
Printed in Canada

ISBN 978-1-4426-4276-8 (cloth)
ISBN 978-1-4426-1153-5 (paper)

∞

Printed on acid-free, 100% post-consumer recycled paper with vegetable-based inks.

Library and Archives Canada Cataloguing in Publication

Kurucz, Elizabeth C. (Elizabeth Carolyn), 1970–
Reconstructing value : leadership skills for a sustainable world /
by Elizabeth C. Kurucz, Barry A. Colbert, and David Wheeler.

(Business & sustainability series)
Includes bibliographical references and index.
ISBN 978-1-4426-4276-8 (bound). — ISBN 978-1-4426-1153-5 (pbk.)

1. Leadership. 2. Sustainability. 3. Social responsibility of
business. I. Colbert, Barry A., 1961– II. Wheeler, David
III. Title. IV. Series: Business & sustainability (Toronto, Ont.)

HD57.7.K87 2012   658.4'092   C2012-906126-3

University of Toronto Press acknowledges the financial assistance to its
publishing program of the Canada Council for the Arts and the Ontario
Arts Council.

 Canada Council   Conseil des Arts
for the Arts   du Canada

 ONTARIO ARTS COUNCIL
CONSEIL DES ARTS DE L'ONTARIO
50 YEARS OF ONTARIO GOVERNMENT SUPPORT OF THE ARTS
50 ANS DE SOUTIEN DU GOUVERNEMENT DE L'ONTARIO AUX ARTS

University of Toronto Press acknowledges the financial support of the
Government of Canada through the Canada Book Fund for its publishing
activities.

Elizabeth and Barry

For our parents, Coleman and Rosemary Kurucz and Bill and Ann Colbert,
whose extraordinary kindness, optimism, and generosity have made
everything possible.
For Cob and Stella whose unwavering companionship
brought great joy and much comfort to the process of writing.
And for Sam, Emily, Elsa, and Wynn – the future is yours to create.

David

For Michelle and Caleb, Claire and William.

Contents

Preface

You have a big problem to solve.

In fact, you have several problems to solve, and they are highly complex and entangled with one another. We are not talking about the problems and challenges that you face in your daily work, though they are likely related. We are talking about the larger playing field on which all of your work happens – along with your relationships, and your nourishment, your obligations and your aspirations: all of the things that sustain your life and make it worth living. The problems you need to solve are ones that threaten to compromise, undermine, and even destroy the conditions that allow you to live that good life. We call these "problems" because they are trends that are heading in the wrong direction and that need our attention and care: issues such as energy generation, clean water provision, food production, a liveable climate, and equitable development for people across the planet. We say that *you* have a big problem to solve because problems for humanity are your problems too and, really, if not you, then who? The big difficulty, the big design challenge we have before us is one of sustainability: how to create conditions for humanity and other life to flourish on earth, while respecting the earth's ability to absorb our impacts so that others can follow after us and continue to thrive.

The good news is that problems, when taken as creative challenges, can be opportunities to create something new and valuable, something that helps make things better and not worse. More good news is that many of these problems stem from our own past behavior, from the systems of energy and industrial production that have propelled us this far, and that have emerged from the logics of growth and consumption that we assume as natural and necessary. If human cooperation and ingenuity built such systems, in the face of the constraints as they were perceived and as they shifted over the past several millennia, then surely we can apply the even greater potential for cooperation and ingenuity that we now possess, enabled by enormous advances in new technologies and social connectivity, to thrive and flourish against our emerging constraints. The leadership challenge at this juncture – and this is a challenge to you, if you are or if you aspire to be a leader in your organization and your life – is to work to understand our major sustainability challenges, to help others in developing a shared understanding, and to engage people broadly in constructive conversation and action towards the goal of all of us living better lives. This is leadership for sustainability, and it is a critical element of the big problem solving we need to undertake.

Why We Wrote This Book

The three authors of this book are management educators, and so this book is aimed foremost at learners in business education, whether in formal business programs or in executive education. We teach in business schools and executive education, mainly in the areas of business strategy, organizational behavior, and organization theory, and, as former organizational leaders and managers ourselves, we hold deep respect and empathy for those in that work. We care deeply about issues in sustainability – meeting today's needs in ways that are just and caring, without compromising the needs of future generations – and we all have children, so these ideas are immediately as well as generally important to us. As management scholars, we recognize that the dominant logics and actions of business and business schools (e.g., an ethos of growth for growth's sake, driven by ever-increasing levels of debt-driven consumption to meet manufactured human wants, powered by take-make-waste production methods) often ignore issues in sustainability, and thereby make them worse. As such we have worked for the past fifteen years to integrate sustainability issues into management education and practice, and this book is a summation of ideas we have developed to date to aid in that integration. At the core of these ideas is the concept of *transformation*: moving to a more sustainable path means transforming our systems of production and consumption, as well as the logics of our personal and organizational lives. This entails that we first question our assumptions about what we value, our understanding of how that impacts our physical and social conditions, and our understanding of the implications of our assumptions and actions now and in the future. The design of this book, therefore, is one of *transformational learning*, where the first task is to lay bare the logics of the current system and to question deeply the implications, so that we can reconstruct our ideas of value. This requires leadership skills in reflective practice: the ability to pause to wonder, probe, analyze, and synthesize what is happening and why, in order to understand more deeply the connections among elements in our world and the effect our actions have on them. There are a number of requisite leadership skills for reconstructing value through reflective practice, and this book is designed to help identify and develop them.

Purpose and Design of the Book

There are several good books on sustainability and business generally and on sustainability issues in particular, and we use many of them in our teaching and reference them here – so why write another? Many books on sustainability are content-rich, and they inform us deeply of the nature of the challenges; others are prescriptive how-to's, full of ideas for organizational initiatives or programs to enhance eco-efficiency, or to improve corporate social responsibility practice. While these are useful, we felt there were three things missing for the purpose of our teaching: first, a fuller acknowledgment of the number, scope, and complexity of the challenges we face, written for the lay manager to comprehend; second, a focus on the collective "social learning" process that is required for transforming our unsustainable assumptions and actions at the levels of society, organizations, and individuals; and third, and related to the first two, an understanding of the leadership skills required to address this complexity and to effectively engage in a process of reflective practice and social learning to reconstruct value. Many books offer prescriptions for getting incremental programs implemented into existing organizational logics. While these can be useful for improving day-to-day operations we think the challenge is bigger than that. We also need to work to understand and transform those logics to place them on a more sustainable ground, while at the same time recognizing that managers are faced with pragmatic organizational realities under the current systems of value creation and trade. Leaders need to be equipped and educated *for* sustainability, and not just *about* sustainability. They need to be able to navigate their current reality while at the same time generating sustainability conversations (the first step towards action) in their organizations, about what matters and why in light of sustainability challenges, and about what might be possible if we think beyond our existing systems and taken-for-granted ways of operating. Therefore, this book is not just a collection of chapters on different topics in sustainability; rather, its narrative arc describes a transformational learning journey, where the lessons from one chapter are carried forward to the next, and together they form an integrated whole.

Outline of the Book

Our model for reconstructing value is built in four parts, which we call the 4R's: *rethinking, relating, responding,* and *reinventing.* In chapter 1 we introduce some background ideas in sustainability and briefly describe the 4R's in relation to the organizing model for the book. The remaining eight chapters are structured in four parts, each with two chapters focusing on one of the 4R's of reconstructing value. In part one, "Rethinking," chapter 2 explores the 4R's more deeply, along with the dominant modes of thinking associated with each, in order to open up possibilities for envisioning new ways of doing business. Chapter 3 draws connections between thinking and learning: by critically delving into underlying assumptions, we set the ground for single-, double-, and triple-loop learning – getting better at playing the game, challenging the rules of the game, and questioning the nature of the game itself. In part two, "Relating," chapter 4 explores the wide array of global issues facing humanity, considering their complexity and their interrelated nature. While not exhaustive, we feel this integrated overview is essential to set the context for our challenges in reconstructing value. In chapter 5 we consider connections among an organization, its stakeholders, and issues in sustainability, with the aim of becoming fully aware of the operating context and taking an integrative approach to considering the relationships between complex issues and the multiplicity of stakeholders at play. For part three, "Responding," we examine in chapter 6 the ways that practicing managers make sense of the idea of sustainability, and we develop a picture of the range of "sustainability conversations" at work in different organizational contexts. Chapter 7 explores the relationships between individuals and their organizational context, which is essential for understanding the barriers and enablers for change. We highlight ways that leaders can recognize and address the social dynamics that emerge within an organization undertaking a sustainability-focused vision, to help to create momentum for sustainable change. Part four, "Reinventing," draws on design thinking as a means to "put it all back together" in a creative and innovative manner that aligns with a sustainability-based view of organizations. Chapter 8 expands on ideas in social learning and considers the requisite skills for undertaking multi-sectoral collaborative initiatives. In chapter 9 we invite you to imagine that you own the whole problem: if the future welfare of humanity depended on you, what would you do? Here we expand on the core of our model by describing design criteria for reconstructing value that is embedded, sustainable, and transformational.

Leadership Skill Building: Process Questions, Leadership Skills, and Skill-Building Exercises

Throughout this book we describe a multitude of relevant concepts and examples in sustainability issues, thinking skills, and learning theory. To help build the necessary skills to put those concepts into practice, we offer a number of learning features that we have developed and use in our own teaching. These begin in chapter 2 and run through chapter 9, and consist of the following elements:

Process Questions

Moving towards more sustainable practice is a process of transformation, and so leaders for sustainability must build skills in process leadership. The challenges highlighted throughout the book hold questions for process, and so we offer many questions to help managers provoke inquiry in their organizations that will result in effective sustainability conversations.

Leadership Skills

Process leadership requires the practicing manager to have a broad array of skills, and so we offer some clearly itemized supporting skills that comprise leadership for sustainability.

Skill-Building Exercises – Learning Team Dialogues and Assignments

To help build those skills, we supply several skill-building features in the form of five in-class Learning Team Dialogues and three Assignments to be undertaken (these are examples of what has worked well for us; many other examples are possible). The Learning Team Dialogues (in small groups of four to six people) give learners the opportunity to engage with the concepts developed in each chapter and to analyze a real world issue or an organization or sustainability initiative. They are an essential component in building capabilities into reflective practice.

There Are No Easy Answers – So Good Questions Are Important!

It has been said that real advances depend not only on answering questions but also on questioning answers. Because there are no pat prescriptions for moving to a more sustainable trajectory, we take a *process* perspective. If we can find general agreement on the objectives and boundary conditions for sustainability, we can generate good constructive questions to help take us there. Good questions are the first steps to innovative design. Good questions provide an opening to a process of engagement, to bring people into a collective conversation about what is important and why. Good questions help us to explore possibilities about how we can live better, and allow others who follow to live better, too.

This is in essence a hopeful book. Not the kind of hope that implies a careless abdication of responsibility to the hand of fate, but rather the hope that comes from the hard work of caring enough for ourselves and for others to pay attention to what is happening, and to question whether what we are doing makes good sense. We believe there are no easy answers to the challenges ahead. But if we equip ourselves with some very good, well-informed questions, and then approach those questions with a mindset and process for collaborative problem solving, then a more sustainable present and future are within our reach. It is our problem to solve, because we *are* the 7 billion people living on earth today. For those of us who choose to take up that challenge, there are new generations arriving, including our own children, who will be grateful that we did.

Acknowledgments

Over the past fifteen years through our research, teaching, and consulting, we have engaged in countless meaningful sustainability conversations with leaders in a wide variety of organizations, at a range of levels, from CEOs to line employees in all functions and facets of organizational life. We appreciate their engagement with, curiosity about, and insight on the particular challenges involved in integrating business practice with sustainability ideals, especially those who contributed personal stories for this book, both anonymous and credited, and those who continue to work tirelessly as change agents in small and large businesses with the hope of building a better world. We are thankful to our undergraduate, graduate, and executive education learners, who have added greatly to our understanding of the practical challenges of sustainability, who have encouraged us in our teaching and whose "aha moments" have compelled us to share our thoughts on reconstructing value with a wider audience through this book. We also owe a debt of gratitude to our colleagues in the sustainability management field for their energetic and inspirational work, for ongoing dialogues at conferences, and for the ideas that they share regularly in journals and books. Elizabeth and Barry are thankful to our friend Lynda Eddy for all of her support in the writing of this book, and all three of us are very grateful to Jennifer DiDomenico for her patience and encouragement, and the whole editorial team at UTP/Rotman Press for their guidance in seeing this project to completion. Thanks also to Jonathan Rivard for his work on the figures. Finally, we want to thank all of our family and friends who have supported us in this work, and we thank each other for making this collaboration a rewarding and enlightening experience.

RECONSTRUCTING VALUE

LEADERSHIP SKILLS FOR A SUSTAINABLE WORLD

CHAPTER 1

New Questions for Business

The mind and the world jointly make up the mind and the world.

– Hilary Putnam, Pragmatist Philosopher

The problem that is usually being visualised is how capitalism administers existing structures, whereas the relevant problem is how it creates and destroys them.

– Joseph Schumpeter, Economist

Sustainability = Change

It seems a paradox that when we talk about sustainability, we are talking about change. "To sustain" usually means to keep something going, to maintain the status quo. But undeniable evidence is mounting that just about every system on which our current way of life depends is under deep duress, due to the *un*sustainable rate of our patterns of consumption of the world's resources and the *un*sustainable way that we finance our social and economic development. Global human population has multiplied more than fivefold over the last 150 years, from 1.2 billion people in 1850 to 7 billion in 2011, and it is projected to swell to over 9 billion by mid-century. The growth in global population coincides exactly with our exploitation of fossil fuels; if we remove the labels from the graphs, the population curve and the oil production curve are indistinguishable over that period. Over the past two centuries – a mere blink in geologic earth time – we have been extremely successful in converting cheap energy into more and more people through advances in agriculture, transportation, housing, and medicine. More people require more power and sustenance, and so population growth in industrial nations is pushing the limits of energy generation, housing, clean water provision, and food production, and altering the climatic balance – the life-giving elements of fire, water, earth, and air. We are confronted with significant challenges in each dimension, and of course they are highly interdependent: energy and water security affect food security; conventional energy generation impacts climate; a change in climate will impact arable land and water availability with consequential effects on human security. The connections are deep and inseparable.

To continue building a prosperous future for humanity, we need to begin to live as though limits matter, which means changing the way that we operate on the planet and in the global economy. The first decade of the twenty-first century witnessed the flatlining in stock market values and living standards across Europe and North America. Arguably, these phenomena were indicative of the beginnings of limits to *economic* growth being experienced in the "old" and "new" worlds that first embraced industrialization. The hard truth about limits is that they make change inevitable: we won't necessarily change because we can, or change because we should, but rather, change because we must, because conditions are changing around us. As in the old saying, "Change is mandatory, suffering is optional," the open question is whether we will proactively navigate towards positive change for our collective well-being or simply carry on with business as usual, hoping for the best until more negative, dramatic change finds us. Either way, a book about sustainability is fundamentally a book about change.

Leadership for Sustainability

This book is also about leadership in organizations and the leadership skills for moving us towards a more sustainable world. The chief difficulty in relating ideas in sustainability to our daily work life is that sustainability deals with broad issues in society, and our work lives are usually bounded by the goals and the activity of a particular organization. Bridging that society-organization chasm is the primary challenge in leadership for sustainability: bringing global issues into the conversational life of the organization and transforming the vision, goals, and actions of our organizations to put the world on a more sustainable path. This is no small feat, because our organizations, and our broader systems of value creation and trade, are designed to work based on foundational assumptions that are inherently *un*sustainable. Transformation at the organizational level requires transformation at the societal level – shifts in the assumptions, rules, and governance mechanisms that define the operating ground for business and other organizations.

Leadership for sustainability is therefore necessarily *transforming leadership*. Eminent leadership scholar James MacGregor Burns defined transforming leadership as "a social process for mutual transformation," in which both the formal "leader" and those being "led" can help each other to live better lives: "it raises the level of human conduct and ethical aspiration of both leader and led, and thus has a transforming effect on both."[1] In transforming leadership, there is a pragmatic focus on improving the societal conditions for human flourishing, and the role of leadership is to bring that into focus, to help direct our conversations and actions towards that end. Transforming leadership is not a heroic act on the part of one individual – it is a social process of democratic engagement; and it is not the responsibility of one or a handful of people in formal leadership roles – it is distributed in the way we engage and interact with each other. Throughout this book we define leadership as a process of social engagement, led by constructive conversation, with the goal of altering our unsustainable assumptions and actions and helping us live better lives.

Organizations and Leaders as Agents for Change

Organizations are powerful forces for change. They constitute the primary structures of our societies and are gathering places for all kinds of resources and concerted action, whether they are for-profit businesses, social enterprises, non-profits, civil society organizations, or governance institutions. Our interest and focus here is on the role of organizations in moving towards greater global sustainability. But for organizations to lead change, they must of course be adept at changing themselves, so we are interested in particular in the role of individual leadership in influencing the directions, decisions, and actions their organizations take.

Leadership for sustainability can happen at both the organizational and individual level, and it is driven by how we think, act, and learn. A critical facet of learning towards sustainability lies in deeply questioning the basic assumptions of our business and institutional structures: understanding as best we can the interconnections that link what we do to the fire, water, earth, and air that sustain us, and to the local and global economies in which we operate. Throughout this book we draw attention to several aspects of leadership for sustainability: how leaders think, how leaders learn, how they help to guide the learning of others, how they conceive of sustainability, and how they lead in building collaboration towards new futures. We focus on leadership as a process of social engagement, the formal organizational leader as reflective practitioner, and the role for the organizational leader in helping to *reconstruct value* – to help collectively redefine what we see as valuable going forward in light of sustainability challenges. But before we can talk about *reconstructing*, we need to think about the "construction of meaning" as an essentially social process – how many of our deeply held "truths" and practices are actually human inventions, which we then treat as our operating reality. We assign value to things by communicating with each other, through all forms of conversation, in an ongoing process of *social construction* of our operating realities.

Constructing Our Social Reality

It is safe to assert that thinking and action are tightly linked: we act on the basis of our own sense of purpose, ambitions, and aspirations, and we are guided by our views of how the world works (our reality assumptions), and how we think it ought to work (our values assumptions). To begin to shift the ways we act in the world, we must first examine the ways we think. But if the fields of psychology, sociology, economics, and organizational behavior have taught us anything, it is that (1) different people think differently, and (2) our various viewpoints interact to form a social reality, which comprises a set of societal norms, practices, and shared values encoded in law and custom. As individuals, we interact with that social reality, as we perceive it, and often we take that reality as a given – forgetting that much of it was made up by other humans and that we are all complicit in maintaining a shared sense of "how things are." We pull up to a red light and stop. We dress appropriately for the occasion. We show up at 7:00 p.m. for a university night class. All the while, we are mostly unconscious of the fact that at some point in the past a group of people sat around a table, barn, or fire and decided that red means stop, tennis shorts are not right for a funeral, and a particular building is part of a university. We also agree that a taking a course leads to a diploma and that a diploma is valuable – only because we all "agree to agree" that it is. If we all decide to agree tomorrow that the university's Engineering Building is now a homeless shelter, it could become that overnight. The physical bricks and mortar remain the same, but the social use and identity of the building is transformed. In sociological and management studies, this is known as the *social construction of reality*,[2] and it is centrally important to discussions of sustainability. What this means is that we continuously negotiate the meaning we assign to things – what we believe, what is right, and what is true – in the social and cultural sense.

Physical reality is different from social reality, though often we treat both as given. We cannot simply all agree to agree that a large oak desk is not a heavy object for one person to lift – there is an undeniable physical reality to deal with. But if you were to tip the oak desk in your office on its side and use the legs to hang your jacket, you might get some concerned reactions from your colleagues. There is a physical reality to the desk, and there is a social reality pertaining to the proper use of it. The distinction between physical and social reality is also centrally important to the pursuit of sustainability: we sometimes fail to see, or we forget, that some things are socially constructed imperatives (such as fashion or economic growth), and we treat them as we would a physical reality (such as cold or gravity). In essence, we often socially construct meanings related to objects in our physical reality in ways that serve and support our belief systems, rather than in ways that are ecologically justified.

Taken-for-Granted Assumptions: Believing Is Seeing

Seeing is believing – or is it? The idea of the "reflexive loop"[3] says that, in fact, the reverse is often true: our beliefs affect what data we take note of in our experiences and thus reinforce our existing opinions. This flips the logic on a widely accepted platitude, suggesting in essence that things need first to be believed in order to be seen. We cannot act without our beliefs – they are the guiding rules with which we navigate our way through the world. We make judgments, form interpretations, and come to conclusions based on the beliefs we have formed, but often we decide what is right or true based on what we already believe. Often we do not do the difficult work of delving into our beliefs to bring our underlying assumptions to the surface, of examining their validity in light of new or changing evidence, and of understanding how our deeply held beliefs affect our ability to see. In order to examine how our beliefs filter what we see, we need to develop the capacity to think critically, and an important part of thinking critically is bringing what is *subconscious* in our thought to the level of *conscious* realization. Only by challenging our surface understanding of the way things happen is it possible to start to deconstruct the assumptions and meanings that give rise to those beliefs, and thus make it possible to shift them to achieve different outcomes. In chapter 2 we will examine alternative modes of thinking in more detail. Here, we will briefly consider some of the various assumptions in management thinking at the organization level in order to illustrate the connection between our assumptions and actions. We will then outline some general "world views" about the relationship between people, the planet, and the economy, and the implications for sustainability. What we *believe* impacts what we are able to *see*, which affects what we *do*. So we need to examine our beliefs carefully.

Metaphors for Organizing: Our Images Are Bundles of Assumptions

Gareth Morgan has written extensively about the ways in which our images of organizations influence the ways we think about management and change.[4] These images are made up of bundles of assumptions we carry in our heads about how organizations work, or at least how we think they should work, and they take the form of general metaphors for organizing. For example, if we see organizations as *machines*, we assume that the land, capital, and human resources are independent, separable, and interchangeable parts – cogs in the machine – that all work together for some pre-designed purpose. Management in this view is a mechanistic exercise of planning, control, and incremental improvement, where change is relatively easy – merely an exercise of setting out objectives, plugging in the right cogs, and executing the plan. If instead we see organizations as *organisms* fighting for survival or symbiosis in an ecosystem of other organizations, we might pay more attention to external contextual factors, and view change as more variable, adaptive, and iterative. If we see them largely as *political systems* of domination and resource control, then we would view managers primarily as political actors, and we would bring issues of power to the foreground when thinking about change.

Morgan describes these and several other metaphors that underpin our major theories and practices for managing in organizations, including organizations as cultures, as brains, as instruments of domination and control, or as processes of flux and transformation, illuminating the strengths and limitations of each. Our mental images are useful for helping us to manage, but they have the power to distort our view as much as they enlighten. In becoming aware of them through reflective practice we can explore them to their fullest potential. Where things become challenging is when you have five people sitting around a planning table who hold five different images of the organization. The "truth" of organizational life lies somewhere in between the perspectives of various individuals, and each underlying assumption we uncover or metaphor we identify results in a different way of understanding physical and social reality. By bringing to the surface the assumptions that drive our actions, we can approach organizational issues and sustainability challenges in a more multidimensional and, hopefully, more creative way. By involving actors outside the organization – customers, suppliers, civil society organizations – further insights may be derived that can help the organization understand its role in the value-creation process and thereby enhance its attractiveness to those stakeholders.

A similar effect occurs when managers think and talk about sustainability. Later in chapters 6 and 7 we will explore some other images – which we call *conceptions of sustainability* – held by practicing managers based on our own research. To first set the ground here, let us explore sustainability as a general concept, as the idea has been described in theory. Organizational researcher Kurt Lewin said in the 1940s, "There is nothing so practical as a good theory,"[5] and quality guru W. Edwards Deming, after a lifetime of studying and improving management practice, wrote, "Without theory, experience has no meaning. Without theory, one has no questions to ask. Hence, without theory, there is no learning."[6] Simple theory helps us to organize, relate, and test the ideas we encounter in daily life. It helps us to learn.

Approaching "Sustainability" as a Concept: What Does It Mean?

What do we mean when we talk about "sustainability"? "To sustain" means "to keep going," but the moment we try to bring that definition off the page into our lived experience, questions start to flow from it: Sustain what? Sustain for whom? Is the thing we are trying to sustain of any real value? How do we determine what is valuable and worth keeping, and what should be changed? The term "sustainability" gains moral and philosophical weight as soon as we start to examine it, and it provokes thinking because it is a value-laden idea. It asks us to stop and consider what we believe is important. It asks us to think about how our world ought to be structured and run. It also embodies an implied critique, in that it says "perhaps the way we are doing things now is not the way we should be doing things; failure is either creeping or imminent, and we should consider exploring alternative directions." It is a word that packs all kinds of meaning for moral philosophers, policymakers, business people, activists, and citizens.

Sustainability as a Contestable Concept

The reason the term contains so much is because sustainability is what is called a *contestable concept*.[7] Art, democracy, liberty, justice – these are all contestable concepts that have a basic first-level meaning based on a core idea (for example, democracy is government of the people, by the people; liberty is freedom from oppression, freedom to exercise one's will; art is creative expression of the human condition). Abraham Lincoln and Mahatma Gandhi refashioned entire societies by reconnecting them with simple core principles at key moments in time; take for example the phrase "All people are created equal." In general, people can find agreement on the first-level meaning because it is so broadly stated. But there is a second-level meaning, where we strive to put the ideas into practice, and this is the ground for practical and political contest over how the ideas are interpreted and implemented. Things get even more interesting at the second level, because it is there that we are asked to call up and debate our values, what we think is important. Just because an idea provokes debate does not mean it is a contestable concept, since people will debate just about anything. *Essentially contestable concepts* fit three basic criteria:[8] they are "appraisive" in nature, which means they signify and accredit some measure of value; they are internally complex, in that they admit a wide range of competing descriptions of their overall meaning; and they are "open" in character, meaning they allow modification of meaning in the light of changing circumstance. Essentially contestable concepts invoke a big idea and then serve as the arena for the values debate that must inevitably follow. They have a core idea that helps to focus the topic, yet they have sufficient flexibility and vagueness to demand that we interpret and reinterpret their meaning in different contexts and over different time periods. Thus, the United States abolished slavery through a civil war in the middle of the nineteenth century but was still working on civil rights one hundred years later. India overthrew British colonial rule, but partition between India and Pakistan remains a source of regional instability to this day.

Like democracy, art, or liberty, sustainability is an essentially contestable concept which will inevitably take many decades and many experiments to evolve. It has a generally accepted first meaning: to keep things going in a way that is internally consistent and resistant to collapse. It also has a generally accepted first-level meaning in the realm of business. In an effort to integrate sustainability ideas into the role of business in society, the World Commission on Environment and Development ("the Brundtland Commission") in 1987 offered a definition of "sustainable development" that is still broadly accepted: "development that meets the needs of the present, without compromising the ability of future generations to meet their own needs."[9] In the business world, the Brundtland definition of sustainable development is frequently taken as the starting point for discussion. The task, then, becomes interpreting that first-level definition in various contexts over time. Some critics have questioned the paradoxical nature of the term, arguing that "sustainable" and "development" cancel out each other's ideas – that is, we can't sustain and develop at the same time because development has traditionally meant degrading the natural environment. They argue that the term "sustainable development" or "sustainability in business" is an attempt to co-opt environmental and social justice agendas into the language and unchallenged objectives of the global economic system; that is, growth for growth's sake (we move quickly to second-level contestation). This critique points out a fundamental clash in basic views of how the world works, which we will explore in a moment, and by striving to merge the "pro-business" and the "environmentalist" or "social justice" perspectives, we can draw focus to the essential challenges of our time. These viewpoints are not entirely mutually exclusive and there is much room for common ground. But the merger does require that we challenge some of our basic operating principles for the planet and the global economy.

Five Principles of Sustainable Development, Assessed against Three Alternative Mindsets

In the mid-1990s, Thomas Gladwin and colleagues[10] examined a broad range of research and writing on sustainable development in an effort to understand some of the key principles and the differing perspectives regarding sustainability. The conceptual framework they offered is still highly relevant and useful today. They summarized threads of research across multiple disciplines concerned with the distinctions between "technocentric" and "ecocentric" world views, and they proposed a synthesis they termed a "sustaincentric" view, which we will call a *sustainability mindset*. Technocentric and ecocentric ways of perceiving the world are in many ways opposed or antithetical to one another. To assess the pragmatic usefulness of each view, they derived a general description of sustainable development from a broad literature, beginning with the Brundtland Commission report. They deduced five principle components of sustainable development: (1) *inclusiveness*, in reference to human development over time and place; (2) *connectivity*, meaning an embrace of ecological, social, and economic interdependence; (3) *equity*, or fairness across generations, within generations, and among species; (4) *prudence*, calling for precautionary care and harm prevention, technologically, scientifically, and politically; and (5) *security*, or safety from chronic threats and protection from systemic failures. They then examined some key features of the technocentric and ecocentric paradigms and compared their underlying assumptions to the ideal principles of sustainable development. They found each

Figure 1.1. Developing a Sustainability Mindset through a Synthesis of "Technocentric" and "Ecocentric" Perspectives

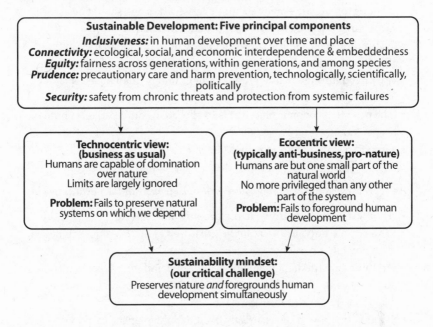

mindset wanting in some respects and proposed a hybrid perspective more closely fitting the notion of sustainable human development. See Figure 1.1 for an overview of the connections, and Box 1.1 for the basic tenets of each perspective.

BOX 1.1

BASIC TENETS OF A TECHNOCENTRIC, ECOCENTRIC, AND SUSTAINABILITY MINDSET

A technocentric mindset: Human dominion over nature

- The earth is inert and available for us to exploit to human ends.
- The natural world has value only in so far as it can be commoditized and valued monetarily and used instrumentally.

- The earth is resilient and changes slowly enough for us to adapt and control it.
- Actions to mitigate potential, but uncertain, damage should be assessed in terms of near-term cost-benefit efficiency.
- Natural capital is highly substitutable because of human ingenuity.
- The economy is a closed system separate from nature, where resources are priced through markets, and waste is largely ignored, except where legislation demands.
- The primary economic objective is to allocate resources to meet human wants (not necessarily needs).
- Growth is good, more growth is better.

An ecocentric mindset: Humans are just one element of the natural world

- The earth is alive, sensitive to disturbance, and sacred.
- Humans are but one thread in the great web of life, no more privileged than any other part of the system.
- All things are fundamentally interconnected and interdependent.
- Intrinsic value also exists outside of humanity in non-human nature.
- Nature is fragile and easily stressed.
- Population growth is has already exceeded the planet's carrying capacity.
- Human capacity to generate and wisely use adaptive technologies is limited, and our judgment is flawed by the bias towards short-term gain versus future survival.
- Resilience depends on small, distributed systems for energy and food versus globalized, densely interconnected value chains.
- Natural capital is only minimally substitutable through human ingenuity.
- Growth must be contained within the regenerative capacity of natural systems.
- The primary economic objective is to maintain steady-state on inputs and outputs, while optimizing human security, material sufficiency, and equality with other elements within the biosphere.
- Collective well-being overrides market forces, on the assumption that not everything of value has a price and can be fairly traded because markets, while useful, are imperfect.

A sustainability mindset: Preserving nature and advancing human development

- The earth is humanity's home and must be well managed to ensure human survival.
- Economic and social systems are embedded within the natural biosphere.
- Birth, growth and maturity, and death and renewal comprise the natural cycle of living systems, and renewal depends on system resilience.
- Humans are immersed in the biosphere in organic and ecological terms, but can transcend natural elements in intellectual terms.
- Ethics apply to the good of human and non-human nature and embrace values of political and cultural human rights.
- Justice is valued between and within generations.
- Material and energy extraction must be limited to prevent the decline of natural systems.
- Waste emissions should not exceed natural assimilative capacity.
- Ecosystem biodiversity must be protected from human destruction.
- Population growth must be curbed.
- Consumption levels in developed countries must be reduced.
- Markets are useful resource allocation mechanisms, but must be subject to policy constraints for sustainable levels of consumption and waste.

Adapted from T.N. Gladwin, J.J. Kennelly, and T-S. Krause, "Shifting Paradigms for Sustainable Development: Implications for Management Theory and Research," Academy of Management Review 20 (1995): 874–907.

Technocentric and Ecocentric Perspectives: Technocrats versus Tree-Huggers

For Gladwin and colleagues, the motivation for constructing a picture of these three world views was the concern that management thinking, and indeed humankind, had become conceptually detached from the rest of the natural world, much to our peril. This dissociation was a result of a long-entrenched technocentric world view, rooted in seventeenth-century Enlightenment thinking and a view of human dominion over nature. A technocentric view holds that the earth is primarily a limitless store of "natural resources" to be exploited to human ends, and that humans can and should exercise full dominion over nature. In contrast, an ecocentric world view draws from some Eastern philosophies, indigenous teachings, and ecological movements that reject the idea of human dominion over nature. An ecocentric paradigm holds that humans are but one element in the biosphere, fully subject to its laws and limits, and are no more privileged than any other part of the system.

Weighing Technocentrism and Ecocentrism against the Principles of Sustainable Development

Judged against the ideal principles of sustainable development – inclusiveness, connectivity, equity, prudence, and security – Gladwin and colleagues concluded that both the technocentric and ecocentric views fall short. Technocentrism represses the fundamental connectivity of life-support systems, largely ignores questions of equity within and across generations and among species, and risks the future viability of humanity by disregarding natural constraints in a precautionary manner. On the other hand, ecocentrism asserts the holistic, interdependent nature of the biosphere, but fails to give any weight to the role of human intellect in managing the balance – while absolute dominion over nature is an overly arrogant proposition, humans must exercise some dominion over nature (i.e., cultivating food, water, shelter) for pure survival. Ecocentrism, in holding ecological sustainability as the overarching objective, discounts the negative effects that social and economic unsustainability have on ecological systems – if people are hungry, cold, or otherwise desperate, they will quickly despoil nature to survive in the short term. In short, technocentrism fails to preserve nature and ecocentrism fails to adequately foreground human development, so both are inconsistent with the notion of sustainable human development – inclusive, connected, equitable, prudent, and secure.

A Sustainability Mindset: Not a Compromise, but a Synthesis

A *sustainability mindset* is more than just a pragmatic compromise between technocentrism and ecocentrism; rather, it is a synthesis, drawing from each the tenets most consistent with principles of sustainable development. Drawn from ideas of responsible stewardship present in most major religions, from ecological economics, and from complexity thinking, a sustainability mindset holds that the key challenge is in advancing human development in areas such as prosperity, justice, and human rights, while at the same time preserving nature and respecting the regenerative limits of the biosphere. The primary "sustainability" challenge to managers in practice is to hold human development as a goal, but to do so within the carrying capacity of the earth. In practice, this is a radical concept: business systems are built almost entirely on a technocentric paradigm, and evidence is mounting that the contradictions and failures of that world view are working to undermine its foundation and stability – most acutely in those parts of the world that first embraced industrialization. Many civil society stakeholder groups, to whom managers are increasingly compelled to respond as we will see in chapters 4 and 5, advocate an ecocentric view. The chasm between the two views of the world is significant, and both have shortcomings when assessed against broad principles for sustainable development. While they may not consider the challenge in these terms, it may be argued that the best that practicing managers can do is to work to implement something resembling a sustainability mindset in their organizations, to hold the resulting paradox, and seek creative solutions that transcend otherwise limiting world views.

Reconstructing Value that Is Embedded, Sustainable, and Transformational

In this book we develop a framework for reconstructing value: a shared human process for redefining what we value and how we can realize it. At the heart of the framework are three design principles to guide the journey: embracing the *embeddedness* of human society in the biosphere; incorporating a *sustainability mindset* as described above; and making a commitment to *transformation* by engaging in a highly participative process to restructure our policies and institutions. Embeddedness means that we acknowledge a hierarchically nested perspective of environment-society-economy, the elements of the triple bottom line first popularized by John Elkington.[11] It has become commonplace for business firms to frame their objectives around elements of people-planet-profit, often depicted as a Venn diagram of three interlocking circles, with areas of overlap. This is a social construction of physical reality that serves our current belief system but is inconsistent with ecological facts. The facets of the triple bottom line are not overlapping realms, but are embedded one within the other – as concentric circles – with economy inside society, which is wholly and practically located inside the planetary domain.[12] This is not to take an ecocentric perspective, but the logic is straightforward: human society exists entirely within the earth's biosphere (even the international space station was constructed from and is sustained by earthly materials and some solar power), and the complex beast we call "the economy," our system of value creation and commercial exchange, is wholly a human creation, meant to meet human needs. The planet can carry on without human society (it did for a very long time), and society can exist outside of commercial trade and the financial system, but it does not work the other way around: we cannot run a business in a society that fails, and we cannot feed and operate a society in a dead ecosystem. Adopting an embedded view means that we accept the basic logic that environment-society-economy are nested systems, and that limits are real. The implications of this are not trivial: it demands that we critically question assumptions of perpetual growth based on linear models of resource extraction, goods manufacture, consumption, and waste disposal, and that we question the things that are externalized in our economic equations and business models. It demands that we seek *transformational* outcomes: results that come from truly integrating business practice with the social and environmental elements of the operating context, and that shift our ideals of constructing value – deciding what we think is important. It means seeking circular models for natural resource use and economic growth where net consumption does not increase and yet the quality of life for 9 billion people is advanced. This is perhaps the central challenge for business – how to decouple economic and social prosperity from natural resource extraction, an idea we will revisit in chapter 9.

The Challenge of Reflective Practice

In order to begin the work of *reconstructing value* so that humanity can develop and thrive within the carrying capacity of the biosphere, leaders and managers need to develop a capacity for reflection, and they need to build reflective practice into their daily lives. Henry Mintzberg emphasizes the central place for reflection in management practice and management skills development:[13] Reflection means thinking about experience to make sense of things, but it is neither idle dreaming nor casual musing. It means wondering, probing, analyzing (breaking down), and synthesizing (putting together) elements of what has transpired against our theories of what we think could or should have happened, in order to understand more deeply the connections and interplay among things. Reflection is hard work. It requires delving into what is elemental in a complex situation, considering things from multiple perspectives, assessing the options against our values and operating constraints, and putting things together to form a plan of action. Reflective practice is when managers do that routinely, and there are many blocks to that happening.

A key challenge to routine reflective practice is the time-constrained nature of day-to-day activity. Organizational life is often so fast paced that leaders and managers get caught in the trap of simply keeping up with current efforts rather than pausing to envision how things might be shifted or improved. However, perhaps an even more significant issue is the bias against reflection and the preference for quick action that organizations impose on their leaders, which is similarly emphasized in business school education.[14] Delaying action to reflect is often viewed as a sign of weakness in organizational leaders, rather than acknowledging how reflection-in-action[15] allows for a process of questioning and self-exploration that enables managers to critically identify their own and others assumptions and beliefs and to broaden their perspective to consider new opportunities. The biggest barrier to reflective practice is often not a lack of time but the disregard that organizational managers have for uncertainty, viewing it in a negative light, and taking great pains to avoid wading into the messiness of such contemplation. However, reflection is an essential part of the learning process. It is an active undertaking that requires a rigorous approach to inquiry, and we cannot assume that practicing managers will have the intuitive capacity for reflection without explicitly working to develop these skills. In order to reconstruct value we need not only to make time for reflection, but also to value and embrace the uncertainty and confusion that will arise once we begin to take things apart. The ability to achieve a high comfort level with uncertainty and to approach critical reflection with confidence are both essential aspects of leadership for sustainability. The practice of reflective thinking is essential in managing organizations to support sustainability outcomes, as it allows us to challenge our underlying assumptions so that "we can develop more collaborative, responsible and ethical ways of managing organizations."[16]

Reconstructing Value: New Questions for Business

Our business schools are traditionally segmented to build specialized knowledge in specific disciplines, such as marketing, organizational behavior, and finance. Each discipline offers a slate of courses to answer questions particular to that perspective of the organization. Traditional business school questions (and their associated disciplines) include:

- What is our value proposition? How do we compete and win in the market? (Strategy)
- How do we find or create a market for our product? (Marketing)
- What is the most efficient procurement/production/service/delivery method? (Operations and Supply Chain Management)
- How do we motivate and manage our workforce (Human Resource Management/Organizational Behavior)
- How do we structure our assets and manage our money? (Finance/Accounting)

These questions are important, and the tools and methods imparted in each discipline are helpful in building essential skills for managers. However, for the most part, these disciplines describe the optimum way to operate within the rules of the current game of business, and the basic game of commerce was designed over centuries when natural limits really did not matter. Rather less frequently do they embrace questions of entrepreneurialism: How do we creatively destroy entire business sectors and replace them with more useful ones? When do oil companies become renewable energy companies? When does private transportation become replaced by public transit? Harvard University admitted its first business degree students in 1908, fully adopted the case method in 1920, and business schools are still using many of the thinking tools and teaching methods that were developed from the 1950s to the 1980s. The game is changing, and society needs the management profession not only to adapt, but to lead in a new and more sustainable direction. Even Harvard's Michael Porter, who more than any management scholar has advocated the principles of competitive strategy that have guided the past forty years of management education and practice, is now exhorting us to think differently about value creation:

> A big part of the problem lies with companies themselves, which remain trapped in an outdated approach to value creation that has emerged over the past few decades. They continue to view value creation narrowly, optimizing short-term financial performance in a bubble while missing the most important customer needs and ignoring the broader influences that determine their longer-term success. How else could companies overlook the well-being of their customers, the depletion of natural resources vital to their businesses, the viability of key suppliers, or the economic distress of the communities in which they produce and sell? ... The presumed trade-offs between economic efficiency and social progress have been institutionalized in decades of policy choices.[17]

A changing game means new ideas of value creation, and new questions for management and management education. These questions flow from an embedded, sustainable, and transformational view of human, social, and natural systems. They are not contained in one discipline or course but stretch across all disciplines. For example, how can we maximize the societal value we create and minimize the negative societal effects of our actions? How will we create value for a broad set of stakeholders? How can we ensure that benefits and harms are fairly distributed? How can we create a just world – not only for moral reasons but for the sake of peace and security? How can we ensure that future generations will have a habitable, thriving planet? How can we be not only eco-efficient, but eco-effective? How can we fully cost our inputs and outputs? How will our natural support systems cope

Figure 1.2. The Process of Reconstructing Value: Reflective Practice Skills for Sustainability

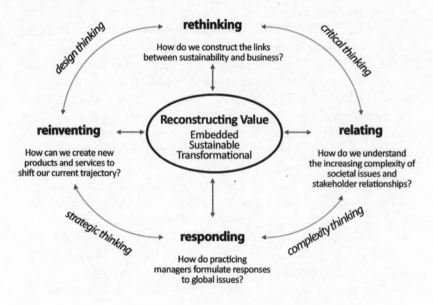

with an exponentially growing population? How will we transform our current trajectory to a path that is more sustainable? These questions require a fully considered, fully integrated approach across not only management disciplines, but also government, business, and civil society sectors. They will require that managers become highly adept as reflective practitioners.

The Process of Reconstructing Value: Reflective Practice Skills for Sustainability

In this book we work to build capacity for reflective practice, so that leaders can help to reconstruct our ideas of value in ways that are *sustainable*, with economy *embedded* in society and society embedded in nature, working towards *transformational* outcomes. We define reconstructing value as a process of the "4R's" of reflective practice: *rethinking, relating, responding,* and *reinventing*. Figure 1.2 presents our model of reconstructing value that will serve as the roadmap for this book.

The 4R's represent four phases of value reconstruction that are sequential, though overlapping and not mutually exclusive, and endlessly iterative, so we show those as connected in a circular loop. *Rethinking* involves examining and digging to the often unstated, underlying assumptions we hold about our actions in the world – what we assume about how the world works and how we think it should work. *Relating* means considering the number and kind of connections between ourselves and others across geographic regions and generations, or connections between the effects of human activity and its natural context, or those between a business and its stakeholders. *Responding* deals with how we formulate strategies and plans for action built on the rethinking and relating work. And *reinventing* entails designing new forms of relationships and new actions aimed at producing novel outcomes to shift our current trajectory. These outcomes are transformational in the sense that they help us to understand a reconstructed definition of value, as well as how we might actually put it into practice.

Underlying the phases are four types of thinking we see as vital to advancing on the journey: critical thinking, complexity thinking, strategic thinking, and design thinking. Each mode of thinking offers unique insights, and we will explore these in more detail in chapter 2. All modes of thinking are always in play, but one or another comes to the forefront depending on which "R" is in focus. Reflective practice is the essential skill that underpins all of these phases. It means regularly stepping back to consider the meaning of what has transpired in order to illuminate assumptions, think about connections, and plan for future actions. Without taking time to do this on a regular basis, organizational outcomes are compromised because managers and leaders fall into a rut of acting that may be increasingly efficient, but may not actually be enhancing organization effectiveness, and also may be compromising societal outcomes. We begin in chapter 2 with an in-depth review of the 4R's, along with the associated modes of thinking in each phase.

PART ONE: RETHINKING

CHAPTER 2

Envisioning a New Way of Doing Business: Thinking Skills for Sustainable Organizations

Every global and social issue of our day is a business opportunity in disguise.
– Peter Drucker,
Pre-eminent Management Thinker of the Twentieth Century

What if change is less about reorganizing, restructuring, and reengineering – and more about reconceiving?
· – Göran Carstedt, Former CEO of Volvo and IKEA

The catastrophic events of 2008 and the subsequent collapse of confidence in how the Western world finances economic growth based on debt and consumption have led to a serious reappraisal of the prospects for global capitalism. Even before these events, anti-globalization protesters and management scholars were calling into question the sustainability of "financial capitalism" itself as a suitable vehicle for securing a transition to a more socially and environmentally benign global economy. Indeed, Stuart Hart and other scholars have described capitalism as having reached a crossroads[1] where our business models need to be completely reconceived in order to ensure that they are creating shared value for a wide range of stakeholders. R. Edward Freeman has long argued for a pragmatic approach for reconciling the values of stakeholders within the capitalist project, and others, including ourselves, have advocated for the inclusion of all forms of capital: human, social, ecological, and intellectual as well as financial into the value proposition for organizations and their stakeholders.[2] The emergence of sustainable value investing and social impact investing as distinct asset classes in recent years is reflective of these arguments where it can be demonstrated that no sacrifice of financial rate of return is necessary for social and environmental benefits to accrue.

While it is clear that there is a different role that business needs to play, both for benefit today, and also to ensure the well-being of future generations, what remains difficult for leaders and practicing managers in organizations is envisioning a process of *how* to successfully engage in business model reinvention. The reinvention of capitalism may be inevitable and even attractive as an exercise in "triple-loop" strategic thinking where all assumptions may be questioned. But as a context for real organizations facing immediate challenges of declining sales or falling stock prices, it is a difficult place to start a conversation. There are many prescriptions for activities that organizations should engage in to become "more sustainable" but very little in the way of guidance for exactly how this might be accomplished or, indeed, details on what "more sustainable" means. It is worth reflecting on how other popular management initiatives over the past few decades such as total quality management, the learning organization, management by objectives, benchmarking, and business process reengineering have been embraced in one culture or type of business and just as quickly discarded when they are transplanted to other settings. Typically, such strategic change initiatives fail because the contextual factors that contributed to their original success were ignored. Similarly, developing a sustainability-focused organization requires attention to context and a process for translating this into each particular situation an organization is facing if the fad/failure cycle is to be avoided. It is for this reason that we have long challenged simplistic notions of a generalized "business case for sustainability"[3] that have been advocated by numerous consultants and commentators over the years. There may well be a universal *societal case* for sustainability, but there is only a specific *business case* for individual organizations in defined market places at a particular time. To pretend otherwise is to potentially mislead leaders and raise false expectations among stakeholders. The challenge then is how business leaders might engage in a process that allows them to translate the societal case for sustainability for use in their own particular organizational contexts to develop a business case for sustainability that will enable both short- and long-term success.

Reflective Practice Skills for Sustainability: Predominant Modes of Thinking and the 4R's

Our framework for reconstructing value (see Figure 1.2 in chapter 1) presents the 4R's in the process – rethinking, relating, responding, and reinventing – and the four modes of thinking that help us move from one phase to the next, namely, critical, complexity, strategic, and design thinking. Here we provide a more detailed overview of the process by highlighting each of the 4R's in turn and describing the predominant mode of thinking. We also identify a number of concepts in management practice and theory that are relevant to each stage, and that are likely familiar to students of business, in order to organize these ideas around our framework for reconstructing value. We illustrate each stage of the 4R's with company examples and brief mini-cases. This chapter provides an overview of the 4R's framework, and Table 2.1 provides an overview of the relationships between the 4R's, the primary associated thinking skills, and the three key design principles at the core of our model: embeddedness, a sustainability mindset, and an ethos of transformation.

Rethinking: The Role of Critical and Self-Reflection in Advancing a Sustainability Mindset

Predominant Thinking Mode: Critical Thinking

Considering organizations from different perspectives can help managers to identify new opportunities and potential constraints. As a reflective practitioner, it is of utmost importance for leaders to develop the skills required to become aware of their own underlying assumptions and to understand how reality is socially constructed in relationship with others, both within the organization and in the broader society. Reflective practice is also essential for sustainability because it is fundamentally about challenging existing business models and developing innovative and entrepreneurial approaches. The importance of critical thinking in sustainability is that it allows us to explore the benefits and limitations of current business practices and to consider possibilities for change. The status quo is not typically supportive of value creation on the multiple dimensions of environment, economy, and society. More

Table 2.1 Reflective Practice Process, Questions, and Thinking Skills for Reconstructing Value

	Reflective Practice *Process* for Leaders for Reconstructing Value			
	Rethinking	**Relating**	**Responding**	**Reinventing**
	Reflective Practice *Questions* for Leaders for Reconstructing Value			
	How do we construct the links between sustainability and business?	How do we understand the increasing complexity of societal issues and stakeholder relationships?	How do practicing managers formulate responses to global issues?	How do we create new products and services to shift our current trajectory?

	Reflective Practice *Thinking Skills* for Leaders for Reconstructing Value			
Design Principles for Reconstructing Value	**Critical Thinking**	**Complexity Thinking**	**Strategic Thinking**	**Design Thinking**
An embedded perspective: society is embedded within and depends upon the ecological biosphere; economy is embedded within and serves society	Challenging reality and values assumptions in existing economic and business models concerning the relationship between environment, society, and economy (i.e., externalities, trade-offs etc.).	Taking an integrative rather than a reductive approach to business and sustainability issues that supports a holistically hierarchical perspective.	Reconsidering the organization's strategic context by acknowledging the holistically hierarchical nature of environment, society, and economy as it relates to their existing and future business models.	Embracing ecological constraints as an opportunity to drive design thinking that will lead to sustainable innovation.
A sustainability mindset: focusing on equitable human development now and in the future, within the regenerative limits of the biosphere	Using critical reflection to explore the reality and values assumptions underlying ideological positions about sustainability in order to rethink social and organizational policies and practices related to sustainability.	Focusing on sustainability as a wicked problem and simultaneously attending to multiple fronts of environment, society, and economy; creatively holding the tension between multiple stakeholder perspectives on multiple issues and striving to optimize human development within ecological limits.	Evaluating the organization's strategy content with a capabilities perspective (i.e., resource-based view) in order to assist leaders with developing the intangible assets in their organization required to support a sustainability orientation.	Shifting the question from "how can we get a particular group to use our product" towards "how do we address a particular human need within the regenerative limits of the biosphere"; considering the feasibility, viability and desirability of innovations developed within this perspective.

(continued)

Table 2.1 (*continued*)

Reflective Practice *Thinking Skills* for Leaders for Reconstructing Value				
Design Principles for Reconstructing Value	**Critical Thinking**	**Complexity Thinking**	**Strategic Thinking**	**Design Thinking**
System transformation: broad engagement in reordering the assumptions that guide our policy decisions	Using self-reflection to reconsider our ways of engaging with the world in order to open up new possibilities for action; exploring the implications of our own beliefs and the meanings that we create around business and sustainability that support our current course of action.	Moving from managing stakeholders to managing for stakeholders; engaging with new stakeholders previously considered fringe or illegitimate and embracing the potential for radically new and emergent outcomes from these interactions.	Envisioning the role of conversation as a core strategic process in the organization that leads to transformation on sustainability issues.	Engaging stakeholders as designers in a conversational approach that embraces complexity and thrives on instability and focuses on creating possible worlds that allow for the emergence of new ideas.

often the view of "trade-offs" arises: we can either do something for the environment *or* for the economy *or* for society. Throughout this book, and in particular in chapters 6 and 7, we will consider how to engage in conversations and activities that will allow us to identify synergies in order to create positive feedback loops between these different elements.

What Is Critical Thinking?

Critical thinking means delving deep to unearth the assumptions that underpin some truth-claim or statement of opinion. We think critically so that we can clearly see the logic laid bare, and assess whether we believe the claim and the line of logic. For example, suppose you are attending a debate on world food production. One party claims that the only way we can adequately feed the world's population is to more broadly adopt modern industrial farming techniques and that relying only on small, locally distributed organic farming will guarantee the demise of millions. The other person claims that industrial monoculture farming techniques are making the problem worse by contributing to soil depletion and that small local food production is the way forward. How do you figure out whom to believe? If you happen to work in the agriculture industry, is your organization's long-term strategy contributing to the problem or making things better? Thinking critically can help to sort out the truth claims, weigh the evidence, delve into the underlying assumptions, and ultimately make policy decisions. We will expand on one critical thinking process later in this chapter.

Critical Reflection and Self-reflection

Two key aspects of critical thinking that are essential in the process of reflective practice towards reconstructing value are critical reflection and self-reflection.[4] In order to be an effective reflective practitioner for sustainability, you need first to be able to identify and problematize taken-for-granted underlying assumptions about the connections between business and sustainability, which requires developing critical thinking capacity. *Critical reflection* involves the ability to think more critically about the way the relationship between business, society, and environment is currently framed in existing business models and the opportunities and challenges inherent in this framing. In order to succeed in this area leaders need to become skilled at challenging *reality assumptions* (about how the world works in practice) and *values assumptions* (moral ideas about how one thinks it ought to work) that are usually taken for granted in the dominant approach to business in our society. For example, a company like Patagonia has moved towards reconstructing value by challenging the reality assumption that unlimited growth is required to make a business successful by continuing to thrive while focusing on "natural growth." This relies on letting customers tell them how to grow without creating an artificial demand for their product, which results in limited growth of about 3–8 per cent per year.[5] The company has also challenged the values assumptions that if a company is doing well it ought to get bigger in order to maximize the potential profits generated. Instead, Patagonia has taken a more holistic view of success and, while profitability is one aspect of this, there are other measures of success on the environmental and social front that are not considered secondary to this narrower pursuit. The organization has experienced great success with this business model. Perhaps most importantly, the company was kept well away from the unforgiving appetites of the capital markets by founder Yvon Chouinard, a fate which was not enjoyed by companies such as Ben and Jerry's (now owned by Unilever) and The Body Shop (now owned by L'Oréal).

Self-reflection involves the leader's ability to reflect on his/her own ways of making meaning around lived experience and to challenge her/his ways of engaging with the world to open up new possibilities for action. In order to succeed in this area, leaders need to become more skilled at challenging their own *reality* and *values assumptions*. Robert Shapiro, former CEO of Monsanto, described the pitfall of not practicing self-reflection and challenging assumptions when considering the reasons for his company's abysmal failure in its initial foray into biotechnology. Failure to appreciate alternative world views resulted in the near-collapse of the organization as European supermarket chains outlawed genetically modified produce and as environmental and international development NGOs campaigned vigorously against the company and its products. Shapiro acknowledged his responsibility:

> Monsanto, and I personally, have to bear our share of responsibility for that situation. We started with a conviction that biotechnology was a good technology, was and is safe, useful and valuable. We've been working on it for 20 years and that's the source of that conviction, but because of that, I think we have tended to see it as our task to convince people that this is good technology. And we've tried to convince people that we're right and that by extension people who have different points of view are wrong or at best misguided.[6]

By focusing outward on convincing stakeholders of what they assumed to be true, rather than directing this examination inward and exploring the implications of the beliefs that were supporting the current course of action, both Monsanto and the sustainability issues it was attempting to address were negatively affected. Later in this chapter we will consider how to build the leadership skills required to identify both reality and values assumptions in day-to-day organizational life. Box 2.1 provides a mini-case illustration of rethinking.

BOX 2.1
MINI-CASE: INTERFACE AND THE PROCESS OF RETHINKING[7]

In 1994, CEO and founder of Interface Carpet Company the late Ray Anderson had an epiphany. He described the realization that his business was harming the environment and creating a toxic legacy for his grandchildren as if he had awoken with a "stake through his heart." Ray's insights were sparked by a book he was reading at the time by Paul Hawken, *The Ecology of Commerce*. The ideas from this book challenged current economic models, suggested they were incompatible with ecological realities, and engaged Ray in a process of *critical reflection*. He began to identify the underlying reality and values assumptions of our existing business models and took particular exception with the idea of "externalities": that there are costs to nature and society that are not accounted for in our current ways of doing business but that clearly exist and continue to accrue even as we deny corporate responsibility for them. This critical reflection sparked a commitment to *Mission Zero*, a sustainability initiative focused on building a company that creates zero footprint by the year 2020. Further *self-reflection* allowed Ray to begin to challenge his own reality and values assumptions in ongoing journey he described as "climbing Mount Sustainability." This process of rethinking led to him to examine his own identity and, consequently, the identity of the organization he created. He asked the question: Rather than thinking of ourselves as a carpet company, what might be possible if executives and employees at Interface thought of themselves as flooring services providers? This line of inquiry resulted in the development of a new business model that was built on leasing and reclaiming carpet, further advancing Mission Zero and also opening up new ways to think more strategically about how the organization might continue to build competitive advantage while supporting sustainability goals. On a personal level, this self-reflection led him to reconsider the legacy that he was leaving to "Tomorrow's Child" and inspired him to move out of the role of dealing with day-to-day business operations in order to become a champion for sustainability. He was a widely sought after speaker on the topic of leadership for sustainability who shared the Interface story with many other executives who were struggling to understand how their own firms might have a positive impact on global issues of sustainability.

Relating: Complex Issues and Multiple Stakeholders

Predominant Thinking Mode: Complexity Thinking

Managers are not confronted with problems that are independent of each other. People are confronted only with dynamic situations that consist of complex systems, of changing problems, interacting with each other. These systems are "messes" and purely analytical techniques will not serve managers. Their job is managing messes, and they need the active, synthetic skill of designing a desirable future and inventing ways of bringing it about.

— Russell Ackoff, Management Scholar[8]

Reconstructing value requires a broader, more integrative perspective that takes into account the multi-faceted relationship between complex issues involving multiple stakeholders working to identify synergies among them, rather than quickly moving to distributing trade-offs, and thus focusing on optimizing value creation for a wide range of stakeholders. In order to build leadership capacity in this domain, the relating skills of complexity thinking can assist with encouraging a process of reflective practice that works to reconstruct value.

The Novel Contribution of Complexity Thinking

Modern approaches to the management of organizations are based primarily on the general systems theory (GST) and the properties of open systems that focus on relationships, structure, and interdependence.[9] The open systems view depicts the organization as an organism that seeks equilibrium, possesses clear system boundaries, and exhibits a stable pattern of relationships within those boundaries. This perspective gave rise to a number of management innovations consistent with a rational, linear world view. The primary goal of many of these approaches that continue to dominate in management thinking today is a focus on management as an exercise in planning, organizing, leading, and controlling. A fundamentally different view of organizations was introduced in the form of "complexity thinking" (alternatively referred to as "complexity science" or "complexity theory") that was drawn from the natural sciences and was applied to organizations in order to generate new insights.[10]

Complexity thinking is built on such fields as chaos theory, cybernetics, and dynamic systems theory. While a focus on process is the essence of complexity thinking, the majority of management approaches that draw on ideas from this field continue to conceive of organizations as systems (in time and space); they simply repackage existing perspectives on management and leadership in new terminology imported from complexity, thereby missing the radical insights of complexity for organizations.[11] We will revisit the limitations of systems thinking theories in chapter 5 and consider more fully the radical implications of complexity thinking for dealing with global issues of sustainability. We will then explore in-depth the relevance of a complexity perspective to the multiplicity of stakeholder views on various sustainability issues. In this section, we will simply focus on two key aspects of complexity thinking that are essential for reconstructing value, namely, an integrative rather than reductive approach to issues that supports an embedded perspective, and a focus on multiple perspectives of sustainability issues that acknowledges the non-linearity and emergence required for a transformational approach to sustainability and that allows for the development of a sustainability mindset within an organization.

Complex Issues: An Integrative Rather than Reductive Approach

Managers in organizations that aspire towards more sustainable business practices struggle tremendously with integrating the complex, societal level ideal of sustainability into their organizations. Part of this struggle can be linked to a reductive, rather than integrative, approach to thinking that stems from traditional approaches to management education. As considered in the previous section, a particular concern is the focus in mainstream management education on pragmatic applications at the expense of critical reflection that would help to build skills of synthesis and integrative thinking, something that is mirrored in management practice. This tension between conventional thinking that strives for simplicity with a focus on solutions-as-trade-offs that will best serve the firm's interests (usually defined by shareholder demands), and an approach to embracing complexity as a means to innovation,[12] is an impediment to the more integrative thinking that is required to fully realize the opportunities that a sustainability ethos offers. Although paradox may challenge everyday efficiencies in an organization and thus the urge to resolve it becomes key, embracing paradox is often an opportunity to enhance organizational effectiveness.[13]

This reductive approach presents particular challenges for integrating sustainability into organizations. The complex "messes" that Ackoff describes are consistent with a view of sustainability issues as "wicked problems," characterized by broad disagreement on both the problem and the solution, and where stakeholders work in various and often opposing directions to frame the situation and the optimal response.[14] The fact that leaders in sustainability-focused organizations need to simultaneously attend to multiple fronts of environment, economy, and society has been described as a proxy for good management, and yet many leaders have not yet developed this capacity to embrace complexity as an opportunity to make better decisions. The premium associated with many organizations considered leaders in sustainability and recognized on indices such as the Dow Jones Sustainability Index and the FTSE4Good Index is that managers within sustainability focused organizations are able to make better decisions because they are required to think integratively on several dimensions, rather than oversimplifying issues with a sole focus on short-term economic concerns. In fact, it has been suggested by stakeholder theorist R. Edward Freeman that the only place where we care if a question is a marketing question or a human resource question or a finance question is in business schools.[15] In the real world there are just business problems, and we need to draw on all of those disciplines to solve them.

HSBC Insurance Brokers in the UK is one example of an organization that claims to be taking a more integrative than reductive approach to the complex issue of climate change. The organization has considered how it might integrate sustainability into its decision making both to address the significant risks as well as to explore the potential business opportunities that are created in a changing climate. The key questions highlighted in this process include:

- Is your product helping or contributing to the problem?
- Do you know the embodied carbon in your products? Does this matter? Is it possible to measure it? What are the risks /opportunities in lending/insuring high carbon activities?
- Are your products and services at risk to a change in climate (temperature, rainfall, sea level rise)?
- Is there a market for new climate products? Can you create a new market?
- Who else is doing this?
- Will it really be more sustainable? What will happen if you get it wrong?

The organization's rationale for integrating sustainability issues is based on the potential impact that they might have both on addressing the cause of the problem and responding to the impacts in a proactive manner. They have encouraged this move away from reductive thinking by drawing together their internal expertise within the organization, the knowledge gained through their involvement with external initiatives and networks such as the United Nations Environment Programme Finance Initiative (Insurance Working Group), and their interaction as part of a larger group of companies with the continuously evolving group-level strategy on sustainable development. Through this interaction and raised awareness of various stakeholder perspectives on the issue of climate change, the organization has identified opportunities to contribute to the move to a low-carbon economy (such as offering services for low-carbon technologies and impacting consumer behavior by "greening" mass-market products) and to respond to the risks posed by growing climatic uncertainty (such as encouraging the development of natural catastrophe risk modeling and considering opportunities for micro-insurance to protect the most vulnerable to climate change).[16]

Complexity and Multiple Perspectives: Broadening Our View of Stakeholders

Stakeholders have been described in various ways; an inclusive definition is anyone who is impacted by or can impact the achievement of the organization's goals.[17] Traditionally, leaders and managers have only recognized and responded to concerns of stakeholders who are perceived as powerful, legitimate, and urgent.[18] Integrative thinking about complex issues requires expanding an organization's field of salience[19] and acknowledging multiple perspectives of diverse stakeholder groups that represent society, the economy, and the environment. Only in creatively holding the tension between those perspectives and not trading off one stakeholder's interests' continuously over time with another can a process of reconstructing value enable the development of a sustainability mindset at the organizational level. Novo Nordisk, a Danish life science company known for innovation in both products and delivery systems in the area of diabetes treatment, is well regarded for its novel approach in the area of stakeholders. The challenge of strategic innovation in life sciences is the growing complexity of the number of factors and the unknown emergent phenomena from the interaction of those factors that organizations in this sector face. In order to find its way through this uncertainty, the firm has successfully built relationships with a wide variety of stakeholders. The innovative model of stakeholder engagement it employs is open-ended and facilitates coevolution and emergent outcomes. In this way the organization has moved beyond simply being recognized for its strong brand and reputation built on its commitment to corporate social responsibility and has become noted for its respect for stakeholders as a powerful source of current and future innovations for the company. This can be seen in a number of its initiatives, including the DAWN program (Diabetes Attitudes, Wishes and Needs), the NDP (National Diabetes Program), and the Oxford Health Alliance, all of which are characterized by engaging multiple stakeholders in ways that both create benefits for them and generate business benefits for the organization. Lars Rebien Sorensen, CEO of the company, described this approach as "moving from intervention to prevention – that's challenging the business model where the pharmaceuticals industry is deriving its revenues ... We believe that we can focus on some major global health issues – mainly diabetes – and at the same time create business opportunities for our company."[20] The complexity of multiple stakeholder perspectives and the non-linear and thus unpredictable nature of the interactions between these various groups is another reason that complexity thinking is so relevant for sustainability. The traditional view of the firm, described earlier as mechanistic in nature, assumes that it is possible to anticipate and "manage" firm stakeholders' reactions to various organizational initiatives. Abandoning this narrow view and acknowledging the potentially radical implications that an organization's various stakeholders can have is important, both to mitigate the risk of emergent collapse and to maximize opportunities for *transformational* outcomes. Complexity thinking acknowledges relationships are not always simple and linear (i.e., 2+2 = 4) but rather can have unintended consequences and unpredictable outcomes (i.e., 2+2 = yellow). While this can create uncertainty and challenge in the belief that a leader's role is to control a situation, it allows for the development of novelty and innovation required to reconstruct value. The concept of stakeholder value[21] and even "radical transactiveness"[22] captures the need for organizations to expand their field of salience and engage with those stakeholders on the periphery who would have previously been considered fringe and non-legitimate. This might include remote communities, the poor, the weak, the non-human and their advocates, among others. Acknowledging that firms operate in a "dynamically complex" context requires the development of skills in complexity thinking in order to proactively and positively move away from *managing stakeholders* towards *managing for stakeholders*.[23] With regard to the complexity of multiple stakeholders, the ability to "fan out" or extend the scope of the firm by acknowledging fringe stakeholders and to "fan in" or integrate the perspective of stakeholders who may challenge the organization's established ways of thinking are both key capabilities that allow a leader to integrate multiple perspectives in order to reconstruct value.

BOX 2.2

MINI-CASE: HONEY CARE AFRICA AND THE PROCESS OF RELATING[24]

Honey Care Africa is an organization that embodies the embedded, sustainable, and transformational approach to relating to complex issues of sustainability and embracing multiple stakeholder perspectives required in order to reconstruct value. The private sector Kenyan firm manufactures and supplies Langstroth Bee hives and related equipment to organizations, communities, and individuals across the country. The organization was launched in 2000 by Farouk Jiwa, a Kenyan-born and raised social entrepreneur, with a key purpose of empowering people in rural areas to take charge of their lives, raise their awareness, and provide them with new options for a livelihood based on a business model designed to support local biodiversity. The organization's model of "Sustainable Bee Keeping," intended to help the rural poor reduce their levels of poverty, operates in ways that are socially, economically, and environmentally beneficial. The organization promotes the use of modern Langstroth Bee hives, provides basic training for bee keepers, and a market for honey. There are many outputs of the initiative, including over 10,000 hives in communities across Kenya, the production of 60–96 metric tonnes of honey annually, and the increased participation of women, rural youth, and rural groups in beekeeping, all representing positive societal level advancements. Economic impacts include over 2,000 households in rural Kenya that now rely on beekeeping as an important source of supplementary income, with the average farmer earning USD$200–250/year, raising many above the poverty line and generating about USD$600,000/year for the rural subsistence farmers involved. Positive bio-diversity impacts include the proliferation of bees that are important pollinators for a wide variety of trees and plants, increased tree planting to conserve Kenya's natural flora and provide a healthy habitat for bees to flourish, and the promotion of the use and protection of local subspecies of bees. The organization developed a "tripartite model" of business with Honey Care Africa (private sector) working in partnership with NGOs (the development sector) and grass-roots communities in a symbiotic "win–win" partnership. The model works because each of the partners has needs that the other partners address and skills and abilities that complement one another.

Responding: Seeing the Organizational Context in a New Light

Predominant Thinking Mode: Strategic Thinking

In order for practicing managers to formulate responses to global issues in ways that enable a process of reconstructing value, how the context of the organization is perceived becomes an important factor in unleashing creative strategic potential. As with other strategic initiatives, in advancing a sustainability vision it is essential to recognize internal organizational strengths and weaknesses in relation to the external context – both the industry and the broader global environment – in order to assess what is possible. Without taking this strategic perspective, many organizations adopt sustainability language and fail to leverage organizational strengths, thus seriously compromising their potential for impact on sustainability issues and the progress already made towards this vision.[25] Many organizations view sustainability or corporate social responsibility (CSR) as a useful PR exercise but do not consider if they have the capabilities to carry off the lofty claims that are being made in their sustainability vision or CSR reports. This ultimately holds the potential to damage rather than to strengthen the organization's reputation and legitimacy. In order to build leadership capacity with this approach of reconstructing value, *responding* skills of strategic thinking are required. In particular we will focus on strategic thinking skills linked to three areas of strategy development that will allow for a process of reconstructing value, and that relate to the central elements of our model (Figure 1.2 in chapter 1) – embedded, sustainable, and transformational. With regard to *strategy context*, leaders need to develop ways to apprehend the holistically hierarchical nature of the environment, society, and economy as it relates to their existing and future business models in order to develop an *embedded* view of sustainability. With regard to *strategy content*, a capabilities view of organizations can assist managers with developing the intangible assets in their organization required to support a *sustainability* orientation. And in relation to *strategy process*, leaders need to develop abilities in the area of stakeholder engagement by acknowledging the central role of conversation as a core strategic process that supports a *transformational* approach to sustainability. For example, this would mean moving beyond a traditional "green marketing" approach to strategy, where the goal is to make normal products green, towards a transformational vision of making green products normal.[26]

What Is Strategy?

There are multiple ways that practitioners define strategy, ranging from a broad view of the overarching philosophy of a company, to the mission statement of an organization to an articulation of an organization's competitive advantage in specific markets, among others. Academics have an equally impressive list of definitions with classic ones from Kenneth Andrews who describes "the match between what a company can do (organizational strengths and weaknesses) with the universe of what it might do (opportunities and threats)"[27] and Michael Porter who describes "a combination of the ends for which the firm is striving and the means by which it is striving to get there."[28] How we define strategy will influence the kinds of thinking skills we deem necessary for leaders to develop. Engaging in a process of reconstructing value means thinking about an organization's strategy as how it intends to collaborate with stakeholders to create mutual value – something which Michael Porter has embraced in the popular management literature, updating his view of strategy from a more organization-centric perspective to one of creating shared value[29] that holds potential for encouraging a sustainability mindset. While some practitioners continue to think of sustainability in terms of Corporate Social Responsibility, taking a strategic perspective on sustainability is more useful for generating mutual value creation that can ultimately lead to a transformation of the status quo. If we think of sustainability as comprising strategic decisions for the organization, then we will begin to move away from this antiquated and limiting focus on responsibility towards the kinds of decisions that can affect the long-term direction of the firm, allow the organization to achieve competitive advantage, align activities to their business environment, build on organizational resources and capabilities, and influence operational decisions of the firm.[30]

The Changing Strategic Context of Organizations

Reconstructing value requires acknowledging that the strategic context of the firm is rapidly shifting. In chapter 4 we will consider more closely some of the complex global issues that organizations increasingly have to address if they want to maximize the opportunities and minimize the risks that they present to their existing and future business. These changes in the external environment in areas such as politics, economy, demography, technology, ecology, equity, and security all invoke parallel shifts in the business environment. Traditional ways of understanding the strategic context of organizations, including models such as PEST (political, economic, social, and technological factors), SWOT (strengths, weaknesses, opportunities, and threats), value chain analysis, and Porter's five forces (threat of new entrants, bargaining power of buyers, bargaining power of suppliers, threat of substitute products or services, and rivalry among existing competitors) can all still be useful analytic tools for understanding the implications of sustainability if they are expanded to acknowledge how this context is changing. In order to apprehend this new context, leaders must develop strategic thinking skills that allow them to take more factors into account than were previously considered relevant to strategic business models. Hart and Milstein describe this new way of understanding the organizational context as adopting a set of sustainability "lenses" that allow for new ways of thinking about how to generate competitive advantage for the organization.[31] For example, moving from a view of a PEST to a PESTLE model that adds "legal" and "ecological" factors as separate categories is one step towards taking a more holistically hierarchical view of the firm's context and acknowledging the significance of ecological and regulatory forces to organizational decision making. Taking a *holistically hierarchical*[32] view of the organization as embedded in society, which is embedded in the natural environment, has particularly significant implications for reconstructing value. In doing so managers can begin to lead their organizations to support broader societal sustainability initiatives rather than focusing more narrowly on sustaining the organization with benefits to society and environment as ancillary. Thinking more integratively about these complex issues means that instead of a trade-offs view a creative solution can be generated. By engaging the tension between these different elements at play and keeping the whole picture in mind when working on individual parts of the problem, positive synergies can be identified.

The Role of Strategy Content

From the perspective of reconstructing value, a critical aspect of strategy is aligning an organization's intangible as well as tangible (financial and physical) assets to the strategy it has undertaken. Intangible assets such as corporate capabilities for learning, reputation building, and engagement with stakeholders, among others, are critical to the success of sustainability-focused organizations. The resource-based view in strategy[33] emphasizes an approach of competing from the inside out. Traditional approaches to strategy have been dominated by an outside-in approach taken in the so-called positioning school where an organization's competitive advantage is determined by how successfully it exploits an existing niche in a particular industry through positioning itself relative to five key forces acting on that industry. In contrast to this, the resource-based view places an emphasis on the role of internal capabilities and competencies in building sustainable strategic value propositions and thus is particularly relevant to the process of reconstructing value. By asking in an iterative way the questions "How do we create sustainable value?" and "What are we good at?" the appropriate competencies and capabilities to support a sustainability focus within organizations may be developed. In order to do this, it is important to consider how capabilities from the basis for competitive advantage and sustainable value creation. An organization such as Campbell Canada has focused its mission statement on a key capability of "nourishing people's lives" to think about how it might nourish consumers, employees, communities, and other stakeholders. In doing so the organization launched a product called Nourish, which is a complete meal with a full serving from three food groups, to help address the issue of hunger within Canada and abroad. The company makes donations of cans to Food Banks Canada with the assistance of key suppliers that donate ingredients and materials. Beyond this Campbell is exploring ways to make the product available at key retailing outlets in a way that will use proceeds from the sale of Nourish to fund future donations. They are working with industry, government, and international organizations in order to explore the potential to make Nourish more widely available to all individuals regardless of their economic situation or geographic location. Because the product is designed to be eaten either heated or at room temperature, has a pop-top lid, a twenty-four-month shelf life, and does not require the addition of water makes it well suited for food banks in Canada or disaster-relief situations globally. This product has the potential to positively impact a sustainability issue while at the same time creating reputational benefits for the organization that will help to strengthen its strategic competitive advantage.

Most simply put, one way of thinking about capabilities is that they determine what we can do and what we cannot do within an organization. Capabilities may come in the form of *values* or the criteria by which decisions get made and determining what is important – morally, economically, socially, environmentally; *processes* or the means by which value is created through communication and coordination – technological, organizational, administrative; and *resources* or the people, equipment, technology, brand, relationships, and cash used to create value.[34] Creating value from intangible assets is different than creating value from tangible assets in that value creation is indirect. Intangible assets such as knowledge, capabilities, and technology seldom have a direct impact on financial outcomes such as revenue; they work through chains of cause and effect relationships. Value is contextual, that is, the value of an intangible asset depends on its alignment with the strategy; and value is potential, that is, the cost of investing in an intangible asset represents a poor estimate of its value to the organization. Thus, intangible assets have potential value but not immediate market value. Potential is transformed through internal processes, and those processes must be aimed at the customer value proposition; and assets are bundled, that is, intangible assets must work in concert with other tangible and intangible assets to create value.[35] Because of this, intangible assets that are essential for reconstructing value in order to build a sustainable organization – such as management skills in critical and integrative thinking, building positive and generative relationships with stakeholders, and valuing ecological, economic, and social outcomes – are necessarily excluded from the balance sheet of organizations because it is impossible to objectively value them; however, these assets are usually the most critical for firm success.[36] We will explore this more fully in chapter 6 when we consider the specific conceptions of sustainability that guide practitioners in creating value for stakeholders and the related capabilities that support reconstructing value in a sustainable manner.

The Role of Strategy Process

Reconstructing value requires a focus on conversations as a strategic process for transforming an organization in its pursuit of a sustainability vision. As with reflective practice, traditionally "conversation" has not held a place of high esteem in either management practice or theory as it is most often perceived as detracting from the true value creation activities of the firm. However, another school of thought suggests that conversations are a core strategic process of an organization[37] and that, in the shifting context of business where workers need to create new knowledge for the organization in order to generate strategic competitive advantage, conversations can be thought of as the most important form of work.[38] Strategizing has been described as being dependent on "creating a rich and complex web of conversations that cuts across previously isolated knowledge sets and creates new and unexpected combinations of insight,"[39] and this way of thinking emphasizes the role of conversation in enabling transformational organizational outcomes. An emphasis on conversation as a core strategic process shifts the focus away from an approach to managing by *results* to one of managing by *means* where there is an understanding that the financial targets and performance objectives that characterize the "ends" and the processes and practices that comprise the "means" co-evolve simultaneously. Conversation is the fundamental "means" by which relationships are built, knowledge is shared and value is created for stakeholders, and so how these conversations are structured becomes critical to the different outcomes that will be possible.

Generative dialogue is a precursor to effective "strategic dialogue" or strategic conversations, which are focused on specific issues and on finding specific solutions in organizational and social systems settings.[40] Strategic conversations can be understood as patterns of dialogue in a broader context. The concept of strategic conversations has been extended metaphorically to describe the general strategic discourse running through an organization.[41] Discrete local conversations, happening continuously and simultaneously across the organization, are given shape at the institutional level *as strategy*, and "this institutional level conversation [i.e., strategy] acts to reshape and redefine corporate intent, based on the knowledge gained in the local conversation."[42] Liedtka characterizes the strategy process as a loop of "gap opening" and "gap closing" between the current reality and some desired future state. Strategic conversations aid in both imagining and designing new value systems and possible futures and in setting about building the necessary capabilities to realize that future. The term "strategic conversations" has been applied to the practice of *scenario planning* developed by Royal Dutch Shell.[43] Scenario planning involves the creation of alternative scenarios about the future, with the aim of preparing the organization to deal with a range of possible futures rather than betting on one scenario transpiring. At the heart of the scenario planning process is dialogue with knowledgeable internal and external commentators, and the resultant organizational learning helps inform possible courses of action for the business. In chapter 6 we will explore more fully the idea of *sustainability conversations* or the specific content of conversations that can enable the reconstruction of value towards transformational outcomes. An assumption behind the priority we place on strategic conversations is that when people are engaged in meaningful discussions about sustainability they will be motivated to organize themselves in ways that will enable the realization of a sustainability vision. And so conversation and action are intimately connected.[44]

Hewlett Packard is one organization that has moved through a series of different conversations on what sustainability means from a strategic perspective. For decades HP has worked to mitigate its environmental impact through the adoption of environmentally responsible practices in product development, operations, and supply chain management. Most recently, HP Canada highlighted this dual focus on both reducing impacts of their business today through recycling and waste reduction initiatives and their lead role in helping to establish Extended Producer Responsibility legislation. At the same time the organization is engaged in sustainability conversations that will allow it to seek more innovative ways to meet longer-term sustainability challenges. Leaders in the organization suggest that it is aspiring to use its influence to help build a sustainable global economy. Recognizing that the information and communication technology (ICT) sector accounts for 2 per cent of the world's carbon footprint and that it could reduce not only its own footprint but also offer solutions to the world's carbon problem represents a shift in the corporate conversation; it suggests how an organization might address these broader global issues of sustainability in a way that is both strategic and supports a transformational, sustainability-based, and embedded approach to reconstructing value. As one of the largest technology companies in the world, HP claims to be firmly focused on playing a key role in finding and implementing these solutions.[45] Similar strategic corporate conversations may now be discerned in a number of ICT firms – for example, Google and Cisco – partly because of the inherently network-based nature of their value propositions with stakeholders and partly because of their corporate values. Cisco UK &

Ireland has become involved in broader discussions with its customers to understand the role that ICT can play in supporting sustainable
business practices. Phil Smith, CEO of Cisco UK & Ireland, reported
that 96 per cent of business people in Britain believe technology can
help the UK meet its carbon reduction targets.[46] Cisco UK & Ireland de-
clares that sustainability must "permeate every level and every facet of
the organization from the boardroom outwards"[47] and describes how
a survey it conducted reveals that ICT leaders are even less "fatigued"
by conversations about sustainability and the environment than the average employee. A large majority of IT leaders are energized by these
conversations and are upbeat about the potentially positive impact of
sustainability on the ICT sector.

In chapter 7 we will consider the social dynamics that emerge from
engaging employees in meaningful sustainability conversations and
how these dynamics can inhibit or enable change towards a sustainability vision. There is an important link between conversations and our
earlier discussion on critical thinking that shows how we ultimately
understand each other depends on what layers of meaning are underpinning our conversations such as inferences, assumptions, values, feelings, and information.[48] Thus, abilities in reflective practice are critical
for the quality of sustainability conversations that take place in an organization, and again highlight the iterative nature of this model of rethinking, relating, responding, and reinventing. This focus on strategy
process as conversation means that strategy making can be thought of
as an organization-wide phenomenon and is not just limited to the CEO
or top executive team. IKEA Canada, recognized as one of Canada's
Greenest Employers for several years for its commitment to sustainability, claims to work hard to create a culture of environmental awareness
throughout the organization. An important element of this is engaging
in new and innovative initiatives by engaging co-workers, customers,
suppliers, and other partners in conversations about what is possible
for the organization around sustainability-focused business practices.
"Job seekers today are looking for more than just a pay cheque – they
want to work for companies that show in action they are looking after
its people, operate their businesses in sustainable ways and provide an
inspiring place to work."[49] The organization achieves this by involving their co-workers in all of their sustainability initiatives. A transformational process of reconstructing value is one that emphasizes social

learning, something that requires participatory approaches to engaging stakeholders in sustainability conversations in order to challenge governing values and norms, an idea that will be explored more fully in the next chapter. Kingfisher/B&Q UK is another organization that has evolved its conversations on sustainability from a focus on sources of wood in their garden furniture in the 1980s to its current engagement in a dialogue with stakeholders about how we need to radically redesign our business models with less emphasis on growth and more on well-being. This shift has CEO Ian Cheshire focused on "our total impact as a business rather than the narrow shareholder value lens, since businesses that do not create broader social value will not survive the longer term."[50]

BOX 2.3

MINI-CASE: VANCITY AND THE PROCESS OF RESPONDING[51]

Vancity is a Canadian member-owned financial cooperative founded in Vancouver in 1946. It distinguishes itself from other financial institutions in that every Vancity employee is a co-owner of the credit union with a say in how the organization is run and is fully invested in its success. The organization's mission is to be a "democratic, ethical and innovative provider of financial services to our members." In order to spark the self-reliance and economic well-being of its membership and community, Vancity is committed to strong financial performance. Its purpose is stated as working with "people and communities to help them thrive and prosper." Working at Vancity is described for employees as an opportunity to live their values every day and to "make a meaningful difference in people's lives." The organization shares over 30 per cent of its profits with members, employees, and the community each year, and it supports innovative projects and activities that are intended to improve individuals' lives, which has earned the organization ongoing recognition as "one of the most innovative, inclusive, dynamic and progressive financial institutions in Canada." The organization is recognized as a leader in sustainability, diversity, corporate social responsibility, and ethical investing. Vancity's approach to sustainability is "the idea that you should not take out more than you put in," and this philosophy focuses the organization on investing members' earnings in order to "make a difference and grow a better world." Vancity aspires to do this by focusing on the following:

- Offering business products that are socially and environmentally responsible.
- Investing in the well-being of the communities served through grants, scholarships, awards, fundraising, and community service.
- Adopting business practices that are socially and environmentally responsible.
- Advocating for social and environmental responsibility in order to make a positive difference for individuals and communities.

Employee engagement is encouraged in a workplace culture that values inclusiveness and diversity and a sharing of creative ideas to inspire innovative practices. Employees are encouraged not to take an "us and them" approach to organizational stakeholders but to focus instead on how they are all members of the same team "working to make our community a better place to live and prosper." Vancity is now using social media to extend this focus on engagement to its online community through its website, www.ChangeEverything.ca. Bloggers are welcome to set their own change agenda and to engage online community members in sharing ideas for making change that is financial, professional, environmental, or global in nature.

Reinventing: Putting Things Together in New Ways

Predominant Thinking Mode: Design Thinking

Along with the other types of thinking that are essential to this process of reconstructing value, the reinvention aspect of our model brings to the foreground the important role of *design thinking* as a key capability that leaders need to develop in sustainability-focused organizations. Design thinking embodies a philosophy of *learning by building*, and so in the cycle of reflective practice we have described, we begin by taking things apart, considering how they relate to each other, formulating ways to understand how our organizations might respond to the new context we are observing and then engaging in a reinvention exercise where we can learn how to rebuild our strategies, products, and services in ways that are aligned with sustainability goals. In this section we will explore elements of design thinking that are most relevant to this reinvention process, namely, acknowledging that design thinking is driven by constraints which, from an *embedded view*, means embracing ecological constraints or limits to growth; a focus on creativity and innovation that unleashes *transformational* outcomes; and a human-centered approach that, when combined with an embedded view, supports the development of a sustainable organization.

What Is Design Thinking?

Design thinking is a systematic approach to problem solving that is distinct in its focus on empathy, invention, and iteration.[52] There are many different perspectives in design thinking that have been captured in various ways. One such categorization contrasts "formula" and "visionary" approaches (where the designer controls the process) with "conversation" and "evolving" approaches to design (which are more inclusive of a wide range of stakeholders and more likely to generate innovative outcomes).[53] A process of reconstructing value draws on design thinking that is more representative of these last two perspectives as they are consistent with a participatory approach focused on shifting the status quo. Business tensions that emerge from engaging in design thinking are provoked by the question of how stakeholders and different forms of knowledge should play a role and how the design process should unfold and prioritize control or creativity. Design thinking and traditional approaches to strategic thinking can be seen as complementary, and these tensions provoke useful questions that can work to advance a sustainability vision.

Whereas traditional thinking in business is based on an objective view of reality that can be quantified and rationally assessed and whereas it is focused on maintaining stability in institutions, design thinking assumes a socially constructed world view and, in doing so, highlights the messiness of human experience by prioritizing real-life behavior over theory and by embracing uncertainty and change. Given the complex issues sustainability-focused organizations are trying to address, design thinking has a particular strength in helping leaders to move beyond coping with uncertainty, towards thriving on it is as a source of innovation and an opportunity to create value for stakeholders. According to Jeanne Liedtka, this focus on experimenting over analyzing is a capability that leaders need to build and "accept that their basic belief that 'analysis equals reduced risk' is just plain wrong in the face of uncertainty. Hiding in your office using questionable numbers extrapolated from the past to predict the future is just about the [most unhelpful] thing you can do."[54]

Design Thinking and Limits to Growth

The reinvention process of reconstructing value is enabled when leaders develop an approach to design that is driven by ecological constraints as a primary force shaping what innovation is desirable, engaging in a process of experimentation to determine if these ideas are also feasible and viable.[55] Design thinking actually encourages an approach to embracing constraints-time, budget, location, materials – and in the case of sustainability – ecological, economic, and social imperatives. Constraints can be thought of in terms of three intertwined criteria that can be used to evaluate the potential success of various ideas: feasibility (what is technically possible in the near term); viability (what has the potential to become part of a sustainable business model); and desirability (what offers appealing solutions to people and for people). In a process of reconstructing value, desirability refers to meeting fundamental human needs within the ecological reality that human society operates within, rather than just responding to random or manufactured desires. The difference between simply engaging in a design process and being a design thinker is the move away from individually resolving constraints towards an approach of bringing them into an integrated state of balance. This is an iterative process that does not result in all factors being given equal weight in different situations; rather, it pragmatically experiments with the factors to generate a solution that works in a particular case, shifting the emphasis away from a particular problem towards working on a specific project and thus ensuring clarity, direction, and a high level of creative energy. By identifying limitations and then experimenting within these, it becomes possible to create the best solution given those issues rather than engaging in the questionable pursuit of attempting to develop a perfect solution that may not be possible amidst such complexity. Frito Lay's compostable chip bags that have recently been redesigned and relaunched for their Sun Chips product may prove to be an example of a useful sustainability-inspired *design process* that has produced an improvement to existing offerings.[56] Pushing further towards more transformational outcomes requires a commitment to *design thinking* that can be found in ideas such as the Aquaduct Bike, a product at the concept stage of development that is intended to meet transportation needs in developing countries with minimal negative environmental impact. In addition, it simultaneously purifies water through the human powered energy generated by pedaling and has the potential to positively improve water-quality issues facing most communities.[57] Playpumps is another design innovation that attempts to harness the natural desire of children to play on a revolving platform and combine it with the need to pump groundwater for a community's water supply.[58] Design thinking is driven and shaped by constraints – the good news from the embedded point of view is that often the best designs emerge under the most significant constraints.

Design Thinking and Innovation

From the perspective of reconstructing value, sustainability is fundamentally about transformation rather than incremental change. However, managers are often most concerned with attempting to maintain stability and control in order to meet their quarterly earnings commitments. Although leaders may declare that innovation is important to their organization, in reality, ambiguity and uncertainty are more often disconcerting to them, and so most business organizations tend to excel at becoming more efficient than more creative. Design thinking embraces complexity and thrives on instability, and this makes it particularly well suited for addressing issues of sustainability. Rather than trying to imitate what leading companies are currently doing or working within the constraints of existing business models, design thinkers focus on creating possible worlds that allow for the emergence of new ideas. Science writer Janine Benyus has advocated industrial design inspired by nature and has popularized the concept of biomimicry:

> In a biomimetic world, we would manufacture the way animals and plants do, using sun and simple compounds to produce totally biodegradable fibers, ceramics, plastics, and chemicals. Our farms, modeled on prairies, would be self-fertilizing and pest-resistant ... In each case, nature would provide the models: solar cells copied from leaves, steely fibers woven spider-style, shatterproof ceramics drawn from mother-of-pearl, cancer cures compliments of chimpanzees ...[59]

Clean technology start-up Calera Cement has designed a process that advances the concept of carbon capture and storage by sequestering a half ton of CO_2 in every ton of cement that it manufactures. Calera claims that this new "green" cement is poised to replace the carbon-intensive Portland cement that is the third largest source of anthropogenic carbon dioxide. The Calera cement process uses flue gas from coal plants, steel plants, or natural gas plants combined with seawater for calcium and magnesium to produce cement, clean water, and cleaner air. Using the product produces benefits on multiple fronts: sequestering CO_2 from polluting plants; displacing emissions from the traditional Portland cement process that generates CO_2; and, because using more of this cement has a positive impact on sequestering CO_2, additional gains can be made through building thicker walls resulting in buildings that are cooler in the summer and warmer in the winter, further reducing energy demands and related CO_2 emissions.[60]

Design thinking is characterized by questioning everything rather than focusing on the most efficient solution and taking risks – with experimentation there is not only the potential for failure but also the opportunity for change. In the context of organizations pursuing a sustainability-focused vision, creative destruction or the breakthrough of innovative upstarts that overthrow established firms has been described as essential for generating the kinds of transformational leaps required to move towards a more sustainable society.[61] However, it is when organizations become good at doing something that they are most likely to lock into a mode of becoming incrementally more efficient rather than looking for transformational breakthroughs.

Design Thinking and the Human-Centered Approach

Another insight that design thinking can offer for reconstructing value is that taking a human-centered approach to design, when combined with an embedded view, will help with the challenging task of building a sustainable organization. In the previous chapter, we discussed how firms developing a sustainability mindset foreground human development while also ensuring the protection and future flourishing of natural systems, thus bridging the technocentric and ecocentric perspectives. However, traditional approaches to business are concerned more with logic than emotion and so the empathy required for a human-centered approach is something that design thinking can bring to the process of reinvention. Human-centered design starts by examining the needs of the people whom designers want to influence with their solutions.[62] Design thinking moves from reflection to action with the experimental focus on learning by building, moving from gathering real observations about people, iterating back to abstract thinking through uncovering insights and themes, and then becoming more concrete again through generating actual solutions; it is a way to envision how reflective practice might be enhanced through developing new capabilities. In relation to sustainability, a design challenge would be phrased in human-centered ways, embracing what is possible given the ecological constraints described earlier – so rather than asking an organization-centered question such as "How do we get a particular group to use our product?" insights can be generated by framing the design challenge in a human-centered way such as "How do we address a particular human need?" For example, IBM's Smarter Planet initiative is intended to create solutions for interconnected problems facing humanity such as potential financial crises, climate change, energy geopolitics, and hazards in the food supply through the development of greater intelligence in the systems and through processes that allow physical goods to be developed, manufactured, bought and sold, services to be delivered, and people, money, oil, water, and electricity to be moved. The company is using an approach that is based on three ideas: instrumenting the world's systems, interconnecting them, and making them intelligent. The conversations initiated thus far with multiple stakeholders have generated potential opportunities that IBM is currently pursuing regarding how to support the development of

Smarter Cities, Smarter Healthcare, Smarter Banks and Financial Services, and Smarter Infrastructure such as Smart Rail, Smart Grids, Smart Sewers, and Smart Buildings. IBM recognizes that these issues require serious consideration and collaborative decision making across multiple stakeholder groups and has indicated that the company is building more than systems – it is also building coalitions that will help to support the Smart Planet agenda.[63]

BOX 2.4

MINI-CASE: BETTER PLACE AND THE PROCESS OF REINVENTING[64]

The design constraints of the depletion of oil resources and the growing issue of climate change have led the organization Better Place to ask the question, How can we address the human need of moving from place A to place B in a more sustainable manner? It has answered this question with a design innovation of electric vehicles (EVs) that are powered by renewable energy. Better Place is an American-Israeli EV company that is attempting to introduce cars that run entirely on electricity while at the same time positively impacting the move towards developing more renewable sources of energy. Improvements in lithium ion batteries have made this concept *feasible* as these batteries now store energy better and will allow the car to travel close to 160 km before having to recharge. The planned concurrent development of installing charging locations at home, parking lots at work, and other convenient locations and having battery-exchange stations where EV drivers can quickly (three minutes or less) replace depleted batteries with fresh batteries for trips longer than 160 km further enhances the feasibility of this design concept. The sustainable business model is *viable* and is based on the mobile phone operator concept where drivers will pay a subscription fee to access this network of recharging locations and battery-exchange stations, just as mobile phone subscribers pay to access cell phone towers and phone networks. Similar to cell phone users who pay per use, EV owners will pay for miles driven. Convenience, reduced environmental impact, reduced exposure to the volatility of oil prices, and a more economical car will all contribute to the *desirability* of this design innovation for consumers. Better Place is taking a two-step approach to addressing the issue of climate change. First, replacing the estimated 700 million cars on the world's roads with EVs would displace about 10 per cent of the roughly 2.8 billion tonnes of CO_2 that they currently produce. Second, the recharge process of the batteries will increase demand for a new and larger market for renewable energy. Since the batteries will be able to be recharged at any time of the day, Better Place will be able to buy the electricity it requires from wind mills or solar cells that are often not used because of their unpredictable patterns of production that do not support the consistency of energy flows demanded by the everyday functioning of the economy. Because the energy demands of the Better Place EV network are a good fit with renewable energy production, this is intended to create greater incentives for energy suppliers to invest in clean energy.

LEADERSHIP SKILL BUILDING:
Process Questions, Skills, and Skill-Building Exercises

PROCESS QUESTIONS AND LEADERSHIP SKILLS CHAPTER 2:
Rethinking–Relating–Responding–Reinventing

Referring back to Figure 1.2, our four major process questions for reconstructing value are (1) How do we construct the link between global sustainability and business? (2) How do we understand the increasing complexity of societal issues and stakeholder relationships? (3) How do practicing managers formulate responses to global issues? and (4) How can we create new products and services to shift our current trajectory? Based on our exploration throughout this chapter, we now consider the leadership "thinking" skills managers need in order to engage more effectively with each of these process questions, and we offer an example Learning Team Dialogue that can help build these skills.

Process Question 1 – Rethinking: How Do We Construct the Link between Sustainability and Business?

Developing Skills in Critical Thinking
In order to build critical thinking capacity linked to reconstructing value, namely, critical reflection and self-reflection, it is essential to develop the ability to identify underlying reality and values assumptions. In doing so, we will be able to challenge

widely taken-for-granted assumptions of existing business models and our own beliefs in order to open up new possibilities for considering the connection between sustainability and business.

Dyer[65] breaks critical thinking into five major parts: (1) It is purposeful – we need to ask, "What are the central claims being made?" (2) It looks at the quality of the data and the reasons that are offered to support claims – we need to evaluate the quality of the evidence offered to us. (3) It acknowledges that claims and evidence are shaped by our basic assumptions and viewpoints – we need to ask, "What are our own underlying assumptions and values?" (4) It challenges inferences about cause and effect – we need to question the validity of the causal claims being made. (5) It considers ways in which ideas are expressed in order to persuade readers and listeners – we need to think about how key concepts are presented, how contradictory evidence is managed, and how words can sway our judgment and evaluate these techniques of persuasion.

There are many resources on critical thinking that can provide useful insight for managers who want to develop this capacity. All of these have some version of developing the ability to assess the claims that are being made and the evidence provided in order to identify the gap in between. In doing so we can find where reality and values assumptions reside in order to allow an individual to make the logical link and reach a particular set of conclusions. An assumption is something we take for granted or presuppose; it is part of our system of beliefs, we assume our beliefs to be true and then we use them to interpret the world around us. Beliefs, and hence, assumptions can be unjustified or justified, depending on whether we do or do not have good reasons for them.[66] They are deeply ingrained and taken for granted and that is why we need to engage in reflective practice and critical thinking to identify them. *Reality assumptions* are our beliefs about what events have taken place, what exists, or how things work in the world – they are our beliefs about reality, the way things really are. *Value assumptions* are our ideals, our standards of right and wrong, the way things ought to be. The following are examples of questions that might be asked to identify assumptions: What must be true if the claim is to follow from this evidence? What general principle might link this particular claim to this particular evidence? What beliefs might I expect from this type of person, that is, linked to his/her role and could someone believe this evidence and still disagree with the claim? Why?

Drawing on insights from our discussion of critical thinking and asking the following questions can help leaders to engage in a process of rethinking to reconstruct value:

1   How is the existing relationship between business, society, and environment currently framed in metaphorical terms outside of our organization (think of media, industry associations, popular culture)? What new metaphors might open up new possibilities for action?

2   How can we describe the reality and values assumptions that currently prevail in the broader society and within our own organizations? In what ways do we think that power interests and ideologies *are* currently dominating the relationship between business, society, and environment and how do we think the dominant perspective conveys that this relationship *should* be structured? How might new opportunities open up by shifting these assumptions?

3   How can we describe our own personally held reality and values assumptions? In what ways do we think that the relationship between business, society, and environment *is* currently structured and how do we think it *ought* to be structured? How might a new course of action open up if we challenge some of these deeply held values and beliefs?

Process Question 2 – Relating: How Do We Understand the Increasing Complexity of Societal Issues and Stakeholder Relationships?

Developing Skills in Complexity Thinking
In order to develop skills in complexity thinking, we need to consider how we might we take a more integrative than reductive approach to viewing sustainability issues that face an organization. Drawing on insights from our discussion of complexity thinking and asking the following questions can help leaders to engage in a process of *relating* to reconstruct value:

1   Consider the broader ecological and social elements of an unsustainable trajectory: energy, food, water, air, population, climate, dignity, justice, and so on. Where might pockets of innovation or societal pressure emerge based on possible opportunities, disruptions, or potential risks that your organization is facing? Look beyond the obvious or widely accepted concerns to consider hidden threats and opportunities posed by issues and stakeholders which have not been thought of as relevant.

2   Think about which stakeholders currently matter most to your organization and receive the most attention? Which are the stakeholder groups that your firm tends to ignore or consider less important? How might you engage in "fanning in" and "fanning out" to gather and integrate new information from these groups that could help to broaden your view of which sustainability issues are opportunities or risks for your organization?

3   Focus on the possibility for emergence over linear and incremental approaches to embracing a sustainability vision in the day-to-day operations of your organization. Embrace complexity as a source of creativity and innovation by identifying several key paradoxes that exist related to sustainability issues within the firm (e.g., we want to build close relationships

with our stakeholders but there is a history of antagonism in our interactions; we aspire to be leaders on environmental issues but our business has a strong environmental impact, etc.). Consider different stakeholder perspectives to help you identify these paradoxes.

Process Question 3 – Responding: How Do Practicing Managers Formulate Responses to Global Issues?

Developing Skills in Strategic Thinking
Reflective practice in the area of strategy context, process, and content will assist leaders in identifying new opportunities for value creation. Drawing on insights from our discussion of strategic thinking and asking the following questions can help leaders to engage in a process of *responding* to reconstruct value:

1   How might we generate a new way of understanding our organizational context by adopting a set of sustainability "lenses" to explore new facets that have not yet been considered?
2   What are the key intangible assets our organization possesses that contribute to our current success? How might we leverage these existing strengths of the organization in order to respond to the new context we have identified?
3   How can we close the gap between our current reality and desired future state by asking the questions, How can we shape tomorrow's value system to create new possibilities, in partnership with other stakeholders? What new capabilities are we committed to developing and learning to care about?[67]

Process Question 4 – Reinventing: How Can We Create New Products and Services to Shift Our Current Trajectory?

Developing Skills in Design Thinking
Drawing on insights from our discussion of design thinking and asking the following questions can help leaders to engage in a process of *reinventing* to reconstruct value:

1   How can we identify constraints within an embedded view of society and environment? Consider what the constraints of feasibility, viability, and desirability mean from an embedded perspective for your organization. Experiment within these limitations and consider how your organization might develop new business ventures that are forward looking.
2   In order to encourage a focus on creativity and innovation within our organization and to promote emergent and transformational outcomes, consider how a shift in involving stakeholders in your organization might enable this. What opportunities are there for us to engage with multiple

stakeholders in a participatory manner, working with them as designers rather than simply informing them of our activities or consulting with them after business decisions have been made? How might we create new opportunities for this type of engagement and what stakeholder groups might we think of involving?

3   In order to promote a focus on human-centered design within an embedded context, how can we move beyond asking an organization-centered question such as "How do we get a particular group to use our product?" in order to generate innovative insights by framing the design challenge as "How might we address a particular human need, given the ecological and economic context we are operating within?"

SKILL-BUILDING EXERCISE CHAPTER 2: Learning Team Dialogue: Reconstructing Value in the Agriculture Sector

Let us revisit the example of the food production debate from earlier in this chapter. Over the past fifty years the face of agriculture has dramatically shifted, bringing with it the positive outcomes of higher yields of food and the challenges that have accompanied the shift in practices that have allowed us to feed more people in a cheaper way. Key issues include topsoil depletion, groundwater contamination, the decline of family farms, continued neglect of the living and working conditions for farm labourers, increasing costs of production, and the disintegration of economic and social conditions in rural communities. The University of California's program in sustainable agriculture research and education provides a good overview of some key issues in this sector.[68] Sustainable agriculture is a movement that attempts to address these various environmental and social concerns while offering innovative and economically viable opportunities for growers, labourers, consumers, policymakers, and other stakeholders in the food system. The intent is to create environmentally sound farming practices and to foster humane animal management while at the same time being economically viable and socially just.[69]

Here are key first steps: adopt the perspective of a specific company in the agriculture sector and apply the reflective process of reconstructing value as detailed in this chapter. This will help you reinvent your organization's strategy in a way that is sustainable, embedded, and transformational. Use the process questions outlined above as a starting point for your discussion.

Conclusion

In this chapter we have described a process of reflective practice that is essential for reconstructing value and building organizations that support sustainability outcomes. We have argued that developing four kinds of thinking skills is integral to this process, namely, critical thinking, complexity thinking, strategic thinking, and design thinking. Managers and leaders who develop capacity in these four areas will generate new insights that will catalyze more transformational outcomes for their organizations. In the next chapter, we will consider how embarking on a participatory process of social learning is critical to moving a company from focusing more narrowly on its own sustainability towards embracing a broader perspective of how the organization might also work to positively impact social, economic, and environmental issues at the societal level.

CHAPTER 3

Learning Our Way Forward: Transforming Organizations and Society

There has been too much incremental change and not enough real revolution. Too many companies have declared themselves responsible while doing little that actually is, and corporate responsibility (CR) has too often devolved into just another form of "greenwashing" and cause-related marketing that companies use to distract us from their uglier operational truths. [Making progress in this area] will mean creating new ways of thinking and operating that allow us to resolve environmental challenges, enhance the living systems upon which we depend, and improve the circumstances of our staff, stakeholders, and communities, all while producing the financial rewards that allow this work to continue.

– Jeffrey Hollender, Co-Founder and
Former CEO, Seventh Generation[1]

Chapter 3 continues our examination of the role of "rethinking" in reconstructing value, with a focus on how different forms of learning can help leaders to fundamentally change the game organizations see themselves involved in playing. "The game" can be thought of as the set of acceptable (often unspoken but understood by all) rules of behavior that comprise a leader's organizational and social expectations. By identifying underlying assumptions, it may be possible for leaders not only to improve or to challenge the rules of the game they are engaged in but also to rethink the assumptions of what the game is about in order to generate breakthrough insights and innovative ideas. In the previous chapter we introduced a model of reflective practice for reconstructing value that is centered on developing four types of thinking skills. We will now delve more deeply into the role of learning in allowing managers and leaders to explore the question "How do we construct the links between business and sustainability?" In order to do this we will explore how the concept of learning has been used in management theory and practice and will then consider the specific relevance of learning for sustainability. We will identify barriers to learning and enablers of innovative thinking in sustainability, and we will consider different levels of learning that allow us to move from more incremental progress towards more transformational outcomes. We suggest that moving to more sustainable business models requires an approach that embodies *triple-loop learning* (i.e., learning that enables paradigmatic reconstruction and is transformative in nature) in order to optimize value creation for a broader range of organizational stakeholders. We will explore the concept of a triple-loop process and societal learning again in chapter 8 in the "reinventing" section, in order to further understand the capabilities required for the leader to function as a reflective practitioner reconstructing value for the organization.

Transformative Learning and Sustainability: Challenging the Status Quo

Over the years there have been numerous approaches to exploring the phenomenon of learning in management theory and practice. "Organizational learning" generally refers to the literature that seeks to understand the process of learning within organizations and is primarily academic in focus. The earliest work on organizational learning focused on this as a part of a model of decision making within the firm and highlighted the role of rules, procedures, and routines that developed in response to external pressures and that were adopted or not in relation to their impact on positive outcomes for the organization.[2] Academics have described organizational learning as (1) new insights or knowledge; (2) new structures; (3) new systems; and (4) new actions; or (5) a combination of the above. Terminology such as "learning," "adaptation," "change," or "unlearning" have all been employed to explore this phenomenon. Despite the diversity of these approaches, in all of them there is a common assumption that learning will improve an organization's future performance.[3] Another area of interest in management theory and practice is the concept popularized by Peter Senge and colleagues known as *the learning organization*, a term used to describe an organization that has the ability to learn effectively and thus to achieve competitive advantage. While organizational learning is more of a focus for academics, the learning organization is emphasized more among those who have an orientation towards practice. It is engaged in order to improve processes that will enhance the learning capacity of organizations, although both concepts are used to some extent by academics and practitioners. Iterations between experience and reflection form the basis for action learning, one of the central mechanisms of the learning organization.[4]

Levels of Learning

In addition to these general fields of study, the concept of *levels of learning* has been widely employed in management theory and practice in the form of single- and double-loop learning,[5] with little attention paid to triple-loop learning.[6] In business school education there is often an imperative to produce work-ready graduates who have developed a skill set that will allow them to instantly contribute to organizations, which results in more of a focus on *training* than on encouraging learning. When envisioning how learning is typically engaged in business schools, technical and practical ways of knowing predominate but "emancipatory" approaches – or modes of learning that inspire a fundamental shifts in thinking and enable transformational outcomes – are not well supported. If managers and leaders are to develop an ecological understanding of the economy and society as embedded in the environment, it will require a commitment to encouraging reflective practice, both within business schools and within organizations, which will allow for a fundamental shift in how we view the world.[7]

"Weak" vs. "Strong" Sustainability

We consider sustainability as a societal-level ideal that has multiple meanings in different contexts, something we unpack more carefully in chapter 6, and so it is useful to distinguish between economic approaches that represent "weak" sustainability and those that are more consistent with "strong" sustainability. "Weak" sustainability is built on the idea that manufactured capital of equal value can take the place of natural capital (a notion espoused in the domain of "environmental economics"). For example, large-scale farming operations have dramatically increased agricultural output by substituting natural fertilizers and soil-replenishing crop-rotation techniques with mineral- and fossil fuel-based fertilizers on large monoculture farms – replacing natural capital with manufactured substitutes. In contrast, "strong" sustainability proponents would charge that such operations are contributing further to soil-nutrient depletion; that following such a path is a short-term strategy that deepens our dependence on finite resources; and that the existing stock of natural capital must be protected and improved because the functions it serves cannot be substituted by manufactured capital[8] (a view typically associated with the field of "ecological economics").[9] Organizations that pursue a sustainability vision are often criticized for taking an approach that represents "weak" sustainability, focusing on rational and incremental improvements to operations and relying on technological solutions to resolve our most intractable environmental and social problems. While incremental change is an important first step in an organizations' trajectory towards more sustainable outcomes, it can be argued that if these commitments are where the sustainability journey begins and ends it is unlikely that business will play a meaningful role in addressing the complex economic, environmental, and social issues that we are currently facing. Similarly, management and leadership development within undergraduate, graduate, and executive education business programs is increasingly scrutinized for how effective these efforts are at developing future leaders for sustainability. Critiques of business school education addressing issues of sustainability are often directed at the incremental nature of this education and how it operates within the status quo. Approaches to sustainability-focused management education and leadership development that emphasizes training leaders with a "toolkit" to impact sustainability issues in their organizations can be described as weak, with a "bolt on" of sustainability ideas that are characteristic of first order change or learning and are often about cosmetic reform. This is evidenced in the growing number of organizations that consistently produce first rate CSR or sustainability reports that highlight activities such as philanthropic pursuits, conservation efforts, or community involvement – all worthwhile endeavours, but tangential to the core operations of the business. In comparison, strong approaches have a "build in" of sustainability concepts to the existing system that represent second-order change or learning by challenging paradigmatic assumptions to develop more sustainable practices.[10] This can be seen in those organizations that engage sustainability as a strategic framework for rethinking the way that they do business and challenge the very kinds of products they sell or the markets they serve (see Box 3.1).

BOX 3.1

MINI-CASE: SEVENTH GENERATION AND TRANSFORMATIONAL CHANGE[11]

Seventh Generation was established in 1988 in Burlington, Vermont, with the intent of providing household and personal care products that help to protect human health and the environment. The name of the company makes reference to the Native American philosophy that reflects the intergenerational justice imperative found in the Brundtland definition of sustainability: "In our every deliberation we must consider the impact of our decisions on the next seven generations."[12] The mission of the organization extends beyond the incremental change implied by a corporate social responsibility approach focused primarily on risk and reputation management and instead is centered on the more transformational objective of how "to inspire a more conscious and sustainable world by being an authentic force for positive change." In doing this, the organization has engaged a "director of corporate consciousness" and strives to have a real impact, both on its own operations and on its competitors, suppliers, community, and government. The organization takes the attitude that while products may be the vehicle for its message, affecting society more broadly is the mission. Founding CEO Jeffrey Hollender consistently challenged the organization to move beyond the PR aspects of sustainability and instead to think about how sustainability could impact all systems in the organization and guide each decision that was made. The organization challenged the foundations of a consumer model of society by declaring that while it is better to buy recycled over non-recycled, it is even more preferable to buy nothing to begin with, and Hollender advised the public that "the first thing you should do is don't buy things you don't need. Even our products."[13] The organization is committed to five principles of "revolutionary responsibility" that inform its decision making:

- An approach to sustainability that is holistic and systemic.
- An acknowledgment that mission matters and needs to be built into every part of the business.
- A focus on creating meaning at work and striving to unleash people's potential.
- A commitment to radical transparency.
- An attempt to build a corporate consciousness that embeds a sustainability ethos in every part of the organization.[14]

Bateson's three levels of learning and change that correspond to increases in learning capacity[15] are relevant to developing the manager's capabilities in the "rethinking" part of our model. In order to reconstruct our ideas of value, we suggest that organizations need to build on all three levels of learning in order to develop reflective practitioners who can work to transform organizations and society.

The Importance of Multiple Levels of Learning in Sustainability

First-order learning is focused on the transmission of information and development of the instrumental skills required to meet the current perceived needs of the economy. This can be thought of as single-loop learning that focuses on incremental improvements within the existing rules of the game, or getting more efficient at what we are currently doing. As we discussed in chapter 2, enhancing efficiency is the predominant objective in many organizations and so, in organizations that are committed to improving, single-loop learning is often the most visible activity. Improving energy efficiency in a carpet factory through better heat management and air conditioning systems might be a typical activity in this realm. Second-order learning and change is less commonly found in management practice as it is directed towards stepping outside the usual frame of reference in order to change the system itself, something referred to as double-loop learning. This might include converting a product to a service, such as InterfaceFLOR is committed to doing in its desire to stop selling carpets and instead sell the service of covered floors through carpet leasing and maintenance arrangements.

Our model of reconstructing value is built on an approach of reflective practice that allows managers to develop the capabilities they need to challenge underlying assumptions that lead to our current actions and behaviors; by doing so, they help their organizations become more effective. In order to truly reconstruct value and develop the sustainable organization, we need to move to third-order learning that enables paradigmatic reconstruction and is transformative in nature,[16] which is also described as triple-loop learning. In this mode we might pose the question "Who needs floor coverings, and what would we sell if the world stopped buying them?" An embedded view of management theory and practice requires a transformative approach to learning where we can challenge underlying assumptions about the relationship between business, nature, and society and reconsider the context within which strategic business decisions are made. Thinking back to our discussion in chapter 1 of how managers have mental maps that they are not aware of but that guide how they plan, implement, and review their actions in various situations, we will now consider more fully how each of these levels of learning helps to reinforce or challenge mental models. In doing so, we will examine their relevance to leadership for sustainability and suggest how organizations might work to incorporate each of them into their management processes.

Incremental (Single-Loop) Learning

Single-loop learning is focused on improving work processes without examining or challenging underlying assumptions. In many organizations, single-loop learning dominates. This first-order approach involves change within the current rules of the game and so encounters the least resistance among organizational members. Strategies are formulated and put into practice, outcomes are assessed, and new strategies are adopted. Within a green marketing framework, for example, this type of learning can be observed within a product brand such as Huggies that continues to produce conventional baby products along with a special line of Pure & Natural diapers that are more environmentally enlightened. Diapers in this product category include features such as organic cotton, a liner that uses renewable materials, and "adorable graphics" with fewer inks. While this product line appears to advance at least incremental change towards sustainability, approaches such as this tread a very fine line between enhanced eco-efficiency and "greenwashing," something Jeffrey Hollender referred to in the quotation at the outset of the chapter. Thus, the claims they are making and the evidence they are providing to support their assertions must be carefully evaluated. Arguably, there is some progress that has been made here by this organization in trying to create a more environmentally sound product. Smaller, more fuel efficient cars that are then marketed as more "environmentally friendly" also represent this strategy of making existing products greener and then using eco-labeling to sell more of them. Consumers are offered a choice between a more green and a less green product in their product lines and can feel good about reducing their overall environmental and social impact, but the system and the organization offering these choices remains fundamentally unchanged.[17]

A focus on the gains to be earned through single-loop learning can be found at Frito Lay Products where commitments to greening its operations have been made through various eco-efficiency initiatives.[18] The company is focused on continuously improving and finding new and better ways to reduce emissions from its manufacturing plants and its delivery vehicles. From 2006 to 2007, changes at its facilities and in its fleet lowered their CO2 emissions by 96 million pounds. Since 1993, at each factory there has been a Green Team established to identify opportunities to further reduce environmental impact. In 1999 the organization established "Big Hairy Audacious Goals" for resource conservation over a ten-year period that included a 50 per cent reduction in water consumption, a 30 per cent reduction in natural gas, and a 25 per cent reduction in electricity usage. The organization has also developed numerous innovations in packaging over the last decade, all of which has been made possible by a strong focus on single-loop learning that allows the company to save money, have a lower environmental impact, and improve its reputation and legitimacy with stakeholders in the process. In organizations that use this as their dominant approach to learning, there is no challenging of the thinking that led to the current strategies but rather a focus on doing things "right" or getting better at what they currently do. The role of the leader in this style of learning can be thought of as an *auditor*. It is more important to assess how effectively certain goals, values, plans, and rules have been operationalized than to question them.

This type of learning is very important for enhancing eco-efficiency and can make an important contribution to advancing an organization's approach to sustainability, but it is not sufficient on its own to reconstruct value. Box 3.2 provides an example of single-loop learning and eco-efficiency.

BOX 3.2
MINI-CASE: SINGLE-LOOP LEARNING AND ECO-EFFICIENCY AT 3M[19]

3M's Pollution Prevention Pays (3P) program has been in operation since 1975. Over the past four decades, the program has prevented more than 2.9 billion pounds of pollutants from being released into the environment and has saved nearly $1.2 billion through a range of 3P projects. Single-loop learning has enabled a focus on eco-efficiency where the 3P program helps prevent pollution at the source – in both products and manufacturing processes – rather than removing it after it has been created. When 3P was launched in 1975, the concept of applying pollution prevention on a company-wide basis and documenting the results was a breakthrough one for the industry. The 3P program was updated about a decade ago in order to provide more opportunities for participation by the company's research and development, logistics, transportation, and packaging employees with the addition of new award categories and criteria. 3P is a key element of 3M's environmental strategy and a cornerstone of its efforts towards adopting more sustainable business practices. The organization has achieved these gains by taking a proactive approach to prevention, which it believes is more environmentally effective, technically sound, and economical than conventional pollution controls. The focus on single-loop learning within the organization has resulted in an eco-efficiency strategy where, rather than using natural resources, energy, and money to build conventional pollution controls and consuming more resources in operating them for a temporary solution, 3P seeks to eliminate pollution at the source through:

• Product reformulation
• Process modification

- Equipment redesign
- Recycling and reuse of waste materials

The 3P program is based on voluntary participation with 3M employees worldwide and has completed over 7,400 projects to date with several innovative projects being recognized with 3P awards. In order to receive recognition, these projects must eliminate or reduce a pollutant, benefit the environment through reduced energy use or more efficient use of manufacturing materials and resources, and save money. The saving of money can be accomplished through avoidance or deferral of pollution control equipment costs, reduced operating and materials expenses, or increased sales of an existing or new product.

Reframing (Double-Loop) Learning

Double-loop learning involves reshaping underlying patterns of our thinking and behavior. This type of learning requires organizational members to think about whether the "rules of the game" themselves should be challenged and changed. The question asked in this approach is "Are we doing the right things?" which enfolds and goes beyond single-loop learning. In the green marketing example this would translate to creating new products that are more closely aligned with sustainability principles rather than just greening existing products. gDiapers[20] is a company that has worked to rethink both the eco-efficiency and eco-effectiveness of diaper options provided to consumers. The company has developed a hybrid model of diapering that attempts to take the best from both cloth and disposable systems and to ensure that everything that goes into their gRefills is reabsorbed back into the eco-system in a way that is either neutral or beneficial to the environment. By challenging the game of disposable vs. cloth diapers they are able to provide an innovative approach that moves beyond that debate to offer an alternative product and ask the more profound questions of how we support parents in their efforts to use less of it. The organization acknowledges that in an ideal world parents would practise "elimination communication" that would effectively reduce the number of diapers needed for their child, and it argues that its product is a compromise that helps to challenge some of the underlying assumptions about diapering while also providing a more eco-efficient and eco-effective approach. From a green marketing perspective, to contrast with the earlier example, this would mean that there are green objectives to selling the product as well as commercial objectives.[21] It is essential for organizations to engage in double-loop learning in order that managers might be able to make informed decisions under the conditions of complexity and uncertainty that characterize sustainability initiatives. Double-loop learning involves a process of inquiry where the mental models, or the deeply entrenched assumptions, generalizations, pictures, images, or stories that influence how managers see their work and how they choose to take action, are themselves reflected upon and confronted. By unearthing these assumptions and challenging this thinking and behavior, leaders are able to be less defensive, more open, and increasingly self-aware. The role of the leader in this style of learning can be thought of as a *provocateur*. The manager in this style of learning inspires reflection in organizational members by identifying and calling into question existing assumptions about the interrelationships between environment, society, and economy in order to identify synergies where previously there might have been trade-offs, with a goal to developing more efficient *and* effective business models. An example of double-loop learning is outlined in Box 3.3.

BOX 3.3

MINI-CASE: DOUBLE-LOOP LEARNING AND ECO-EFFECTIVENESS AT CARSHARING ASSOCIATION[22]

In 2011, eighteen carsharing organizations from around the world representing approximately 100,000 members founded an association that lays out the ethical, social, and environmental standards for the carsharing industry. The principles of the new CarSharing Association (CSA) focus on environmental and social impact and responsibility, education, research, and ethical practices. The association is committed to reducing the number of cars on the road, relieving congestion, and increasing transportation options. The various carsharing organizations participating in CSA provide members with twenty-four-hour access to a fleet of cars stationed around cities. Carsharing significantly helps to decrease emissions that contribute to air pollution and climate change by helping each member reduce his/her driving by as much as 50 per cent, which means a reduction of 1.2 tonnes of CO_2. Every shared car in use replaces six to eight private cars on the roads. Carsharing organizations are not simply a "cars on demand" service but are also "transit-oriented" in that they encourage carsharing as part of a sustainable transportation network of choices that include walking, cycling, and transit and thus maintain a focus on creating sustainable communities. In challenging the underlying assumption that car ownership is required to get from Point A to B, the CarSharing Association enhances eco-effectiveness by moving away from providing a product that has significant negative impacts on sustainability. Instead, the CSA offers a service that is based on providing transportation options that are more supportive of outcomes such as reduced greenhouse gases, improving urban land use and development, and addressing the social issue of providing access to vehicles when they are required for those individuals who could not otherwise afford it.

Transformational (Triple-Loop) Learning

This approach to learning involves managers shifting the context of their point of view through engaging in a participatory process with multiple stakeholders to ask the question "How do we decide what is right?" Reconsidering the values and principles that guide actions and assessing the whole context or the inter-relationship between problems and solutions and the patterns that have led to the status quo are critical for the creative breakthroughs required to enable global sustainability. This involves questioning "the game" itself in which organizations are engaged;[23] for example, identifying business opportunities through engaging in collaborative and generative dialogue with stakeholders. Carrying forward the green marketing example, this would represent a situation where there are cultural, green, and commercial objectives to selling the product or service. Triple-loop learning supports innovation and helps to reshape culture by "making green seem normal"[24] and, as such, many triple-loop initiatives are entrepreneurial in nature. An example of this can be seen in Kiva Microfunds (Kiva.org),[25] a non-profit organization with a "mission to connect people through lending." Kiva. org works with microfinance institutions in fifty-nine countries across five continents to provide loans to people who cannot secure them through traditional banking systems. Challenging the cultural notion of a gift as an object that is purchased, wrapped, and delivered to someone, Kiva inspires individuals to give microcredit loans to people as gifts or simply to make a loan to help an entrepreneur succeed in their venture. When the loan is repaid, the giver can choose to finish the transaction or to reinvest in another entrepreneur. Since its founding in 2005, the organization has facilitated $307 million in loans with a 98.93 per cent repayment rate to date. The Kiva.org business model can be described as representative of Development 2.0, a conversation that is taking place between ICT technologies and international development.[26] Development 2.0 is the application of Web 2.0 thinking to development studies with principles of facilitating citizen participation and voice, encouraging collaboration, increasing transparency, and enabling relationships towards sustainable, human-centered development,[27] a triple-loop process that leads to transformative outcomes.

Another example of a triple-loop approach can be found in E+CO,[28] a model of clean energy entrepreneurship in developing countries. The organization's philosophy is that "there is a demand for clean and affordable energy in developing countries and this demand can be satisfied by local entrepreneurs." E+CO invests services and capital in small and growing clean energy businesses, an innovative business model to address energy poverty and accelerate green energy adoption for the poor. Launched in 1994, this model of financing local solutions that fit the needs of specific communities was a significant departure from top-down approaches by traditional finance institutions (e.g., the World Bank and the IMF) centered on high visibility, major power plant operations that focused on major cities but not the rural poor. It was also an alternative to rural interventions by civil society groups that offered technical solutions that were most often not economically feasible for communities or financially sustainable.[29] Through the E+CO approach, communities are able to generate combined heat and power options from sustainable sources, thereby increasing energy security and reducing costs for fossil-fuel based alternatives, a transformational outcome around energy production results. The *sustainable local enterprise network* model (SLEN)[30] involves dense networks of for-profit businesses, local communities, not-for-profit organizations, and other actors working together in a self-organized manner in order to create social, ecological, and economic value. Its structure embodies an entrepreneurial approach and a triple-loop participatory ethos that challenges existing business models of producing products and services and leads to innovative outcomes through an engaged and inclusive reconsideration of the interrelationships between complex problems and proposed solutions.

Triple-loop learning depends upon the ability to envision future opportunities through a process of "generative dialogue", building creative potential for what might be possible. In chapter 5 we will consider how creative destruction is enabled through a broader dialogue with a wider range of organizational stakeholders, and in chapter 6 we will explore a process of generative dialogue specifically related to sustainability, which we call "sustainability conversations." The role of the leader in this approach to triple-loop learning can be thought of as a *meaning-maker*.[31] Leaders are identified by the group as those who manage meaning through reframing and structuring organizational members' experiences in an engaging way. From this perspective leadership is an ongoing *social process* defined through the interactions between the leaders and the led. Through their use of words, images, symbolic actions, and gestures, leaders draw attention to different priorities and encourage action in new directions in organizations. Box 3.4 describes an example with potential for triple-loop learning.

BOX 3.4

MINI-CASE: THE POTENTIAL FOR TRIPLE-LOOP LEARNING AND TRANSFORMATION AT MARS[32]

Chocolate manufacturing company Mars has embarked on an initiative focused on improving the lives of more than 500,000 cocoa farmers in Côte d'Ivoire where the organization sources a large volume of its cocoa. While it is yet to be seen what this initiative will substantively accomplish in terms of transforming the kinds of products that the company produces, that is, towards those of greater societal benefit, this multi-sector partnership has the potential to catalyze triple-loop learning and societal transformation on a range of sustainability issues. Mars has been involved over the years with a number of industry efforts in West Africa, including the Sustainable Tree Crops Program and the Bill and Melinda Gates Foundation/World Cocoa Foundation Cocoa Livelihoods Program, but views the signing of a Memorandum of Understanding between Mars and the Côte d'Ivoire Ministry of Agriculture as providing the opportunity for a new and different type of collaboration. Better farming practices and improved plant stocks are being explored with the intent of tripling the yield per hectare, both increasing the income of farmers in the region and enhancing the sustainability of Mars' supply chain. This initiative is called "Farmers First" and is intended as a grass-roots program that will work directly with farmers to address sustainability issues. In order to accomplish this, the company has worked to coordinate effective collaboration between multiple organizations, including the Côte d'Ivoire government, which needs to provide more agricultural extension workers; the World Bank that needs to finance new roads; and bilateral donors, who need to support NGOs in improving health care, nutrition, and education in cocoa-growing communities. In addition to these government and non-governmental organizations, Mars is exploring ways that it can work with its direct competitors on a variety of "pre-competitive" issues in order to extend its reach to farmers outside of its own supply chain. The current ban on exporting cocoa in the Côte d'Ivoire region due to political turmoil has at least temporarily slowed progress on this initiative, but the model is certainly one that has the potential to generate triple-loop outcomes by bringing together a wide range of stakeholders in a collaborative manner and thus challenging the governing values and norms of the cocoa-production industry in this region.

In chapter 8 we will consider the relevance of single-, double-, and triple-loop learning for sustainability in avoiding suboptimal societal outcomes – or the "tragedy of the commons" – and supporting innovation and the development of more sustainable business models.

LEADERSHIP SKILL BUILDING:
Process Questions, Skills, and Skill-Building Exercises

PROCESS QUESTIONS CHAPTER 3: Developing Learning Capacity in Sustainability-Focused Organizations

In order to develop the learning capacity required to reconstruct value, leaders need to engage the following process questions in their day-to-day operations:

1 *Single-Loop Learning* – Are we doing things right? Are we doing things as eco-efficiently and socially responsibly as possible? How effectively have the various goals, values, plans, and rules around the organization's sustainability vision been operationalized? What areas for improvement in the company's internal operations can be identified?

2 *Double-Loop Learning* – Are we doing the right things? Are we doing things as eco-effectively and socially beneficial as possible? How have the mental models or the deeply entrenched assumptions, generalizations, pictures, images, or stories in the organization influenced how people see the situation and how they are choosing to take action? How are these assumptions being reflected on and confronted?

3 *Triple-Loop Learning* – How do we decide what is right? Are we selling products and services that will positively impact societal well-being and that will lead to more sustainable outcomes at the individual, organizational, and societal level? What are the values, principles, and norms that guide the organization's actions? What is the inter-relationship between problems and solutions and patterns that have led to the status quo? How might we interact with stakeholders in a participatory process that will enable transformation to take place?

LEADERSHIP SKILLS CHAPTER 3: Capabilities to Develop Learning Capacity in Sustainability-Focused Organizations

In order to engage in these process questions identified above, leaders need to build the following capabilities at each level of learning:

1 Capabilities for Catalyzing Single-Loop Learning:
   a) developing capacity in quality management and other continuous improvement processes by acknowledging the environment and society as the embedded context of business operations, and thus as drivers for enhanced efficiency in the organization;
   b) focusing on internal systems improvement or increasing efficiency of existing operations;

   c)   the leader functioning as an "auditor," assessing how effectively certain goals, values, plans, and rules have been operationalized within the organization

2 *Capabilities for Catalyzing Double-Loop Learning:*
   a)   developing capacity in reframing and critical thinking by challenging the assumptions of existing business models for providing products and services that are not sustainable;
   b)   re-examining the relationship between the organization and context with an intent to enhance the effectiveness of what is being offered in a way that is consistent with an embedded view of organizations;
   c)   the leader functioning as a "provocateur" by developing a model of shared leadership in which the leader invites participation and inspires reflection in organizational members by identifying and questioning existing assumptions and mental models.

3 *Capabilities for Catalyzing Triple-Loop Learning:*
   a)   developing capacity for collaborating across multiple sectors;
   b)   invoking a participatory process of engaging multiple stakeholders in order to challenge governing norms and values of the company in a way that can enable the transformation of both society and the organization;
   c)   the leader functioning as a "meaning-maker," treating leadership as an ongoing *social process* of interaction between leaders and stakeholders, working to engage stakeholders and reframe experiences and thus draw attention to different priorities and encourage action in new value-creation opportunities for organizations and their stakeholders.

SKILL-BUILDING EXERCISE CHAPTER 3: Learning Team Dialogue: Averting a "Tragedy of the Commons" in the Rapa Nui Role Play

Ronald Wright is a historian, an archaeologist, and a writer who authored the book *A Short History of Progress*. In this book Wright introduces the idea of "progress traps," where human societies pursue the "myth" of progress that is enabled by their inventiveness and then end up creating problems which they cannot solve because they lack the resources or the individual or political will to do so. We will explore this phenomenon of the "tragedy of the commons" and its relevance to societal learning more fully in chapter 8. In his chapter "Fools' Paradise,"[33] Wright offers an interpretation of story Rapa Nui, the place known in the West as Easter Island, in which he describes the collapse of the society on the island as a result of the depletion of resources.[34] In Wright's story, the efforts of the people of Rapa Nui to honor the Moai, giant stone statues that they erected and worshipped, blinded them to the effects on their environment. The decline of natural resources, especially food and wood for fishing boats, led to civil war and the collapse of the society. In this learning team dialogue, consider the role of single-, double-, and triple-loop learning in the situation of the people of Easter Island. In particular, focus on the role of leaders as "auditors," "provocateurs," or "meaning-makers" as this relates to enabling change towards outcomes that destroy or optimize value for stakeholders.

The Scenario

Traveling back to circa 1200 CE, imagine that a senior member of your community has a dream highlighting the problems that he/she foresees on your island. Engage in a discussion with your group members that is a role play of a community meeting of the people of Rapa Nui. Assume this is a culture where all of you are leaders and must engage in dialogue to achieve a consensus on what to do about the situation that the dream seer has identified.

Phase 1: The Leader as "Auditor" (10–15 min)

The discussion in Phase 1 should take an approach of single-loop learning. The dialogue should focus on an incremental change within the current "rules of the game" in order to address the existing problems as identified by the dream seer. The focus should be on how effectively certain goals, values, plans, and rules in the community have been operationalized rather than questioning them.

Phase 2: The Leader as "Provocateur" (10–15 min)

The discussion in Phase 2 should engage a process of double-loop learning. The conversation should focus on whether the "rules of the game" should be challenged and changed to address the existing problems as identified by the dream seer. The focus should be on engaging in a process of inquiry where the mental models or the deeply entrenched assumptions, generalizations, pictures, images, or stories that influence how the people in the community see the situation and how they are choosing to take action, and how they are themselves reflected on and confronted.

Phase 3: The Leader as "Meaning-Maker" (10–15 min)

The discussion in Phase 3 should take an approach of triple-loop learning. The conversation should focus on whether "the game" itself should be challenged to address the existing problems as identified by the dream seer. This involves asking the question "How do we decide what is right?" Community leaders should consider the values and principles that guide actions and assess the whole context, the interrelationship between problems and solutions, and the patterns that have led to the status quo. The focus should be on framing the experience of others in ways that enable actions to occur that are guided by a commonly held view. Through your use of words, images, symbolic actions, and gestures you should draw attention to different priorities and encourage action in different directions.

***Phase 4: Relevance to Your Own Organization* (10–15 min)**
Phase 4 is a debrief of the role play. Consider the insights gained from the role play concepts from chapter 3, and draw on your own organizational experience when engaging in a conversation on this topic in your learning team dialogue. Examine how and why other complex decision-making processes that involve a range of stakeholders in your organizations might also flounder and thus lead to suboptimal outcomes. Be sure to consider how fundamental underlying assumptions might block triple-loop learning within organizations aspiring towards more sustainable business practices. Try to challenge your own underlying assumptions and values when you are interacting with your learning team members and respectfully encourage others to do the same. What would happen to the "dream seer" in most normal organizations? Would she/he be listened to or dismissed for being off message? For this rethinking module ensure that the conversation does not focus on the level of opinions and beliefs – you should not be trying to "prove your point," but rather should be exploring how shifting underlying assumptions might encourage outcomes that create value for a wider range of stakeholders.

Conclusion

In this chapter we have examined ideas of individual and organizational learning and considered the role of leadership within single-, double-, and triple-loop approaches. We have discussed how these different modes of learning lead to different levels of change and how triple-loop learning is essential to optimizing value creation for a wide range of stakeholders. In order to encourage organizations to take a fundamentally creative and innovative path that will generate radically different outcomes enhancing organizational effectiveness, the three modes of learning – single-, double-, and triple-loop – must be engaged. Leaders then must acquire the capabilities required to lead this change and acknowledge that shared leadership and more participatory approaches are essential for success. In the next section we will begin our exploration of the theme of "relating" and consider how different models of change, in particular self-organization and complexity, are helpful in envisioning the role of the leader as a facilitator of decision making with regard to the complex global issues of sustainability.

PART TWO: RELATING

CHAPTER 4

Complex Global Issues as the Context for Value Creation

The twenty-first century will, in fact, be the Age of Nature. We'll learn, probably the hard way, that nature matters: we're not separate from it, we're dependent on it, and when there's trouble in nature, there's trouble in society.

> – Thomas Homer-Dixon, Political Scientist, 2006

Whereas international conflict was until recently governed by political and ideological considerations, the wars of the future will largely be fought over the possession and control of vital economic goods – especially resources needed for the functioning of modern industrial society.

> – Michael Klare, Author of *Resource Wars*, 2001

Humanity is facing a complex set of global challenges that are converging on an unprecedented scope and scale – population growth (with its associated human insecurity, debt, and youth unemployment), growing water scarcity, threats to food security, diminishing fossil derived energy resources, and a changing climate – each of these factors is enormously challenging on its own. Adding to the complexity is the fact that all of these phenomena are not amenable to simple, short-term political solutions. Indeed, they are multi-sectoral (involving governments, business, and civil society), multi-level (local to global), and highly interdependent: more people and more industry require more food and water; global-scale food supply requires massive inputs of fresh water and energy for production, processing, and delivery; burning fossil fuels negatively affects climate; a changing climate is leading to acidification of the oceans and desertification on land, which impairs food and water provision. The connections are deep, circular, and highly complex – we really cannot know if all of the causal linkages and, at the same time, the small changes we do implement will have long-ranging impacts making outcomes more unpredictable as they emerge.

Paradoxically, this complex mix of "wicked" problems also forms the context for new modes of sustainable value creation. The two key questions for managers of organizations are How do we begin to apprehend the major forces at work in the full picture, and How do we formulate strategic intentions towards making things better and not worse while staying in business? It is in the latter domain that ideas for reconstructing value will be born.

In this chapter we explore five major systemic drivers – population growth, water scarcity, food insecurity, energy supply constraints, and climate change – in order to paint a broad picture of some of the "sustainability issues" that will drive business decision making in the future. This overview provides context for our discussion in chapter 5 that focuses on managing for stakeholders and discusses three levels of stakeholder value creation – organizational, value communities, and societal. In that chapter we will consider the complexity of these ideas in order to help us inform our thinking on how practicing managers can navigate these complex global issues.

Given space constraints, in this chapter we will attempt to strike a balance between comprehensiveness and brevity – to give a sense of the scope of the challenges of the issues in just a few pages each, supported by several source notes and ideas for further reading in the appendix. For each we will provide a brief *synopsis* of the major issue, along with some *key challenges and process questions* to guide inquiry and dialogue. In appendix 1 we list some *resources* to begin further investigation on each issue. We conclude by addressing the implications for leadership in a complex world, including the need for managers to understand the underlying systemic drivers and their interdependencies, which we carry forward and expand upon in chapter 5.

Global Issues: Population Growth, Water Scarcity, Food Insecurity, Energy Supply Constraints and Climate Change

Population Synopsis: How Many Are We?

Ask people in your circle of family and friends how many people are on earth and it's likely that most could give an approximately correct answer of "7 billion."[1] Now test their demographic knowledge further by asking some of these questions: When did we hit 7 billion? How many people were on earth in the year 1800? What about 1920? When are we expected to cross 8 billion? What is the projection for 2050? Is the rate of population growth steady, increasing, or declining globally? The answers are, respectively: 2011 (the United Nations estimates say we crossed that mark in October 2011), 1 billion, 2 billion; 2028, 9 billion, and declining – the *rate* of percentage growth peaked in 1963–4 but the overall population is still increasing. While most people have a sense of the current level of global population, many do not see it in the context of the broader picture: that 7 billion people co-habiting earth is a relatively recent event in the history of human experience, and that our numbers are still climbing rapidly. Confronted with the trend line of population growth of the past two centuries, the more curious among your family and friends might form a few questions of their own: How did that happen? What are the underlying causes for the exponential growth of humanity on the planet? Where is growth occurring? Where is total human population going? What are the implications – for today and tomorrow? There are years of estimated data and explanatory theories to answer the first few questions and some educated but uncertain projections to address the latter two. To help us focus our thinking on the implications, let us first look at the overall picture of global population over the course of human history and at some projections for the future. We will then consider some theories on the factors and forces acting as drivers and limits to population growth. Then, finally, we can address the potential implications of how the population picture relates to global issues today and how things might evolve in the future.

Figure 4.1. World Population Growth throughout History

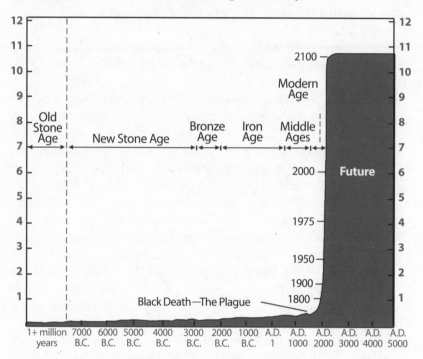

Source: Adapted from J.A. McFalls, "Population: A Lively Introduction," *Population Bulletin* 58(4) (2003): 33.

Human population through history. Figure 4.1 shows world population growth estimates over several millennia, and Figure 4.2 shows the rapidity with which we have added each billion more recently. Historically, human population stayed relatively flat with slow but steady growth over several centuries, which meant that the birth and death rates were roughly equal. Sudden fluctuations were usually attached to some significant event, such as the plagues of the fourteenth and seventeenth centuries. It is generally accepted that growth was kept in check by natural "Malthusian" limits, so named for English political economist Reverend Thomas Robert Malthus, whose influential 1798 book *An Essay on the Principle of Population* advanced the theory that agricultural production was the primary constraint on growth. Malthus identified "preventive" checks (moral restraint, abstinence, delayed marriage)

Figure 4.2. Time to Successive Billions in World Population: 1800–2050

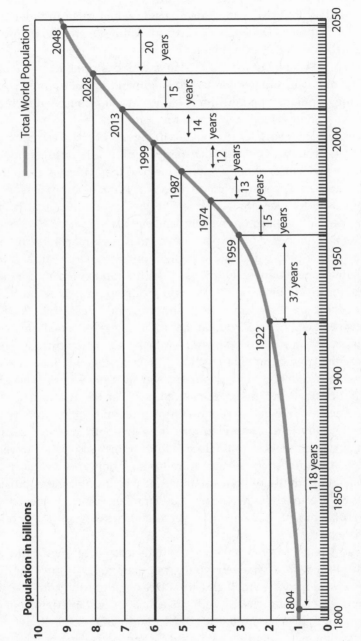

Source: U.S. Census Bureau, *Global Population Profile 2002* (Washington, DC: U.S. Census Bureau, 2004), 11.

and "positive" checks (disease, famine, war) on population growth, and he advocated policy towards managing the former in order to return population to sustainable levels and avoid catastrophe. He did not foresee the major advances in food production that have occurred over the past 200 years, but a "Malthusian crash" has come to take a more general meaning and today refers to an impending collision between a growing population and the limits of the natural resources on which it depends – energy, food, and water, for example.

Demographic transition. The picture in Figure 4.1 changes pretty dramatically around 1750 – so what happened? It is worth considering the basic mechanics of population growth so that we can start to think about causes and potential effects. Levels of human population are determined by two key measures: fertility and mortality – that is, how many people are born on average, and how many die. The "fertility rate" is the number of births per woman; the "birth rate" is the number of births as a proportion of the population in a given year, and both measure the rate of new additions to the human family. To demographers, the crude birth rate (CBR) is typically expressed as births per 1,000 people over a given period, and the crude death rate (CDR) is deaths per 1,000 people. Population grows, logically, when the rate of births exceeds the rate of deaths. Over the past three centuries we have undergone "demographic transition," the term given to the collection of theories explaining how populations grow as societies develop.[2] At its most basic, demographic transition theory states that societies that experience modernization progress from a regime of high fertility and high mortality to a postmodern one in which both are low.[3] Because mortality rates tend to fall before fertility rates as societies develop, there is a natural increase and overall population grows rapidly and exponentially until both rates stabilize, at which point the population levels off at a much higher steady-state number. Figure 4.3 depicts the model of demographic transition over four stages of change in developing societies.

Stage 1 is considered *pre-modern*, characterized by high birth and death rates, with a relatively young population. Birth rates are high since contraceptive technologies are scarce or culturally scorned; child-rearing is relatively cheap, with no education or entertainment expenses, and children are useful to help with subsistence chores such as collecting water and firewood. When grown, offspring provide farm

Figure 4.3. The Classic Stages of Demographic Transition

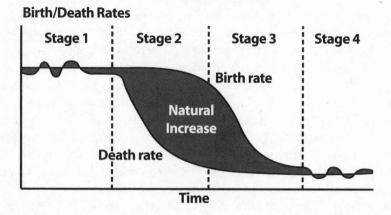

Source: Adapted from J.A. McFalls, "Population: A Lively Introduction," *Population Bulletin* 58(4) (2003): 34.

labor and elder care, particularly sons, as daughters would likely be married off to other families. Mortality rates are also high, including infant and child mortality, due to drought, famine, disease, and other Malthusian "positive checks." Population levels stay relatively flat within the carrying constraints of the environment.

In Stage 2 societies are urbanizing and industrializing, and mortality rates decline rapidly. Better practices in agriculture and food preservation and distribution, cleaner water and waste management, new medicines and education help decrease mortality rates in infants and children, and help to extend life expectancy overall. A decline in birth rates tends to lag behind mortality rates, and so birth rates stay high, leading to a natural increase in population levels. Stage 3 is the mature industrial period, where urbanization, expanded education and roles for women, modern contraception, and an increased relative cost of raising children all contribute to a declining birth rate; rates of population increase begin to decline, and absolute increases in population levels begin to flatten. In Stage 4, both birth and death rates are low and population stabilizes. Some demographers have proposed a fifth stage of population aging and even a sixth of fertility rate rebound when development levels are high.[4]

Factors and projections. This model allows us to consider what factors drove the great global population boom beginning around 1750. In a broad sense, the answer is straightforward: technology, which was driven by abundant, cheap energy. The start of the boom coincides with the onset of the industrial revolution (James Watt improved Thomas Newcomen's steam engine in 1763), and the discovery and exploitation of fossil fuels on a large scale. This led to advances in agriculture, resource extraction (especially coal and iron ore), manufacturing, transportation, medicine, and mass education, with more free time to pursue it. With more abundant food and advanced medicine, mortality rates in the industrializing countries fell into decline, birth rates stayed relatively high into the twentieth century, and the exponential multipliers played out. In effect, we have turned fossil fuels into food and food into people, which accounts for the uncanny similarity between the coal and oil production curves and the population curve from 1750 to today. As fertility rates continue to fall around the world in the coming decades, the population is expected to level out at around 9 billion, with a three-scenario range of 7, 9, or 11 billion, reflecting the real uncertainty over how fertility and mortality rates will actually perform and whether our support systems for food, water, and shelter can sustain 9 billion. Uncertainty is amplified by the fact that fossil fuels play an enormous role in maintaining our support systems, and they are in finite supply. Beyond 2050, estimates vary even more wildly. The UN Population Division projects three possible population scenarios for the year 2300: a low of 2.31 billion, a medium of 8.97 billion, and a high of 36.44 billion.[5] One of these scenarios is probably close to correct!

Fertility rate and mortality rate vary greatly in different regions of the world, and so while the demographic transition model applies globally in aggregate, it also unfolds nationally and regionally at different rates, with a variety of underlying causes driving fertility and mortality.

Varying regional dynamics mean that as we move from 6.8 to 9 billion by 2050, the composition of the global population will look different from today, with much of the growth occurring (as it has over the past century) in less developed regions. Table 4.1 shows the 2050 projections for the major global regions, and Table 4.2 lists the top ten most populous countries from 1950 to 2002 to 2050. More developed regions are expected to grow by approximately 1 per cent (growth in the United

Table 4.1. Projected 2050 Population Size for Major Regions – Three Scenarios

Region/Country	2010 Population (Millions)	2050 Population (Millions)		
		High	Medium	Low
World	6,896	10,614	9,306	8,112
More Developed	1,236	1,478	1,312	1,158
Less Developed	5,660	9,136	7,994	6,954
Africa	1,022	2,470	2,192	1,932
Sub-Saharan Africa	856	2,204	1,960	1,732
Asia	4,164	5,898	5,142	4,458
China	1,341	1,479	1,295	1,130
India	1,225	1,953	1,692	1,457
Japan	127	121	109	96
Latin America/ Caribbean	590	869	751	646
North America	345	501	447	396
Europe	739	814	719	632
Oceania	37	62	55	49

Source: UN Population Division, 2010 Data Projections (http://esa.un.org/unpd/wpp/index. htm).

States will offset decline in Europe and Japan, where fertility rates are already below the replacement rate of 2.1 children per woman), and less developed regions should see a 49 per cent increase over 2004 levels in the medium scenario. According to the U.S. Census Bureau (see Table 4.2), six of the top ten most populous countries in 1950 were more developed countries; by 2050, the United States is expected to be the only more developed country on that list. In other words, practically all future natural population growth will happen in the less developed regions of the world, which will have enormous implications for energy demand, food provision, water scarcity, urbanization, and migration patterns, and place greater demands on the production of consumer goods to support a burgeoning population moving through Stages 2 and 3 of its demographic transition. In cases where consumption is prevented or youth unemployment rises, we can expect more anger and

Table 4.2. The Top Ten Most Populous Countries: 1950, 2002, 2050

Less developed countries will dominate the list of the world's ten most populous countries by 2050		
1950**	**2002**	**2050**
1. China*	1. China*	1. India*
2. India*	2. India*	2. China*
3. United States	3. United States	3. United States
4. Russia	4. Indonesia*	4. Indonesia*
5. Japan	5. Brazil*	5. Nigeria*
6. Indonesia*	6. Pakistan*	6. Bangladesh*
7. Germany	7. Russia	7. Pakistan*
8. Brazil*	8. Bangladesh*	8. Brazil*
9. United Kingdom	9. Nigeria*	9. Congo*
10. Italy	10. Japan	10. Mexico*
11. Bangladesh*	11. Mexico*	14. Russia
13. Pakistan*	13. Germany	16. Japan
15. Nigeria*	21. United Kingdom	24. Germany
16. Mexico*	22. Italy	29. United Kingdom
32. Congo*	23. Congo*	35. Italy

*Less developed countries
**Current boundaries
Source: U.S. Census Bureau, International Programs Center, International Data Base (http://
www.census.gov/population/international/data/idb/informationGateway.php).

frustration from these populations that in turn will place greater pressure on politicians and armed forces to secure resources beyond their
boundaries.

Population: Key Challenges and Process Questions

There is a complex interplay between population and sustainability
issues. Fertility and mortality rates are driven by forces that are cultural, economic, technological, political, and environmental, and the
causal connections are not always clear, and so most of our working assumptions on population dynamics are based on speculative
theories. If our key challenges are to be framed within a sustainability
vision – advancing human development within the carrying capacity
of the biosphere – we would focus on keeping population at sustainable levels (which requires working out what that means), and directing our attention towards building resilience in our life-supporting
systems.

We can think of the complex challenges as opportunities for environmental, societal, and business value creation. The following are fundamental process questions that will need to be considered:

- What standard of living is attainable for a planet of 9 billion, given our natural constraints?
- What goods and services will a population of 9 billion need and which businesses and government agencies will provide them?
- Does equity matter, or do we adopt a more laissez-faire, Darwinian ("survival of the fittest") approach and simply sell products and services to whomever can buy them?
- How will population projections impact demand for energy, food, and water provision? How will this vary by region, and over what time periods?
- How will businesses and industries of the future balance their requirements for energy and water with the competing demands of domestic consumers?
- What social and cultural factors, by region, impact population and therefore market growth?
- What are the implications of an aging population in more developed countries due to declining fertility rates?
- How will consumer credit and household debt constrain or enable market growth in different populations and regions of the world?
- How will youth unemployment and other drivers of human insecurity and tension introduce political risk into markets in the future?
- What will the markets of the future look like, both demographically and geographically?
- What are the implications by region of the resilience of our food system?

See appendix 1 for a starting list of resources for further investigation into these population issues.

Water Synopsis: Water, Water Everywhere?

Water is the stuff of life: it sustains most every living thing on earth, and depending on your age and gender, it comprises 55–80 per cent of your body. Earth's integrated water cycle extends from the depth of the world's oceans to the moisture in our atmosphere, enveloping every lake, river, pond, and puddle in between. The health of our oceans and rivers determines the health of the planet and of the people and industries that depend on them, since the global food chain, the water supplies, and the trading systems are rooted in the water cycle. But the pervasive and essential role of water in supporting our global ecosystems is largely invisible to us – we take it mostly for granted. Our more immediate daily concern is having enough freshwater (i.e., non-salt water) to drink, wash, and grow our food. The surface of our "blue planet" is covered by 70 per cent or close to 1 billion cubic kilometers of water. How could we possibly be worried about a shortage?

In fact, the availability of freshwater is a concern occupying the attention of governments, researchers, and private sector organizations worldwide. Population growth, industrialization, and poor-use practices are leading us towards what has been called a looming crisis in fresh water scarcity. Hunger strikers have gone more than six weeks without food, but if you go five days without water, the fifth could well be your last. Dehydration due to diarrheal disease remains the major killer of children under the age of five worldwide.

Current global shortages. For many people, the water crisis has long arrived, as the distribution of available clean water on the planet is highly uneven. According to UNESCO, a human requires 20 to 50 litres of clean water per day for basic needs, depending on whether we use it for drinking and cooking only or also for basic sanitation – bathing, washing clothes, wastewater disposal, and cleaning households. The average North American uses 575 litres per day; citizens of France and Spain consume around 300 litres; people in the UK and India around 150; the Chinese are at 85; and those in the countries of Bangladesh, Kenya, Cambodia, Ethiopia, Haiti, and Uganda fall below the "water poverty threshold" of 50 liters per day. Those in Mozambique use 5 litres per day.[6] These are averages, so some people use more, some less.

Water can be physically scarce or economically scarce, or some combination of both. Physical scarcity means there just is not much around or that supplies are drying up; economic scarcity means that there is water available, but it is too expensive to access and to process to be fit for human use. Currently, 2.5 billion people, more than 35 per cent of the world's population, do not have improved sanitation (a facility that ensures hygienic separation of human excreta from human contact), and nearly 1 billion people lack access to clean water entirely. Millions of women and girls spend most of their day searching out, queuing for, and carrying large containers of water over several kilometres, often from unclean sources, which means that other opportunities are closed to them.[7] Each year about 3.6 million people, 84 per cent of whom are children in developing countries, die of water-related diseases, and at any given time these patients occupy about half of the world's hospital beds.[8] The Waterkeeper Alliance puts the issue succinctly: without water there is no life, and without clean water there is no healthy life.[9]

Growing shortages in developed countries. Water scarcity is not only a problem for developing countries. Water researcher Sandra Postel writes of the present and growing problem in the relatively water-rich United States, where "we are meeting some of today's food needs with tomorrow's water."[10] Overdraws from river systems mean that the Colorado and Rio Grande Rivers discharge little or no water to the sea for months at a time, and groundwater overpumping has led to historic low levels in the massive Ogallala Aquifer, which lies beneath parts of eight states from northwest Texas up to southern South Dakota, and provides 30 per cent of the groundwater used for irrigation in the country. So while demand is increasing, supplies are diminishing. Climate change, growing population, and an increased demand for food are combining to put pressure on freshwater supplies globally. And in a new twist on the energy–water resource conflicts in North America, novel ways of extracting natural gas through "fracking" of underground rock strata are accused of endangering groundwater resources on a massive scale.

Of the water blanketing the earth, 97 per cent is saltwater and only 3 per cent is freshwater. Two-thirds of the freshwater is held in ice caps and glaciers, with 1 per cent in circulation; one-fifth of that is in remote inaccessible areas, far from human population bases. This leaves us less than 0.1 per cent of the water on earth for human use, and we use it in just about everything we make and do: our current use is distributed roughly as 70 per cent for agriculture, 20 per cent for industry, and 10 per cent for municipalities and other water suppliers. We hear a lot about the "carbon footprint" of our everyday lifestyles and consumer choices, but not as much about the embedded "water footprint" in the things we use. Most people would be surprised to learn that it takes

70 litres (a litre is about a quart) of water to produce an apple, 40 litres for a slice of bread, 150 litres for a pint of beer, and 2,400 litres for a hamburger.[11] Most of the water is consumed in growing the grain and feeding the livestock, and some in processing and transporting the food to our plates. Of the water that enters our homes in North America, roughly one quarter is used to flush toilets, where we routinely use 13 litres (3.4 gallons) of potable water to rinse away 150 ml (5 ounces) of urine. About a third goes to watering lawns.[12]

Water as a business issue. Many large corporations, especially those with a significant water footprint, are acutely aware of water issues and impending challenges. The 2030 Water Resources Group (WRG) is a consortium of food and beverage producers (Coca-Cola, Nestlé S.A., The Barilla Group), big agribusiness firms (New Holland Agriculture, Syngenta AG), brewers (SABMiller plc), and financial institutions, with project management from McKinsey & Company, and advice from recognized experts in water issues, "who are concerned about water scarcity as an increasing business risk, a major economic threat that cannot be ignored, and a global priority that affects human well-being."[13]

The 2009 report *Charting Our Water Future: Economic Frameworks to Inform Decision-Making* from the 2030 WRG offered an assessment of demand and supply of water resources to 2030. The group projects that under an average economic growth scenario, and if no efficiency gains are assumed, global water requirements would grow from 4,500 billion m^3 today to 6,900 billion m^3 (a cubic metre of water is about 264 U.S. gallons), which represents demand growth of 40 per cent over today's available supply (see Figure 4.4). In some basins that supply one-third of the world's population, concentrated in developing countries, the projected deficit is larger than 50 per cent. If supply increases on its normal historical path through infrastructure build-out and the rate of improvement in water productivity remains the same, there is still projected to be a global shortfall of 1,500 billion m^3 to meet the needs of a burgeoning population – demand will outstrip supply by 28 per cent.

Water: Key Challenges and Process Questions

The water crisis is a design problem of enormous and complex proportions, because the macro problem described above is really an aggregation of countless local and regional situations. The challenges are

Figure 4.4. Projected Fresh Water Supply Shortfall, 2030

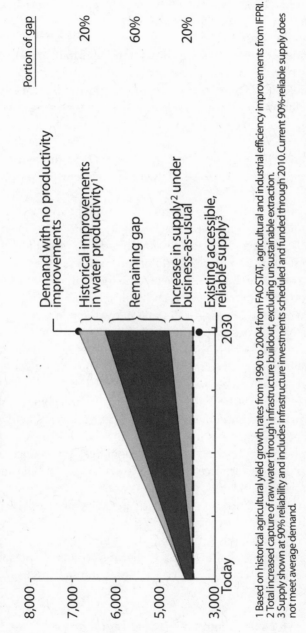

	Portion of gap
Demand with no productivity improvements	
Historical improvements in water productivity[1]	20%
Remaining gap	60%
Increase in supply[2] under business-as-usual	20%
Existing accessible, reliable supply[3]	

1 Based on historical agricultural yield growth rates from 1990 to 2004 from FAOSTAT, agricultural and industrial efficiency improvements from IFPRI.
2 Total increased capture of raw water through infrastructure buildout, excluding unsustainable extraction.
3 Supply shown at 90% reliability and includes infrastructure investments scheduled and funded through 2010. Current 90%-reliable supply does not meet average demand.

Source: Adapted from The 2030 Water Resource Group, *Charting Our Water Future: Economic Frameworks to Inform Decision-making* (2009), 7, exhibit 2; http://www.2030waterresourcesgroup.com/water_full/Charting_Our_Water_Future_Final.pdf

technical, cultural, and sociopolitical: technical in terms of water capture, cleaning, and efficient use; cultural in that we require a shift in awareness, attitudes, and behavior around how we use water; and sociopolitical in the sense that rivers flow and rain falls without concern for the national borders we have drawn, and shortfalls in water will undoubtedly bring potential for conflict.

We can think of the complex challenges as opportunities for environmental, societal, and business value creation. Here is a good starting list of process questions to consider:

- How can technology help to increase supply, productivity, and efficiency of water use to close the projected demand/supply gap?
- How can water-dependent businesses and industries work with governments to ensure areas currently living in "water poverty" can increase access to potable water in order for populations to remain healthy in both rural and urban environments?
- In what ways can businesses overcome the challenge of water transportation, to free women and children from the daily grind of searching and fetching water and allow them to be more economically and socially productive?
- How can businesses work with civil society organizations and their own employees to raise awareness of impending water issues in regions that are relatively water-rich?
- How can businesses work with governments and civil society organizations to implement the right incentives to shift cultural attitudes and behaviors regarding water use?
- How can we identify and address geopolitical governance issues on shared water resources (e.g., the Great Lakes, the Nile and the Euphrates Rivers)?
- How can we balance public and private investment and management of water resources?
- How can we make clear the connections among water, energy, food, and climate change, in particular the economic and social threats if we fail to make the connections, and the opportunities if we do?

See appendix 1 for a list of additional resources for further investigation into these water issues.

Food Synopsis: Is There Anything to Eat?

Feast and famine have coexisted simultaneously on earth for countless millennia, and still do today, but with two modern twists. Never have the numbers of those in surfeit and those in deprivation been so many, and never has the global food system that keeps the fortunate ones fed been so integrated, so interdependent, and so vulnerable to shocks – due mainly to heavy reliance on fossil fuels and global supply chains for its ongoing maintenance.

The UN's Food and Agriculture Organization (FAO) estimates that in 2010 there were 925 million people who were chronically hungry – those considered undernourished, meaning they lacked secure access to the minimum caloric intake (1,800 kcal energy intake per day on average) to maintain minimum attained body weight and a moderately active life. While that figure is down from the peak in 2009 of over 1 billion, it is higher than the historical average since 1970, and about 150 million people higher than the low in 1995–7 (see Figure 4.5).[14] As world agriculture commodity prices have doubled since 2002 (Figure 4.6), hunger has risen in step. The dramatic rise in 2009 was a lag effect of the global food price spike in 2007–8,[15] and the vast majority of those undernourished were in developing countries (Figure 4.7). Twenty-two countries are considered to be in protracted crises, leading to chronic hunger among 166 million people. Recurrent natural disasters, long-term conflict, and weak governance all contribute to an ongoing state of food insecurity, as do unsustainable livelihood systems impaired by institutional breakdown or poor environmental conditions.

Stuffed – at a cost. At the other end of the scale, there are roughly 1 billion obese people in the world, largely in developed countries.[16] Somewhat counter-intuitively, many of the obese are also poor, relative to their developed country context; obesity levels derive from diminished nutrient value in the cheaply produced processed foods that are most affordable and the rise of chemically derived substitutions. Civil society activism is growing in developed countries to raise awareness of the system of food production and distribution.[17] Plentiful cheap food has come at a cost: a much-reduced nutrient value due to large-scale monoculture and a surge in the use of artificial fertilizers; vulnerability to disease and contamination; degradation of land and rivers from waste run-off from factory farmed livestock; and the ubiquitous presence of corn, in the form of high-fructose corn syrup, in everything from meat

Figure 4.5. Global Hunger

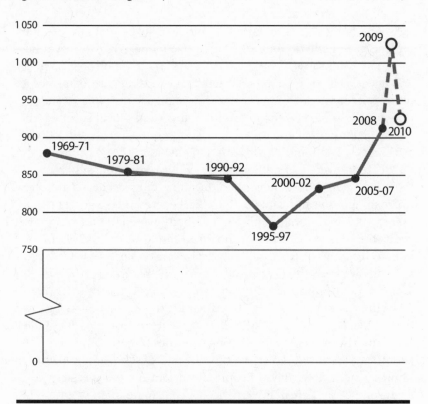

Note: Figures for 2009 and 2010 are estimated by FAO with input from the United States Department of Agriculture, Economic Research Service. Full details of the methodology are provided in the technical background notes (available at www.fao.org/publication/sofi/en/).

Source: Adapted from "Number of Undernourished People in the World, 1969–71 to 2010," in Food and Agriculture Organization of the United Nations, *The State of Food Insecurity in the World* (Rome: FAOUN, 2010), 9.

to milk to Coke to ketchup to peanut butter. Along with claims of its contribution to obesity and poor health, a primary critique of the modern food production system is that it is unsustainable: peak oil, peak soil, peak phosphorous from artificial fertilization, and diminishing freshwater resources are all looming threats to ongoing food security in

Figure 4.6. Global Food Price Index

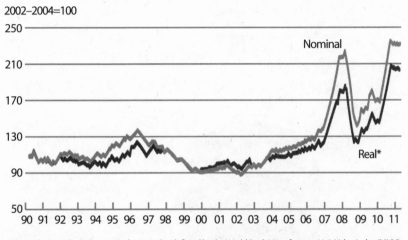

2002–2004=100

*The real price index is the nominal price index deflated by the World Bank Manufactures Unit Value Index (MUV).

Source: Adapted from "FAO Food Price Index 1990–2011," in Food and Agriculture Organization of the United Nations, *Food Prices: From Crisis to Stability* (Rome: FAOUN, 2011), 6.

the developed world. The UK's scientific academy, The Royal Society, says of the future of food:

> Food security is an urgent challenge. It is a global problem that is set to worsen with current trends of population, consumption, climate change and resource scarcity. The last 50 years have seen remarkable growth in global agricultural production, but the impact on the environment has been unsustainable. The benefits of this green revolution have also been distributed unevenly; growth in Asia and America has not been matched in Africa. Science can potentially continue to provide dramatic improvements to crop production, but it must do so sustainably.[18]

Global food security 2050. Science journalist Julian Cribb highlights the complexity of the food challenge in his comprehensive examination of the global food system.[19] He draws on the lessons of past famines, most recently the widespread commodity boom and spike in global food prices in 2007–8, and points to the futility of searching for a

Figure 4.7. Undernourishment in 2010, by Region (millions)

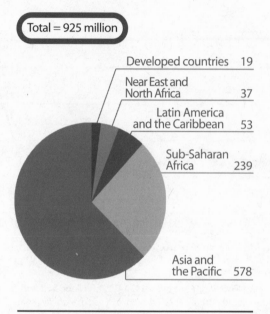

Total = 925 million

Developed countries   19

Near East and
North Africa   37

Latin America
and the Caribbean   53

Sub-Saharan
Africa   239

Asia and
the Pacific   578

Note: All figures are rounded.

Source: Adapted from "Undernourishment in 2010, by Region," in Food and Agriculture
Organization of the United Nations, *The State of Food Insecurity in the World* (Rome: FAOUN,
2010), 10.

single cause or solution. Various commentators have blamed speculators (investment money fleeing from the unfolding credit crisis), soar-
ing energy prices, ineffective or protectionist governments, growing
population numbers, climate-related weather events, and the shift to
biofuel technologies for the crisis of 2008. Cribb contends that none of
those was the single trigger, but together they combined to produce
emergent outcomes that left millions hungry in a crisis that material-
ized in a matter of weeks and days. Because the global food system
is so deeply integrated, with a myriad of interdependencies that are
often invisible until something goes wrong, it is impossible to devise
simple policy levers to fix the problem. The drivers of such crises are
only growing in strength and interdependence, converging towards a

deep and protracted global food shortage around the midpoint of this century that will exhibit similar complexity:

> The coming famine is also complex, because it is driven not by one or two, or even a half dozen, factors but rather by the confluence of many large and profoundly intractable causes that tend to amplify one another. This means that it cannot easily be remedied by "silver bullets" in the form of technology, subsidies, or single-country policy changes, because of the synergetic character of the things that power it.[20]

Box 4.1 outlines the key drivers in Cribb's analysis on the demand and supply sides. World demand for food calories is expected to be 70–100 per cent higher than today, driven by population growth and changing diets. Serious supply constraints will make it exceedingly difficult to meet that demand. Scarcer freshwater and fertile land, nutrient loss, diminishing stock of mineral fertilizer, especially phosphorous,[21] escalating fuel costs, acidifying oceans, spreading drought from a changing climate, and international governance and policy conflicts are all modern Malthusian checks limiting our capacity to feed the future.

BOX 4.1
SUPPLY AND DEMAND DRIVERS OF "THE COMING FAMINE"

Demand side drivers:

Population. The present upward trend of 1.5 per cent (100 million more people) per year means about 3 billion more than in 2000. Most of this expansion will take place in poorer countries and in tropical/ subtropical regions.

Consumer demand. As people rise out of poverty the strive to improve their diet, seeking more protein foods such as meat, milk, fish, and eggs – demand for these is rising rapidly in India, China, Southeast Asia, and Latin America, which requires vastly more grain to feed the animals.

Population *and* demand. This combination of population growth with expansion in consumer demand indicates a global requirement for food by 2050 that will be around 70–100 per cent larger than it is today.

Supply side constraints:

Water crisis. Farmers presently use about 70 per cent of the world's readily available freshwater to grow food. Growing megacities (with 30+ million people) are competing with farmers for this finite resource. Farmers will have about half of the world's currently available freshwater with which to grow twice the food.

Land scarcity. A quarter of all land is now so degraded that it is scarcely capable of yielding food. Cities are sprawling, smothering the world's most fertile soil in concrete and asphalt. A third category of land is poisoned by toxic industrial pollution.

Nutrient losses. Annual losses in soil erosion alone probably exceed all the nutrients applied as fertilizer worldwide. The world's finite nutrient supplies may already have peaked. In most societies, up to half the food produced is trashed or lost; so too are most of the nutrients in urban waste streams.

Energy dilemma. Advanced farming depends entirely on fossil fuels, which are likely to become very scarce and costly within a generation.

Oceans. Marine scientists have warned that ocean fish catches could collapse by the 2040s due to overexploitation of wild stocks. Coral reefs – whose fish help feed about 500 million people – face decimation as the climate warms and oceans acidify.

Technology. Investment in technology has declined, leading to reduced productivity gains.

Climate. The climate is changing: up to half the planet may face regular drought by the end of the century. Storms, floods, droughts, and sea-level rise are predicted to become more frequent and intense, impacting food security, refugee waves, and conflict.

Economics, politics, and trade. Trade barriers and farm subsidies distort world markets, sending the wrong price signals to farmers and discouraging investment in agriculture and its science. The globalization of food has helped drive down prices received by farmers, and speculators have destabilized commodity markets, impacting farmers' production decisions.

Source: Adapted from J. Cribb, The Coming Famine: The Global Food Crisis, and What We Can Do to Avoid It (Berkeley: University of California Press, 2010), 10–12.

Food: Key Challenges and Process Questions

Addressing global food challenges requires a collective, planned approach with a holistic view. Focusing on one challenge and neglecting others leads to cross-purpose, self-defeating solutions (e.g., desalinating sea water with high intensity fossil fuel inputs to use for agriculture). We can begin to frame our questions using the supply and demand drivers from Box 4.1:

- How can business work with governments and civil society organizations to help connect population policy to food policy?
- What are the elements of a healthy global diet, and how can businesses work with other actors to begin to influence the requisite cultural norms to lead in that direction?
- How can global agribusinesses reinvent their value creation models to more explicitly address the challenges and opportunities represented by the need to feed a world of 9 billion people?
- How can businesses contribute to dramatically reducing the energy intensity and carbon footprint of our food production and transportation systems?
- What *sustainable* and *societally acceptable* business opportunities lie in novel areas such as nutrient recycling, salt water irrigation, biofuels, and genetic modification?
- What sort of societal discourses would be required at international, regional, and national levels to allow for novel solutions to the food crisis to emerge?

See appendix 1 for a starting list of resources for further investigation into these food issues.

Energy and Climate Synopsis: Powering the Future within Climatic Bounds

The last two major global issues we will describe are energy and climate change and they are inextricably linked. By energy we mean the various ways in which we power our world – our transportation, illumination, manufacture, agriculture, heating and cooling, and generally operating the big machines and small gadgets that make our world run. By climate, we refer to the chemistry and temperature of the atmosphere, as the operating sink for much human, oceanic, and geological activity. We could examine each issue separately, but energy supply and use is a significant climate issue, and vice versa. We cannot fully consider energy challenges and proposed solutions without also factoring in the impact of those actions on climate change and the impact of the changing climate on our energy policies for the future. Energy and climate have always set the conditions for human and industrial development, and our deep dependence on both means that changes will fundamentally shape our operating context going forward.

The twin issues of energy and climate are each vast in scope, and so for this brief synopsis we can only sketch the major contours of the problems and challenges. We will first take the issue of declining energy stores – is there a problem, and if so, how deep and how soon? Then we will outline the key parameters in the climate challenge: what is the scope, and what are the implications? Following a discussion of the climate parameters, we will briefly sketch the connections between energy and climate, and will then consider some key questions and challenges for businesses.

Are we running out of oil? In 2008, our global energy supply had the following mix of fuels: 34 per cent liquids (oil, natural gas-to-liquids, coal-to-liquids, and biofuels); 28 per cent coal; 23 per cent natural gas; 10 per cent renewables; and 5 per cent nuclear.[22] The last four are largely used to generate electricity, and the liquids mainly drive transportation. Diminishing oil supplies would seriously affect our ability to move things – food, goods, and people – around the planet as cheaply and efficiently as we do today. "Peak oil" is often called a "theory" or "thesis" based on the work of former Shell geologist M. King Hubbert,[23] but there is broad consensus that supplies of conventional oil (i.e., light sweet crude that is tapped from underground stores) are peaking and set to decline over the next several decades. Peak oil is not the point where we run out of oil. It is the point at which the daily supply of oil begins to fall while demand continues its steady rise, and a gap grows between the two, leading to shortages and upward price pressure. Common sense tells us that would happen at some point – oil is a finite resource – and so the question is: When? In 1956 Hubbert calculated the production curve for a finite resource and applied the formula to U.S. oil production. He presented his findings to the American Petroleum

Institute in 1956 and, amid some controversy, predicted that U.S. production would peak between 1965 and 1971. It peaked in 1970, and has declined steadily since (see Figure 4.8 for Hubbert's U.S. curve).

Others have applied Hubbert's curve to global oil production,[24] and have placed the predicted peak sometime between 2000 and 2015, typically about 2007. Estimates from the International Energy Agency (IEA), the energy research arm of the Organization for Economic Cooperation and Development (OECD, or "the G28" of developed countries), appear to bear that out. The IEA's 2010 World Energy Outlook[25] (see Figure 4.9) placed the peak of production from currently producing fields in 2008 at about 62 million barrels per day (mb/d), with a fairly steep decline to 2035 to less than 20 mb/d. We currently burn about 82 million barrels of liquid fuels each day, and other sources fill that gap, mainly liquefied natural gas and "unconventional oil" from heavy oil feedstock, oil sands, and oil shale. In the future, drilling for oil in the Arctic will be another "frontier" resource, but it will not be without significant ecological risks. So, we can predict that more production is expected to come online from fields found but not yet developed, and also from fields not yet found, to hold conventional crude production constant at about 60 mb/d (considering that it normally takes a decade or more for newly discovered fields to start producing crude, we could question the geometry of the curve and the assumptions underpinning it).

The IEA is not a fringe "peak oil" alarmist group; to the contrary, the IEA has been accused in the past of painting a too-optimistic picture, and in 2009 *The Guardian* reported a whistleblower story of IEA staff who claimed they were pressured to do so by the U.S. government, so as not to destabilize world markets.[26] According to the IEA's 2010 forecast (see Figure 4.9), total equivalent energy production is expected to reach 96 mb/d by 2035. The Energy Information Agency (EIA) of the U.S. Department of Energy forecasts demand for such liquid fuels in 2035 of 112.2 mb/d – a daily difference of 16 million barrels from the IEA forecast – and expects production to ramp up smoothly to meet that demand. Geoscientist David Hughes, who spent thirty-two years assessing resources and reserves with the Geological Survey of Canada, asserts that both the IEA and the EIA

invariably paint a view of the future that is barely distinguishable from the past ... because consumption growth trends from the past are projected

Figure 4.8. Hubbert's Curve: United States Oil Production: Forecast at 1956

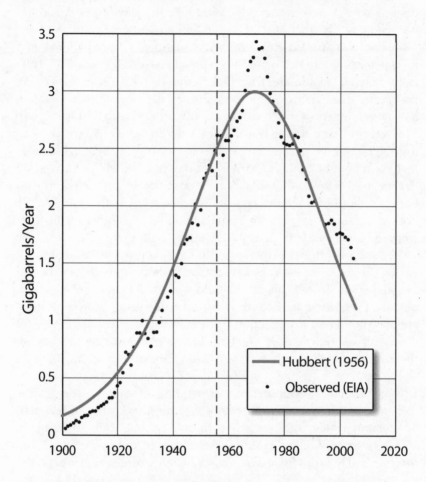

into the future – and it is *assumed* that energy supplies will be available to fill in the gap under the demand projections. The concept that non-renewable resources are finite at some level and that *rates of supply* are approaching their maximum for geological and geopolitical, not economic, reasons does not factor into their analysis.[27]

There is general agreement between energy policy and advocacy groups and official public sources that we are around the midpoint of

Figure 4.9. Liquid Fuels Production Projection

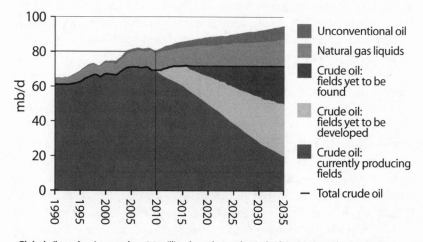

Global oil production reaches 96 million barrels per day (mb/d) in 2035 on the back of rising output of natural gas, liquids, and unconventional oil, as crude oil production plateaus.

Source: Adapted from International Energy Agency, *World Energy Outlook 2010* (Paris: IEA, 2010), 122, fig. 3.19.

conventional oil production – the easily recoverable resources – and that our supply going forward will be supplemented by more and more of the hard-to-recover resources: unconventional oil, liquefied gas and coal, and also conventional oil in places more difficult to access, such as the Arctic. These resources are generally more expensive and have a greater carbon emission footprint than conventional oil in their extraction and processing. Before we think about the interplay between energy and climate, let's look at a few basic facts and ideas surrounding the climate change issue.

Climate: Changes and impending impacts. On climate, we take two points as scientifically established beyond reasonable dispute, despite an ongoing, largely manufactured "debate" on climate change: first, that the climate is changing and the global atmosphere is warming beyond the normal fluctuations of historical record; and, second, that human activity is a chief cause of this anomaly.[28] Two further points are more uncertain: the scope and timescale of the impacts, and whether it will be all bad for all people. These are more matters of informed speculation, but there is a high degree of consensus on the speculation, and most of it is not good. The Stern Review of 2006, commissioned by the British government and led by Sir Nicholas Stern, professor at the London School of Economics and former chief economist of the World Bank, concluded that inaction on climate change mitigation could cost up to 20 per cent of global GDP by mid-century.

The climate problem is mainly focused on the increasing levels of greenhouse gases (GHGs) in our atmosphere, such as carbon dioxide (CO_2), ozone, methane, nitrous oxide, human-made gases such as CFCs (chlorofluorocarbons), and the correlation of GHGs to global surface temperature (CO_2 is the most prevalent, but methane has the greater warming effect). The Intergovernmental Panel on Climate Change, a global consortium of about 2,000 climate scientists, issues a study every six years to track climate developments and make policy recommendations.[29] The science is subject to extensive peer review and consultation and while the policy recommendations are directed by the science, they are also subject to global political influences, so the statements that are issued are sometimes presented more conservatively than the science might warrant.[30] Among the conclusions of one IPCC working group in 2007 was that "most of the observed increase in globally average [surface] temperatures since the mid-20th century is very likely due to the observed increase in anthropogenic [human made] greenhouse gas concentrations."[31]

The key figures around which there is broad scientific consensus (along with much educated guesswork and some range of uncertainty) are 350, 450, and 2. A global concentration of CO_2 of 350 parts-per-million is regarded as the "safe zone," the level at which earth's ecosystems can sustain a relative balance.[32] By 2011, global CO_2 levels were at 389 ppm. A level of 450 ppm is seen as the tipping point into the "danger zone." It is predicted that 450 ppm will lead to a global temperature rise of two degrees, at which point other positive feedback loops are expected to kick in, such as the melting of the peat fields of Siberia, which contain vast amounts of frozen methane. This scenario is often called "runaway climate change," since at that point we will have lost control of the emissions source. A level of 560 ppm, double the mid-nineteenth century preindustrial level of 280 ppm, is likely to lead to a temperature increase of between 2°C and 4.5°C.[33] A joint report by the U.S. Center for Security and International Studies and the Center for a New American Security presented three scenarios – expected, severe, and catastrophic climate change – each deemed "plausible" given certain event trajectories. The "expected" scenario has a temperature change of 1.2°C by 2040, "severe" has a gain of 2.6°C by 2040, and "catastrophic" is 5.6°C by 2100, and each scenario contained a description of potential international impacts and security risks, including a rise in the sea level of 0.23, 0.52, and 2.00 metres, respectively.[34] What is the potential for such an increase? Figure 4.10 shows a sketch from the non-governmental organization Climate Interactive,[35] which charts the progress of CO_2 emissions proposals against the low-emissions path goals and against the "business as usual" scenario. The low-emission path goal is 450 ppm with an estimated associated temperature rise of 2°C by the year 2100; confirmed proposals to date put us on track for 885 ppm and a temperature rise between 4.5°C and 8°C; and business as usual leads us to 975 ppm and a temperature rise between 5°C and 8.9°C.

Energy and climate. In dialogue with those concerned about the future of energy and climate (setting aside those who deny either is a problem), there are a few major lines of thinking, not all of them in agreement. A conversation might go something like this:

"Oil supplies are peaking and beginning to diminish; we are running out of oil, and since our society is so integrally dependent on cheap energy supplied by oil, life as we know it will change dramatically over the next few decades."[36]

"Yes, production of conventional oil may be at peak and on a downward path, but we are not running out of fossil fuels; there are vast reserves (i.e., stuff we can get to now, with current technology) and even more vast further resources (i.e., material that is in the ground but currently out of reach until technology improves) of other fossil fuels such as coal and natural gas. These can be converted to synthetic fuels and serve as gasoline, or converted to electricity. We also have unconventional oil sources such as bitumen in the oil sands, heavy oil in Venezuela, and oil shale."[37]

"But much of the potential fuel to be derived from those unconventional sources is much more expensive than what we are used to; the EROI (energy return on investment) of a gusher near the surface is about 100:1, meaning we get the equivalent energy of 100 barrels of oil out for every barrel we expend to get it. The EROI of oil sands is 5:1 – it is much more

Figure 4.10. CO_2 Concentrations by 2100

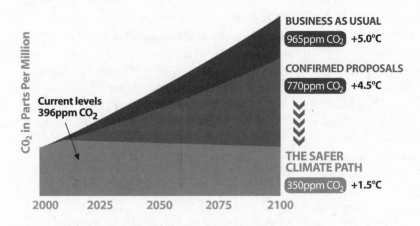

Source: Adapted from 350.org using more recent data from climateinteractive.org

expensive to access and process. Some of the unconventional hydrocarbons will never be burned, because it is uneconomical to do so: even if technology improves and we can get to it, the EROI is below 1:1, meaning that we have to expend more energy to locate, extract, and process the resource than it gives us back. It is not really a matter of resources, but of the rate of delivered supply – how fast we can get it out of the ground – to meet the expected 50 per cent growth in demand in the next two decades. So we will be confronting an energy shortage, or at the very least, escalating prices for energy from alternate sources."[38]

"Market forces will bring alternative fossil fuels online at rates that will not dramatically affect our lives. It's true that energy security is a major concern, but the real threat is climate change. Our agricultural support systems have evolved over several millennia, and will not be able to adapt to a climate that is on track to change four times more in the next 100 years than it did in the last 1,000. Not to mention the effect on coastal regions of rising sea levels, and the millions of climate refugees that would create. Our efforts to renew our energy system should be driven by a focus on drastically reducing carbon emissions to mitigate climate change."[39]

"We simply cannot sustain the energy consumption patterns of a 'Western' lifestyle even in the developed north and west, let alone in the developing east and south. Our world(s) will change from both diminishing energy and a changing climate, and the transition will be more painful and traumatic if we wait to change reactively rather than taking action proactively. We're asleep at the switch."[40]

The texts cited in the endnotes provide rich detail and reams of data to support these assertions. While they differ at points in their analysis and policy recommendations, what they all have in common is a focus on the pinch-point between energy and climate and an emphasis on the imperative to provide security in both. These claims vary along a spectrum from technocentric to ecocentric (i.e., from "we need to rely on technology to sustain our development path" to "we are greedy and should be ashamed of the damage we've wrought, and need to make redress to future generations by voluntarily reverting to an earlier stage in human development"). Elements of both are valid. The central challenge in the energy/climate dilemma is the one we outlined in chapter 1: How do we take a sustainability-based approach, where we foreground human social and economic development within the carrying capacity of the biosphere? That would require finding the right combination of energy provision, efficiency, conservation, carbon emission reduction (which might mean total negation), and global lifestyle shift to allow for a reasonable standard of living for all, and to work towards Gladwin and coworkers' sustainable development principles (see chapter 1) of *inclusiveness*, in reference to human development over time and place; *connectivity*, meaning an embrace of ecological, social, and economic interdependence; *equity*, or fairness across generations, within generations, and among species; *prudence*, calling for precautionary care and harm prevention, technologically, scientifically, and politically; and *security*, or safety from chronic threats and protection from systemic failures.

Should we regret the day that oil bubbled up through the ground and became the lifeblood of modern civilization? Not if we value the idea of human development flourishing, and the changes that cheap, portable energy has brought: extended lifespan, warm shelter, extraordinary mobility, clean water, medicine, escape from daily hunger (for about half of us, at least), and freedom to pursue a life of richer meaning. In fact, paleoecologist (or environmental historian)

Curt Stager says that if we had not discovered fossil fuels, our biggest concern would be the next cyclical ice age, and that news reports would be filled with exhortations to take material from the ground and burn it to stave off the next freeze (assuming we had developed energy and technology to create news reports, absent of fossil fuels). While a warming planet will vastly change our living (or dying) conditions, a "full glacial advance is a total wipeout," he writes. "Compare it to what most experts expect modern warming to bring ... and you'll understand why a paleoecologist's panic button might not be so easily pressed."[41] Our challenge now is to extend the human experiment by recognizing the full potential implications of our actions and to find the sustainable synthesis by advancing our goals in recognition of natural limits.

Energy and Climate: Key Challenges and Process Questions

Climate and energy are highly complex and interrelated challenges. Business leaders can meet them by first working to build awareness of the potential impacts and to seek opportunities for making things better and not worse. Here are key process questions for business leaders to consider:

- What are the implications of future energy scenarios for our operations: costs of energy, security and availability of appropriate and reliable energy supplies and competition for energy with other users?
- Where will be the areas of positive opportunity to help meet the challenges in energy generation and distribution?
- What goods and services might we sell more of in the future because they are less energy intensive?
- What goods and services might we sell less of in the future because they are more energy intensive, including in transportation and distribution?
- How can we meaningfully engage with our employees, governments, and the academic and civil society sectors to learn about the energy and climate implications of our business model and to explore new opportunities for value creation?

- How can we optimize our energy security and financial returns from energy efficiency and renewable energy investments to reduce the carbon footprint of our operations to near net zero?
- What opportunities and threats might exist in other industries (e.g., transportation, agriculture, and water) that will be significantly affected by climate change and energy prices, and how will those affect our operations?

Complex Interdependence of Global Issues

We hope that at least two things are clear from these short overviews of some major global issues. First, that each is highly complex on its own – which means more than just "complicated." A complex system is one that has innumerable component parts, all operating with some measure of autonomy while interacting with other autonomous agents – that is, independently and interdependently. For example, think of a beehive, a populist street protest, a mosh pit, or a stock market. There is no central command, and the behavior and outcomes of the system are impossible to predict ahead of time. Second, that each of the issues is deeply connected to all of the others, and solving problems in one area could make another worse; increasing energy production will have positive and negative impacts on the other issues, for example. A third element, which we will explore further in the next chapter, is that attached to each of these issues are multiple players with multiple perspectives on what is important. How can an organizational leader take action in such a tangled, swirling, uncertain environment?

LEADERSHIP SKILL BUILDING:
Process Questions, Skills, and Skill-Building Exercises

LEADERSHIP SKILLS CHAPTER 4: Integrative Thinking and Action

The thirty-two process questions offered in this chapter present significant challenges and potential opportunities for sustainable value creation. Reacting to individual events is likely to invoke simplistic, non-strategic responses that may distract from real solutions or exacerbate the situation. Pouring trillions of dollars of public money into banks did not solve the credit crisis. Investing in carbon capture and storage may simply postpone more fundamental reforms in our profligate use of fossil fuels for power production. Building sea defenses against a modest sea level rise will be a complete waste of time if the polar ice caps slip into the oceans under a runaway climate change scenario. Making sense of observations and responding effectively to the systemic drivers underpinning them invariably requires collaboration with multiple actors, and thus invokes as much humility as it does dynamism. Dramatically reducing domestic debt requires unprecedented civil society, political and business collaboration – particularly from the financial services sector. Reducing the use of coal in power production requires the U.S., Chinese, and Indian governments to all agree this is essential and work with their industrial and domestic electricity users to find cost effective alternatives. Reducing the risk of runaway climate change is likely a more cost effective approach to sea level rise than building ten-metre walls around the world's coastlines. But this will require intelligence from large industrial power users, informed by the insurance and reinsurance industries, coupled with a level of political wisdom and global social engagement that is well within our reach but that we have yet to witness in human history.

Complexity thinking offers insights to help approach these questions. The primary role of the organizational leader is to help embrace the complexity by seeking out and connecting to broad sets of stakeholders, while nurturing innovative capacity in their organizations. In chapter 5, we continue looking at the art of *relating* and outline a skill-building exercise to develop integrative thinking and action.

CHAPTER 5

Managing for Stakeholders in a Complex World

The trouble with our times is that the future isn't what it used to be.
— Paul Valéry, Poet, 1944

The future is already here, it's just not very evenly distributed.
— William Gibson, Science Fiction Writer, 1999

Who Are the Stakeholders in These Complex Global Issues?

In chapter 2 we provided an overview of stakeholder management concepts. Without doubt, some companies have been relatively successful at integrating stakeholder concerns into their businesses – and some have not. In addition to the benefits that accrue from engaged and loyal customer, supplier, and shareholder relationships, leadership research has shown that a stakeholder orientation in CEOs leads to a perception of visionary leadership, resulting in increased effort and engagement from followers and better organizational performance.[1] In the spirit of visionary leadership, here we take the idea of stakeholder management further into the future by applying stakeholder thinking to the kinds of global sustainability issues we discussed in chapter 4.

Stakeholders in an organization are "the groups and individuals who can affect or are affected by the achievement of the organization's goals," and the role of managers is to build relationships with stakeholders such as customers, suppliers, employees, financiers, governments, and communities in order to create mutual value.[2] This is a highly inclusive definition, and one that can apply over a wide variety of geographic, cultural, and time horizons. To connect today's business concerns to tomorrow's challenges, we can think in terms of stakeholders: who are an organization's stakeholders in relation to these complex global sustainability issues? To answer this question we would first need to ask: Will the average business organization affect or will it be affected by these issues going forward? As business organizations are the primary engine for growth and resource consumption, and the effects of diminishing resources, continued environmental impacts, and increasing demands will be keenly felt by them, these issues will need to be included in business planning to avoid potential risks and to optimize value creation. Second, who are the stakeholders in the big sustainability issues? All of human and even non-human life, certainly, to a greater or lesser degree, depending on one's place in the world. It follows, then, that for the average organization, the stakeholders are everybody and everything, and the effects are multiple. How does the average manager begin to apprehend and process that in business terms?

To generate some insight into this practical challenge, we draw connections among concepts from stakeholder theory, the complex global issues outlined in chapter 4, and ideas from complexity thinking. The key point that we will work our way towards in this chapter is this: we can think about stakeholders on various levels of time and distance from the organization, and exploring these levels raises the potential for longer-term sustainable value creation. As leadership thinking moves from concern for stakeholders who are directly connected to the organization in the present, to broader value communities of stakeholder networks (perhaps within cooperative joint ventures, value chains, or "institutional ecosystems" supporting innovation), to society-as-stakeholder in terms of the global sustainability issues such as population, water, food, energy, and climate, the nature of the value proposition changes. And the opportunities to create value on multiple levels (without destroying value on others) increases immensely. We argue that the way to move up the hierarchy of value creation is to shift organizational thinking – through sustainability conversations – into more expansive domains of stakeholder management: from *managing stakeholders*, to *managing for stakeholders*, to *managing for humanity and the global commons*. To describe this process, we begin with a few key concepts from complexity thinking, and then outline how those ideas can help managers think about processes of stakeholder value creation.

Managerial Stories

Throughout our discussion of stakeholders and complexity thinking in this chapter, we intersperse six real stories of practicing managers working in different industrial sectors: oil production, mining, forestry products, the financial industry, home improvement retail, and manufacturing. Each of these people had as part of his or her job the task of implementing sustainability programs or initiatives, which entailed articulating value creation propositions for the organization's stakeholders. See Box 5.1 for the first of these. We offer these as windows into the organizational challenges faced in practice, and we will relate them to the stakeholder value creation framework we present later in this chapter. In chapter 6 we move further into the experience of practicing managers and present our model of conceptions of sustainability based on our in-depth research in this area.

BOX 5.1

NINA'S STORY: A GLOBAL MINING COMPANY WITH CONFLICTED NARRATIVES*

Public commitment to stakeholders

Nina worked for a large mining company whose general message via internal and external publications was that "sustainable development" was strategically very important to the company, its public reputation, and the management of its operational risks. However, it was clear to Nina from her first day on the job that there were many internal tensions around efforts to incorporate sustainability as a core value, still less any strategic intent to transform the organization into a sustainable corporation.

The conflicting priorities, assumptions, and values within the organization created major disconnects within the company and its internal stakeholders, which Nina witnessed firsthand. While many ordinary members of the company held on to traditional mining engineering assumptions, others – including Nina – tried to change how the company built and operated mines to reflect socially and environmentally responsible values. But in Nina's experience, the dominant conversation of senior managers was to seek the highest rate of return with little regard for any sustainability issues; and so the company, its workers, and its leaders appeared to her to be stuck in an identity crisis.

A hollow commitment

Mining the earth's resources is not an especially sustainable activity. A "sustainable mining company" would need to strive to minimize harm to natural and human environments while at the same time maximizing the benefits that the company's activities would contribute to local economies. This was the primary intent of Nina's work at the company. But as Nina soon learned, the company's main goal was actually to maximize profitability and shareholder value. Since the latter far outweighed her organizational mandate, Nina's work was, in her words, "relegated to the metaphorical dark corner of the basement. Our work was not supported, recognized, nor communicated to key people because it was considered, by many managers, to be subversive to the company's real goal – making money. Minimizing harm and maximizing benefits implies a larger upfront cost with stronger, longer-term benefits that managers were seldom willing to contemplate."

Discussions taking place at the senior leadership level did sometimes include social and environmental problems at its operating sites – particularly when they were being highlighted in the media and tracked by environmental and social activist organizations. The company's strategy for managing these problems was usually reactive, for example, using paid media campaigns to limit damage to the company's reputation. Some executives recognized that Nina's colleagues could add value in these circumstances and, perhaps, even help reduce the potential for further problems in the future. Unfortunately, disagreements and tensions due to conflicting priorities at the leadership level resulted in very little mobilization of Nina and her team's expertise to address the reputational challenges. Instead, a consistent lack of support for their work translated into repeated disappointment, which quickly lowered the morale of the team.

Sustainability as a core value

Mixed messages trickling down from the leadership also created confusion and anxiety within the broader employee base. As Nina describes it: "From my team tasked with building corporate strategies for social-environmental sustainability, to the site teams that needed clear leadership on the priorities to guide their decisions in the field, the result was chaos and frustration.

"At this company I learned that instilling sustainable development as a core value cannot be done unless *all* members of the senior leadership team are on board and support the workers who are hired to build and implement the sustainability systems. To say that it was a challenge to do the job I was hired to do is a massive understatement."

Today, Nina consults for companies on a project-by-project basis while keeping arm's length from similar corporate identity crises; close enough for her to observe but far enough to keep from getting entangled. However, she is continuously seeking new understandings of how corporate systems can be made robust enough to operate successfully in a sustainable way and where the sustainability conversations need not be so strikingly divergent.

*This is a true story. The name has been changed and the company is anonymous.

Complexity Thinking: Complex Adaptive Systems and the Difficulty of Social Systems

In chapter 2 we introduced ideas in complexity thinking. Recall that the study of complex systems arose out of recognition that some situations or phenomena are simply too difficult to understand using the linear, scientific management theories of the early 1900s,[3] or the general systems theory of the 1940s, or the cybernetic systems of the 1950s, or even the mapping of dynamic systems in the 1960s. Scientific management breaks problems down into manageable bits, and the sum of the parts are assumed to make up the whole. Think of Henry Ford's automotive production lines, with component tasks analyzed by time and motion studies. Of course, it was this thinking that first informed the birth of management education at the Tuck School of Business at Dartmouth College in Hanover, New Hampshire, with the strong encouragement of Frederick Winslow Taylor, and to which today's degrees in "business administration" owe much of their original philosophical grounding. General systems theory sees systems as self-regulating, seeking order and stability, with boundaries that are open with some regulating boundary – the human body for instance, which takes in and expends energy, yet maintains a relatively constant temperature and internal equilibrium. Cybernetics is the study of "steering" systems, like a thermostat on the wall of your house: there is a target and adjustments are made towards that target (e.g., your heat system comes on) until the target is reached or overshot, and then corrective action in the opposite direction occurs (the heat shuts off and your house cools).

If you have ever participated in a "gap analysis" problem-solving exercise, in which a preset target (e.g., sales) is compared to an actual outcome, and then strategies are developed to close the gap between them, then you have used a cybernetic process. Systems dynamics approaches work to mathematically map the changes in a system using causal loops and stocks and flows, but do not assume the system is settling to equilibrium, it may sustain or break down. All of these theories are still in use in organizations today, and they have entered management education through disciplines such as operations, marketing, and even organizational behavior. But scientists in biology and chemistry recognized that there is another kind of system that none of these theories explains well – a complex adaptive system (CAS).[4]

A complex adaptive system is one with no central command but many associated parts or "agents," each acting according to its own local rules and logic. When the parts interact, the behavior of the whole system evolves and takes shape – a shape that is unpredictable ahead of time. This phenomenon is known as *emergence*. Think of a flock of birds that moves in the shape of a wavelike swell, without collision, though certainly with some kind of collusion regarding direction and apparent group-intention and purpose.[5] No one is in charge, there is no grand plan or prescription for their behavior, but a shape does emerge at the system level: the agents self-organize into patterns that give the overall system its shape and identity. System behavior is defined by the *interactions* between the agents in the system. The agents are independent and interdependent at the same time – free to act on their own, but their actions are influenced by, and in turn influence, the actions of those around them.

BOX 5.2

LOUISA'S STORY: A CONSERVATIVE INTERNATIONAL OIL AND GAS COMPANY TRYING TO "DO THE RIGHT THING"*

Building organizational value by managing stakeholder relationships

Louisa worked for several years in different roles in a major oil company with operations in Europe, North America, and the Middle East. The company had developed a culture of "doing the right thing," which was not well defined, but was an aspiration widely held in the company. Louisa's roles had spanned several corporate services roles, including environment, health, and safety, and she was widely understood to be the sustainability champion within the organization. Unfortunately, for her, the CEO at the time had a somewhat negative view of the term "sustainable development." This was based mostly on his subjective opinion rather than any understanding of what the term really meant, or could mean, to the business. His leadership style was conservative and did not support significant organizational changes. The corporate culture was one of "evolution not revolution."

Nonetheless, Louisa felt that the leadership did have a clear understanding that business could only succeed if stakeholder concerns and interests were addressed. This included not only regulatory approvals but also the realization that the company's "license to operate" depended on being a good neighbour, having a positive reputation, and treating all stakeholders with respect. Therefore, each operational unit and facility did good things with respect to environment, health, and safety. The company also maintained active local and corporate community investment programs.

Connecting with new constituencies brings a shift in perspective: Peer forums and a new operating context

Given this operating context, two things happened that Louisa believed should provide the impetus to take the company to the next level:

- First, a senior environment, health, and safety leader and the head of community investment joined a forum of companies learning from each other about how to drive social responsibility into mainstream business.
- Second, the company made an acquisition that included assets in countries with little or no environmental regulation, and in some cases with poor human rights records. The company knew from the experience of other oil companies that its reputation could be tarnished even by a suspicion that the organization and its investors condoned or benefitted from poor social and environmental practices.

The need to address the risks of operating in these countries, coupled with the desire of a few, highly respected people to find a better way to integrate corporate social responsibility into mainstream business, motivated Louisa and others to develop a roadmap that could be endorsed by the executive team.

Building an integrated approach internally and shifting the conversational themes

The company was participating in external conversations through its membership of various corporate forums. And the company commissioned two benchmarking studies to determine how other companies managed their strategic sustainability approaches. The studies showed Louisa's company that the "leaders" in sustainable development were either companies whose CEO had a strong personal belief in the concept and thus drove the strategy or companies which had had major accidents or other events that had ruined their reputations and so they looked to sustainability as a way to better manage their businesses and improve their standing.

Louisa's company's sustainability strategy was based on business need, risk management, looking for opportunities, including leveraging what they were already doing right, and better supporting business success. One of the interesting things that caught the attention of the senior leaders was how much the company was already doing, albeit in a very inefficient and fragmented fashion, each department doing its own thing, issue by issue.

So Louisa and her team sought approval for a more integrated approach whereby a steering group of senior individuals representing each function and business unit were given responsibility for specific tasks:

- Ensuring the company was moving towards meeting its publically stated sustainable development principles and that it publically reported on progress.
- Agreeing on key priorities for sustainable development for the next three years.
- Aligning and integrating the components of sustainable development while still maintaining individual functional and business unit roles.
- Guiding the design and content of the annual sustainability report and ensuring the function or business unit produced accurate and timely data and information for the report.
- Dealing with difficult and controversial issues as they arose.

This steering team was supported by a senior corporate responsibility manager who was essentially the staff resource and content expert for the team.

Begin in a familiar place and stretch from there

This approach led the company to make great strides in taking the organization to a new level of performance and understanding. There were many benefits from this. In retrospect, Louisa's explained the learning from her experiences as follows:

> Integration of sustainable development into a company will not be successful as an idealistic or moralistic objective, unless perhaps the CEO is the true believer. Instead, it must be based on business need and strategy. There are many intersection points between doing right for society and the environment, and doing right for business. Helping business leaders see those intersection points and taking advantage of them is a good place to start. There are lots of mistakes that other companies have made that also make for good learning points.

* This is a true story. The name has been changed and the company is anonymous.

Much CAS work examines the behavior of a defined system, such as genetic algorithms and evolving computer programs,[6] cells in a Petri dish,[7] or light bulbs strung together in what is called a Boolean network, in which each bulb has local blinking rules that depend on and influence those around them, and the network settles into unprogrammed patterns.[8] Scientists observe the relationships between individual agents and how that relates to system behavior in an effort to learn about the rules of complex systems and the relationship of parts to the whole. In complex systems, the behavior of the whole is more complex than the behavior of the parts. It cannot be "managed" in any conventional sense, due largely to the presence of non-linear effects (i.e., a lot of effort that has little effect – like throwing great sums of money at an illiquid bank or a failing economy and not solving it; or a little cause with great effect – the proverbial butterfly wings that trigger a hurricane).

Clearly, human social systems and organizations qualify as complex systems, and there has been a great deal of work done in trying to transfer the learning from biological systems to social systems. But the transfer is complicated. In many applications of complexity science in management, the "system" is typically assumed to be a group of individuals (groups, teams, or organizations), and individual humans are the agents; or sometimes at a higher level, the organization itself is cast as the agent, and the system is the industry sector or competitive field of other organizations. For social systems, this is problematic at both the system level and the agent level: no amount of systematic "stakeholder mapping" by management consultants can eliminate the uncertainty in human beings and relations between them.

BOX 5.3
ABRAHAM'S STORY: AN ENLIGHTENED NORTH AMERICAN
FINANCIAL SERVICES FIRM*

A mandate to build a coherent approach

Abraham was hired by one of the largest and most powerful financial institutions in the world – a bank with more than 70,000 employees across the globe. He was given considerable freedom to make an internal business case, to involve people across the organization, and to reconstruct the sustainability mandate for the entire institution, a brief which he describes as "a dizzying and exciting task."

Abraham's first priority was to assess the state of play with respect to sustainability and related issues in the bank. While he found evidence of a number of strong initiatives in various parts of the organization, three clear observations emerged: (1) sustainability programs existed mainly to satisfy external regulatory and reputational requirements; (2) internal awareness was low and, consequently, innovation and initiative were limited; and (3) there was little to no strategic or systemic alignment.

So Abraham took a step back to reflect on his role and the bank's expectations of his contribution. He concluded that his personal mission was to "influence capital market decision-making processes and to redirect capital to an economic model that supports sustainable development." But for the bank, the expectations were more modest – to support risk management with respect to financial, brand, and reputational issues. With these different perspectives in mind, he set off to weave personal and organizational agendas together. He undertook numerous consultations both internally and externally and found that there were two sets of opportunities for action. First, he was able to identify the priority issues that needed to be addressed. And, second, he discovered individuals who could help him and his team remove the many roadblocks that had held sustainability back in the organization.

Sustainability as a legitimate conversational theme

Fortunately for Abraham, environmental and social responsibility was an increasingly legitimate conversation within the bank, fostered by the prominence of climate change issues in the media, the success of the Carbon Disclosure Project, and the emergence of international charters such as the Equator Principles for project finance and the UN Principles for Responsible Investment. Increasingly, the bank understood the connection between value creation, brand, and customer attraction and retention. The chief operating officer of the bank was sympathetic to the agenda, and Abraham's line manager saw the opportunity to use sustainability as a platform for considerable advancement. Even the legal department required that all sustainability and social responsibility disclosures be auditable and material. Everything was set fair – Abraham's team developed a strategic framework for sustainability at the bank that raised the level of awareness within the organization to a height never before seen. Numerous ideas and innovations emerged. The bank's competitors and peers were racing to keep up by adopting major policy statements and programs, and Abraham's team was busier than ever.

Challenges in moving beyond risk-management and on to building societal value creation

But this apparent success story has to be tempered by business realism. In retrospect, several years after leaving the organization, Abraham believes that sustainability remains a tangential part of the corporate strategy and mission of the bank. He believes there are two main reasons for this: (1) beyond some immediate cost reduction opportunities, the bank has still not figured out how to realize greater profits from its sustainability initiatives; and (2) to this day, the bank's sustainability programs are still directed primarily at external audiences as part of the brand-value proposition.

Abraham reflects: "Has the bank continued to innovate and prosper, even though it has not fully recognized how to enhance its ability to profit through better decision making with their capital through sustainable development? This is a yes/no question. Will sustainable development ever be truly understood and integrated in to the bank? Only time will tell."

* This is a true story. The name has been changed and the company is anonymous.

The Difficulty of Putting Boundaries on "the System" and "the Agent"

Such mapping is difficult because system-agent descriptions assume the agents are "homogeneous," meaning that all agents are the same and will behave in a similar way in response to a similar set of circumstances – and we know that is not true for people. Individuals are themselves complex and sometimes unpredictable. So, if each person is a bundle of complexity, then the "agent" in a social system must be some subset of a person: a person's thoughts? his or her intentions? his or her actions? And what is the "system": the person, the team, the organization? Are not all organizations open and permeable? Are not the boundaries of "the organization" really just a distinction that we socially and artificially construct? The chief difficulty in applying lessons from complex adaptive systems to a social system is that we really do not know what is the agent and what is the system – both are arbitrarily defined, and so we can draw the boundaries anywhere.

Complex Responsive Processes

Ralph Stacey and colleagues suggest a different approach to applying complexity thinking to human social systems.[9] What drives the behavior and shape of a complex entity is the interactions at a lower level, and the richness of those interactions is driven by "micro-diversity," or the many small differences among the lower-level components. Thus, to assume that all agents are the same is unhelpful and inconsistent with complexity. What matters are the processes of relating, rather than the systems' boundaries. Stacey shifts the focus away from systems thinking (thinking in space and structure) and towards process thinking (thinking in time and interactions). A process perspective of complexity draws attention to the way the sublevel components respond to and influence one another. Rather than looking at complex adaptive systems, Stacey focuses on *complex responsive processes* (CRP) and the ways that such processes create patterns in relationships that define the shape and behavior of the system (however we wish to define it). That makes sense when we think of a stock market, or a flock of starlings: processes of information flow and communication among the components are what makes the higher level entity change and take new forms. Stock prices are unpredictably determined through interactions among countless investors; and the fluidly morphing, often astounding shapes assumed by a flock of starlings are a result of the innumerable communications and responses expressed among the individual birds.

For organizations, a CRP view describes the patterning of relationships among people. We can observe the patterns by examining the things people talk about, and how they construct meaning within the organization. Some beliefs and viewpoints are seen as legitimate (these Stacey calls "dominant" themes), and some are seen as illegitimate or subversive (these are the "shadow" themes – water cooler, hallway talk about what might be wrong within the organization or what could be changed). All of these themes are observable in the ongoing communication in the organization. In *complex responsive processes* thinking, they are the result of the give-and-take of daily conversation. Here "conversation" means all of the ways that people communicate in organizations (e.g., meetings, presentations, lunchroom debates, gossip, rituals, speeches, and hallway chatter, and rules and values expressed in management systems and processes).

BOX 5.4
JIM'S STORY: CLASHING CONCEPTS OF SUSTAINABILITY AT A
FOREST PRODUCTS FIRM*

Jim worked for a major forest products company as vice-president for environment. He had worked for the parent company before joining the subsidiary and came with a clear mandate to help reform and improve environmental practices following a couple of serious incidents that had caused significant corporate concern.

Corporate strategy was overseen by George – a highly intelligent and influential member of the executive team. Someone with a quantitative background and known for his somewhat argumentative approach, George carefully analyzed the strategic initiatives of the company using more or less conventional business techniques.

About two years into Jim's mandate and while he was making solid progress on compliance and environmental management standards, another legal case emerged at one operation that necessitated a wholesale rethinking of corporate policy and practice. At this point George was very positively engaged in the topic of environmental management and liabilities for legal non-compliance.

Definitional wrangling

At the same time "sustainable development" was beginning to enter the wider corporate lexicon as a strategic opportunity – especially for resource-based industries like forest products. So Jim began to insert the concept into the work of repositioning the company. Unfortunately, at this point, he met considerable and specific resistance from George to the phrase "sustainable development." George's position was that the concept was "oxymoronic" and that development for an ever-growing population bent on living ever-more comfortably could not possibly be sustained.

The conceptual debate significantly affected the framing of the proposed draft environmental policy. Notwithstanding the general move of the forestry industry to embrace the societal ideal of sustainability, George vetoed the inclusion of the term "sustainable development" until it was insisted upon by one board member. Other executives watched this debate play out but took a passive stance.

At one point in the conversation, the three pillars of sustainable development were under discussion. There was no management resistance to improving environmental performance as a means of improving compliance and reducing risk; indeed, industry leadership initiatives were supported. Similarly, there was no reluctance to ensure economic measures were improved, including profit and benefits for local communities where operations existed. Making social factors a part of the conversation proved to be a greater challenge.

Finding consensus in action

Then, Jim arranged for a major presentation on corporate risk communications and relationships with stakeholders to be made at an annual meeting of company leaders. After that session it was clear to everyone, including George, that relationships with stakeholders of many types did indeed have strategic relevance for the company. With the three pillars now clearly understood, Jim made another attempt to bring George around to finally accepting the language of sustainable development. But it proved to be of no avail. George was strongly in favor of corporate actions on environmental, economic, and social topics … it was the language of "sustainable development" that he found unacceptable.

The corporation downplayed the language of sustainable development for internal discussions while emphasizing corporate activities that enhanced environmental performance, improved economic outcomes, and developed close relationships with stakeholders. In other words, the company wanted to enact sustainable development without actually saying it ... at least internally. But under Jim's influence, external corporate environmental reports embraced sustainable development language as shorthand for the company's collective activities. The company was later identified by a corporate environmental magazine as the leading environmental performer in the industry.

Jim eventually left the company with his integrity intact but with a few scars and many lessons from the battles with George. It is not clear to this day why George was so troubled by the concept of sustainable development. Was it "political"? Or was it the absence of a clear, uncontested definition perhaps – anathema to the mind of someone with such an analytical and quantitative mindset? Jim reflects now that "in results-based organizations it is important not to allow overly intellectual discussions of professional or managerial concepts to get in the way of actions that have their own merits – especially when they are widely apparent to the internal audiences."

This is a true story. The name has been changed and the company is anonymous.

The themes in these conversations give meaning to organizational life, and these themes and patterns change in unpredictable ways. Themes pertaining to what is important and meaningful are formed and perpetuated through what people talk about; we talk about who we are, what we are doing, or what we have done (*narrative* themes, where we weave stories to explain how things are); and we talk about who we might become, or what we might possibly do (*propositional* themes, in which we make proposals for the future). Conversation is the engine of change. The direction of the whole is a self-organizing result of the ongoing interchanges between people. Through narrative and propositional themes people construct the identity and the activity of the organization (who we are, who we might become; what we do, what we could do). It is also how people in organizations construct strategy; Stacey contends that *strategy is the emergence of organizational identity*. Strategy is also called "business policy," and so we could say the same thing at the level of "public policy" – government policy is the emergence of collective public identity. The kinds of policies we enact are an expression of who we are.

Conversation and meaning-making are mechanisms by which we navigate the complexity of the world. From ancient traditional storytelling and songs, to religious systems of thought, to coming and going trends in popular culture, humans have always interacted with each other with the aim of making and remaking identity. For organizations and for people within them, a central driver of these narratives is the relationships with stakeholders and the quality of the conversations.

Stakeholder Theory: A Genre of Stories about How We Can Live Better

Leading stakeholder theorist R. Edward Freeman has said that stakeholder theory exists as a set of narratives, as a genre of stories about how we could live.[10] The goal of a good management theory should be pragmatic and experimental, and it should help managers create narratives of cooperation and mutual value creation, in order to live better lives. In a complex responsive processes view, the kinds of stories we tell and our propositions for a better future depend on the dominant and shadow themes in organizational conversation. In our six narrative vignettes describing the experience of real, practicing managers, various dominant and shadow conversational themes are evident at points where there is stagnation or movement forward – where ideas are seen as legitimate or not. From the relegation of sustainability concerns "to the metaphorical dark corner of the basement" in Nina's story, to the central place of sustainability, storytelling, and social value creation in Nadine's story, we can see that the nature and quality of the sustainability conversations are critical to progress. We will examine that idea in even greater depth in chapters 6 and 7.

BOX 5.5

**ALAN'S STORY: MOVING FROM UNAWARENESS TO A
SUSTAINABILITY FOCUS IN RETAIL SUPPLY CHAINS***

Alan's story began when a journalist asked the marketing director of
home products retailer B&Q, "Where does your timber come from?" He
did not know and could not readily discover an answer; so the journalist
responded, "If you don't know, you don't care."

Thus Alan was recruited by B&Q in 1990 to sort out "the timber issue." He
was certainly not hired to make an impact on global deforestation. His job
was to protect the business from harm that was felt would emerge if the
company did not have a better handle on the origin of its timber.

A hands-on approach to supply chain audits

Looking back on those times with the benefit of hindsight Alan believes
he was lucky. Even in his early days he had the support of senior executives and board members. His conversations within B&Q were invariably
business-focused and "win-win." He was able to identify those high
profile product areas where B&Q needed to improve and present cases
for action. From timber ranges to brass door fittings, doormats and light-
shades, he was given freedom to visit suppliers around the world and
speak directly to relevant NGOs to find out exactly what the environmental and social issues were and what B&Q could do to help improve
the situation. This was not just about public relations insurance through
audits. Alan's work with the brass suppliers in India reinforced the need
to create a direct sourcing program so that B&Q could be more closely
linked to product development and reduce costs – in addition to seeing
through improvements in working conditions.

B&Q's hands-on nature differed from many other companies where the
focus was desktop supply chain audits – encouraging suppliers to tick
boxes on standard questions, some of them relevant to individual suppliers and some of them not. What was *not* happening in most cases was the
development of challenging continuous improvement plans where companies asked themselves what were the critical issues in their supply chains
and set objectives for what they wanted to achieve in defined timescales.

Sustainability – beyond corporate social responsibility

At B&Q, the main challenges were timber, factory working conditions, solvents in paint, and peat. The driver was always about reducing the negative impacts of current business practices; it seldom fundamentally challenged the business or the business model.

Over the past two decades Alan has worked with businesses on sustainability challenges, and the major change he has witnessed is the emergence of sustainability as a strategic part of business operations. He believes that leading companies have come a long way from the old mix of philanthropy, reducing environmental harm, and working conditions in developing countries. Today, the most progressive companies understand that they need to move from "less bad" to understanding the true business significance of resource constraints and eco-services. As Alan says, "Sustainability is replacing CSR. It is no longer about giving a reassuring message to shareholders, governments, and consumers, it is about creating businesses that, through their products, are aligned to helping everyone create a sustainable global economy where 9 billion people can live quality lives, with low carbon emissions, and within one planet's worth of renewable resources. The question has become, What good can our products do to help address the world's most pressing challenges?"

Today, Alan is the sustainability director for business in the community and a leading player in an organization he helped found in 2010, the Global Association of Corporate Sustainability Officers (GACSO, www.gacso.org). This is one of the world's first professional bodies to support the positive evolution of sustainability conversations in corporations.

This is a true story. Alan and B&Q are the actual names.

Stakeholder Value Creation: Three Kinds of Value and Their Anchor Points

Led by Freeman's work, the conversation in stakeholder theory over the past three decades has taken shape around three "problems"[11] relating to business:

- *The problem of value creation and trade:* In a rapidly changing and global business context, how is value created and traded?
- *The problem of the ethics of capitalism:* What are the connections between capitalism and societal values?
- *The problem of managerial mindset:* How should managers think about management to (1) better create value, and (2) explicitly connect business and societal values?

The executive's role is to nurture these relationships to create as much value as possible for stakeholders and to manage the appropriate value distribution among them. The incorporation of societal values and ethics are made central to business, since every business decision is an allocation of benefits and harms among stakeholders, and is therefore an ethical question. Perceived tradeoffs may arise (say, between workers and stockholders), so executives must allocate the benefits as appropriate and figure out ways to avoid having to make tradeoffs in the future. Central to doing that is to focus on creating greater mutual value – to improve the arrangement so that all stakeholders are getting more, not less, from the sum of relationships supported by the organization. A wider range of potential value creation opportunities comes into view when the geography, time horizon, and the field of stakeholders are expanded. From a CRP perspective, innovations arise out of the diversity of conversation, and this is very evident in Nadine's story: "I am hopeful that these course corrections will be more easily facilitated as Interface develops its capacity for collective learning and exchange. As Interface learns its way into the future, not only will the business enhance its capacity for innovation, but just as importantly, for resilience."

In Figure 5.1 we show a picture of the relationship between three kinds of value, and the points at which the value is anchored.[12] The first mode is organization-centered, focused on mitigating risk to the company. Stakeholders are seen as primarily threats (or at best sources of unpredictability) to the core value goal of maximizing investor return; in that sense, "stakeholder management" means *managing stakeholders* – ensuring that relations with customers, suppliers, the community, or employees are carefully controlled, and that the organization comes out on top of the value-capture competition. Examples would include keeping the unions away from strikes because of workplace safety concerns and customers away from class-action suits for faulty products. The second mode is centered on value communities,[13] which recognizes

Figure 5.1. Three Modes of Stakeholder Management and Value Creation

greater interdependence among stakeholders and sees value creation as necessarily a mutual exercise. In highly integrated value chains, cooperative research and development as is common in biotechnology, or in industrial clusters that comprise a value "ecosystem" of skills, services, and suppliers, as it is in the Silicon Valley technology sector. In this case stakeholder management means *managing for stakeholders* – the focus is on creating value for stakeholders with the understanding that benefit will accrue to the organization if relationships are fruitful. Starbucks selling fair trade coffee; mining giant Rio Tinto building community facilities near its mines; Walmart and Unilever eliminating unsustainable fish from their supply chains; all of these represent serious "nods" in the direction of customers' sustainability values in return for customer loyalty and continued sales.

The third mode, as yet underdeveloped, is centered on the societal commons, and stakeholders are seen as all of humanity and non-human species alike – those who will be affected by global sustainability issues both today and in the future. The range of value creation opportunities expands tremendously, as the organization's strategic planning becomes much more anticipatory than reactive. As ice hockey great Wayne Gretzky said about his uncanny ability to make plays and to always be where the puck is: "I skate to where the puck is going to be, not where it has been." A soccer equivalent for our European readers would be the uncanny ability of former Everton (and now Manchester

United) star Wayne Rooney to anticipate and receive passes from apparently nowhere before scoring.

Stakeholder management ranges from dealing with a few individual or small-group stakeholders that are powerful, legitimate, and urgent[14] towards acknowledging a wider range of undeclared or "fringe stakeholders"[15] that promise greater potential for building value communities. For business organizations, a third step towards greater integration with global issues occurs when deep and broad social needs are put to the foreground in reimagining business strategies – when strategic planning exercises are driven from an intensive exploration and understanding of complex issues in the near and not-so-distant future. An organization can be working in all of these modes simultaneously, and indeed different parts of the same global organization can emphasize different levels according to geographical and cultural expectations. In the progression from one mode to the next, nothing is lost, but there is an increase in integrative capacity – bringing more stakeholders and issues into the picture and perhaps lengthening the time from for the value creation process. Conventional management thinking, driven by short-term efficiency, would advise towards focusing on fewer stakeholders and issues; but *embeddedness, sustainability,* and *transformation* are longer-term concepts. Cognitively connecting to stakeholders over longer time horizons raises the potential for creative innovation and more sustainability-aligned decision making. Thus, some smart global corporations such as Shell, Unilever, and DuPont sometimes draw attention to their "long-term shareholder value" proposition rather than their ability to maximize short-term returns for flighty investors. This helps manage expectations; it also helps to ensure that institutional investors commit for the longer term, thereby reducing volatility in stock prices.

BOX 5.6

NADINE'S STORY: CARPET MANUFACTURING IN AN ASPIRATIONAL ENVIRONMENT*

Sustainability as a dominant conversational theme

Nadine works for a company that has embraced sustainability as a core value. This profound commitment along with a fierce sense of entrepreneurialism and innovation helped InterfaceFLOR address many challenges in the early years of the twenty-first century. These included two global recessions, competitors advancing their sustainability efforts, and the death of the company's founder, Ray Anderson, whose personal epiphany and vision for a restorative enterprise changed the course of the business in the mid-1990s.

Interface has now lost its heroic leader, its charismatic storyteller, the man who could tell the story of Interface's transformation in the first person – the self-described plunderer who finally "got it." Many in the business community may wonder about life at Interface after Ray Anderson. How will the company maintain its sustainability leadership position without its iconic ambassador, and what new conversations may emerge?

Sustainability as a driver of innovation

Nadine describes how despite these challenges, bold goals to eliminate any negative impact the company might have on earth by the year 2020 remain at the forefront of Interface's strategy. Sustainability has continued to evolve from an operations focus into a source of innovation and new market development. Senior leaders agree: innovation is needed not only in product development and research but also in all aspects of the business.

In 2011, Interface launched a global engagement process to tackle the question, How do we accelerate our progress towards our 2020 goals? As Nadine describes it: "Using principles of appreciative inquiry, employees from across the globe were asked to share their insights on how and where to innovate, and to explore ideas and solutions to achieve the company's sustainability vision. The feedback collected indicated that we needed to become better communicators, collaborators. and learners, not just within our global business but also within our partnerships with external thinkers."

Building integral relationship with nature and society

"I am learning that Interface's sustainability journey is not just about rethinking the business' relationship with the natural world, but our relationships with each other across geographies and cultures. There is a clear desire within the organization to be better connected globally. This will require more time for reflection, listening, and storytelling. This is not always easy in the fast-paced world of carpet tile manufacturing. It will mean confronting some tough questions about how we shape and are shaped by global inequalities. It raises important questions about how we learn as an international organization. There is agreement among senior leadership that organizational learning is important; however, what's lacking is a common understanding of what this means and what it looks like in practice. Figuring this out is a key part of Interface's evolving story."

To Nadine and many others at Interface, Ray Anderson's epiphany was a gift. It was the beginning of a powerful, shared story. It was an invitation to participate in an unprecedented journey to transform outdated notions of the industrial enterprise. The journey itself is ever-changing as it adapts to changing environments. The world is a very different place from how it was in 1994 when Interface began its famed "mid-course correction," and it will be an entirely different place in 2020.

As Interface continues to evolve, it will likely undergo additional course corrections – perhaps some more subtle than others, as Nadine explains: "I am hopeful that these course corrections will be more easily facilitated as Interface develops its capacity for collective learning. As Interface learns its way into the future, not only will the business enhance its capacity for innovation, but just as importantly, for resilience." The Interface sustainability conversations still reflect a unity of purpose in what is and what could be.

This is a true story. Nadine and Interface are the actual names.

Summary

A *complex responsive processes* (CRP) perspective says that narrative conversational themes are vital to shaping the direction and actions of an organization, and stakeholder theory tells us that relationships with stakeholders are the prime value generation mechanisms. In this chapter, we expanded the notion of organizational stakeholders towards integration of the global sustainability drivers outlined in chapter 4. We will pick up these themes throughout the rest of the book: chapter 6 looks in depth at conceptions of sustainability in a framework for sustainability conversations; chapter 7 extends this framework to examine the social dynamics of sustainability within organizations; and chapter 8 examines social learning as a mechanism to broaden out towards social integration as depicted in Figure 5.1.

LEADERSHIP SKILL BUILDING:
Skill-Building Exercises

ASSIGNMENT: Roundtable Dialogue Role Play on Sustainability Issues

In chapter 4 we outlined some major global sustainability issues and we offered thirty-two process questions to lead dialogue towards problem identification and problem solving. We also identified integrative thinking as a core leadership skill to pull together various perspectives on these issues. This exercise is designed to challenge learners to consider each issue from multiple perspectives, and then to build integrative thinking skills by synthesizing the various perspectives into a sustainability mindset and craft "design questions" as challenges for business value creation. This assignment is to be prepared ahead and presented in a class or in an executive learning environment in a live dialogue format.

Purpose

1   To explore topics in sustainability through roundtable dialogue, so that everyone comes away with a better understanding of the depth and complexity of the issues.
2   To consider the various levels of stakeholder value, and the opportunities for business, environmental, and societal value creation.

Process

1   An individual signs up for a topic of his/her choice. Some examples are set out below. In an executive learning situation, a real life example from the challenges faced by the organizations represented could be just as powerful. Each participant in the roundtable will be responsible for articulating a particular point of view on the topic of the roundtable, as a member of a business organization, a social enterprise, a community group or civil society organization, or government.
2   Each session should have most or all of those perspectives represented (four to six people per session is ideal). Role assignments should be real people in real

organizations (e.g., the executive director of the World Resources Institute), and the participant researches that organization ahead of time and brings the policy perspective of that organization to the dialogue. A role assignment might also be an individual with some expertise in the area (e.g., an academic or an author of a book on the topic). All should be roles that have ample information on the web or in books and articles. Along with researching their own roles, participants should look at the other perspectives represented around the table.

3　In student learning environments, participants might submit a 750–1,000 word position paper on the topic to the instructor based on their research. Each can bring four illustrative slides to help communicate his/her perspective and can ask for them to be called up through the discussion as necessary. The instructor reviews the submissions ahead and prepares the line of questioning. In executive learning situations, a one-page brief might be provided the night before for participants to work from.

4　The instructor/facilitator acts as the moderator of the dialogue and poses questions to the participants and facilitates the dialogue (the objective is not to "stump" the panel, but to help bring forth the research that participants have done).

5　The dialogue is not planned or rehearsed. Each participant comes prepared to engage, without conferring with others on the panel in advance. Panelists are permitted to bring notes to work from. This is not necessarily a debate (although sometimes disagreement will surface); rather, the focus should be on a constructive exchange of ideas to raise the level of literacy of all participants and observers (the rest of the class is the live studio audience).

6　The roundtable runs thirty minutes, with a further thirty minutes for questions from the studio audience. Alternatively, both could be combined so that the audience asks questions throughout for greater engagement.

Evaluation Criteria (for Students)

- **Individual Preparation**
    - Quality of written preparation: position paper and slides

- **Individual Performance in the Session**
    - Demonstrate depth of understanding of the issues
    - Initiate new lines of discussion
    - Engage with others' ideas in a meaningful way

- **Group**
    - Overall quality of interaction
    - Overall quality of discussion

Exercise Debrief

The goal of this exercise is to surface the richness of perspectives surrounding each of several major global issues. Following the dialogue, the full group can consider these questions:

1   Applying critical thinking skills, what claims, evidence and underlying assumptions did you hear from the various participants?
2   What do you see as the major challenges and points of tension among the perspectives?
3   Did you hear different mindsets evident in the participants' perspective (i.e., technocentric, ecocentric, or sustainable)?
4   What would a sustainable synthesis of the perspectives look like (i.e., focusing on equitable human development now and in the future, within the regenerative limits of the biosphere)?
5   Summarize the main challenges by posing some "design questions," beginning with "How might we ...?" or "What if ....?"
6   What are some business opportunities for sustainable value creation stemming from these design challenges?

Possible Topics and Roles

Here are some ideas for structuring the roundtable dialogues, though this list is not exhaustive.

Water Wars: Blue Gold, or Common Good?

Private firms seek permits for bulk extraction and export of water resources, while critics warn of impending global water shortages and the need for international governance over water supplies.

Aspects to explore:
- The outlook for world water security
- Regional disparity in water security
- Water in relation to other sustainability issues, e.g., food, climate, population
- Private/public ownership of a common good
- The responsibilities of government, business, civil society in the issue

Panelists (a generic sample list of global stakeholders – identify and research real roles):
- An economist in support of water exports
- A government official with jurisdiction over water use
- A researcher from an environmental non-governmental organization
- A well-known activist on water issues
- A representative from a bottled water company

Powering the Future: Electricity Generation

Nuclear, coal, hydroelectric, wind, solar, biomass – all of the above? Electricity demand is projected to rise steeply over the coming decades. What is the right mix of energy to fuel the future?

Aspects to explore:
- The current energy supply picture
- Demand forecasts for the coming decades
- The pros and cons of various power sources in meeting demand
- The responsibilities of government, business, and civil society in the issue

Panelists (a generic sample list of global stakeholders – identify real roles):
- A government official with jurisdiction over energy policy
- A researcher from an environmental non-governmental organization
- An executive from a power generation organization
- An author or activist on energy issues
- A representative from the coal/nuclear/renewable energy industries

Carbon Policy: Cap It, Trade It, Tax It – or Leave It Alone?

We are caught between the twin crises of diminishing energy stocks and a changing climate. What energy mix and policies will drive the future?

Aspects to explore:
- Projected impacts of a changing climate
- The effect of various fuel sources on climate
- An overview of various mitigation options
- The responsibilities of government, business, and civil society in the issue

Panelists (a generic sample list of global stakeholders – identify real roles):
- A researcher/policy analyst from an environmental non-governmental organization
- A scientist who is member of the Intergovernmental Panel on Climate Change
- An author or activist on energy issues or carbon policy
- A government official with jurisdiction over energy and/or environment policy
- An executive from the oil and gas industry
- A representative from the International Energy Agency

Population and Poverty: Problems and Potential Solutions

World population is rising exponentially, especially in developing countries. What are the problems brought about by population growth, how is that tied to poverty, and what can we do about it?

Aspects to explore:
- The population picture: past, current, and future
- The causes of population growth, the causes of poverty
- The relationship between population and poverty
- The effects of development aid, pro and con
- The merits and pitfalls of top down "base of the pyramid" development approaches for corporations
- The responsibilities of government, business, and civil society in the issue

Panelists (a generic sample list of global stakeholders – identify real roles):
- A leading author on base of the pyramid development approaches
- A critic of base of the pyramid approaches
- An advocate for increased aid to developing countries
- A critic of increased aid to developing countries
- A member of a civil society organization working on poverty
- A social entrepreneur working on poverty issues
- An author/academic proposing other solutions to poverty
- A representative from the UN Population Division

Transportation and Design of Sustainable Cities

With urbanization increasing worldwide, the convergence of three issues is gaining importance: population growth, transportation, and urban design. Here we explore these issues and how they interact.

Aspects to explore:
- The role of cities in adapting to sustainability issues: climate, population, food, water
- What is a sustainable city?
- Who are the stakeholders in sustainable cities?
- Policy perspectives on transit
- The responsibilities of government, business, and civil society in the issue

Panelists (a generic sample list of global stakeholders – identify real roles):
- Executive from a major regional transit authority
- Executive from a business organization active in sustainable cities (e.g., IBM)
- A government official with jurisdiction over policy for transit or city design
- A representative from a cities association (e.g., the C40 Cities Climate Leadership Group)
- A leading commentator/author on sustainable cities

The Food Issue: Feeding the Future

Food production is facing mounting challenges in both developed and developing regions of the world: factory farming, monoculture soil depletion, the impact of biofuels, and the relationship between diet, oil, and climate change, to list a few.

Aspects to explore:
- Where our food comes from
- The dominant methods of production and delivery
- The problems with our food system or threats to supply in the future
- Alternative systems for food supply
- The potential effect of other issues on food security – water, climate, population
- The responsibilities of government, business, and civil society in the issue

Panelists (a generic sample list of global stakeholders – identify real roles):
- A leading author on food issues
- An expert/author/academic on threats to future food supply
- A representative from the UN's Food and Agriculture Organization
- An executive from a major agribusiness
- An operator of a Community Supported Agriculture organization
- A leader in organic or biodynamic methods

PART THREE: RESPONDING

CHAPTER 6

Sustainability Conversations: Conceptions of Practicing Managers

I'm really struggling with this "sustainability" stuff – I can't get it all in my head at once. I think of it differently now than I used to: I can't think of sustainability just in the context of a company anymore, it's a global idea. I can think of some *implications* for an organization, but company-by-company, the response tends down towards compliance. We can see the bigger picture, but haven't been successful yet in developing an integrated sustainability strategy, one that unites the environmental with the social and economic in a way that drives our behavior and decision-making differently. But we're talking about it, we're working on it.

– Manufacturing Executive, Primary Metals

In part one, we examined modes of thinking and learning as mechanisms for *rethinking* the relationship between economy, society, and nature. In part two, we examined various means of *relating* the myriad components in a complex system, focusing on the role of the leader, and on connections among an organization to its stakeholders. Here, in part three, we look at *responding* – the ways that the societal idea of sustainability is brought into organizational thinking. In chapter 6 we explore the ways that practicing managers work to form "conceptions of sustainability" in connection to their daily challenges, and in chapter 7 we examine the "social dynamics of sustainability," or the ways that tensions between differing conceptions can create blocks to change, or positive momentum, depending on how they are addressed.

A "conception" is a collection of principles which when taken together exhibit a stable scheme of cohesion and cooperation – often such principles are implied in the way that people speak or act rather than in an explicit set of articulated guidelines.[1] Here we use the term conception to mean a way of thinking and talking about sustainability that is coherent and consistent across a number of subthemes. We have constructed conceptions of sustainability by observing, listening, and talking to managers who were working on interpreting sustainability concepts for their organizations. These conceptions can form frames for "generative dialogue," in which organizational members uncover their operating assumptions and beliefs about sustainability, and "strategic dialogue," through which organizational leaders set direction for action. A generative and strategic dialogue on sustainability combines into "sustainability conversations" – the prime mover of organizational thinking and action towards more sustainable outcomes. In the introduction to the book we outlined some theoretical ideas on sustainability in a way that was derived top-down from existing theory – technocentric, ecocentric, and sustainability mindsets, and the connection to the definition of sustainable development. Here we work from the ground up, from the experience of practicing managers: looking at managerial perspectives on sustainability and building those into a descriptive framework that is grounded in real experience.

Sustainability in Practice: Managerial Perspectives

In the first ten years of the new millennium, ideas on business and sustainability moved very much into the mainstream of the popular management press and into the strategic and operational dialogue within organizations. Consulting firm KPMG reports that sustainability reporting (i.e., combining environmental, social, and economic performance metrics in annual reports) has gradually displaced exclusively financial reporting since 1999, to the extent that almost 80 per cent of the Global Fortune 250 companies routinely offer a multidimensional perspective of their strategy and operations.[2] The past few years especially have seen tremendous growth in the number of surveys reporting what is happening in organizations with relation to sustainability efforts and initiatives. It is relatively easy now to find useful survey benchmarks on the kinds of activities being undertaken – and those that should be – to enhance corporate responsibility and to advance global sustainability. Ideas come from all directions, including international agencies, consultancies, academic institutions, government and non-governmental organizations, and for-profit corporations. To cite but a few examples among many: as of 2010, the United Nations Global Compact had more than 6,000 members in 135 countries expressing their support for 10 principles of social and environmental responsibility, and which were required to report annually on their progress against those principles; they now poll the members annually for their thoughts on progress. Consulting firm KPMG publishes a triennial survey on trends in corporate responsibility reports that reflect strategic intent in corporate communications; U.S. consultancy and think tank Business for Social Responsibility (BSR) and CSR polling firm GlobeScan produce an annual poll of business leaders in their "State of Sustainable Business" report; Canadian CSR magazine *Corporate Knights* and its collaborators publish an annual list of the world's 100 Most Sustainable Corporations which is released at the Davos summit of the World Economic Forum each year; *MIT Sloan Management Review* magazine ran a CEO survey in the fall of 2009 and launched a special issue and a website to report on attitudes and action trends in business and sustainability to be updated continuously; McKinsey & Company's *McKinsey Quarterly* offers a steady stream of short, useful articles related to sustainability issues; the World Business Council on Sustainable Development (WBCSD), a consortium of large for-profit corporations, provides research and analysis across a broad range of issues and industries; and Walmart has developed a web portal for companies to share success stories in sustainable management.[3]

Periodic surveys like these and the benchmarking they represent are highly useful for understanding *what* managers and executives think, what they believe is strategically important (if only for reputational reasons), and what they do at a given point in time, under the social and economic pressures of the day. Particularly where benchmarks reflect corporate trends, they also stimulate opportunities for membership-based knowledge sharing (e.g., within the Global Compact, the WBCSD, BSR, and others) to help organizations learn and replicate successes. We will not report on those activities here, since they change daily and are accessible via social media feeds. Instead we do want to focus on *how* managers think, based on our own in-depth research. We accept the simple premise that how people think determines to a large extent what they think, and what they think will drive what they do. If they reflect on what they do and make adjustments, then that is called learning; and as we saw in chapter 3, learning can happen at multiple levels through iterative recursive loops. Our framework of *conceptions of organizational sustainability* describes various managerial mindsets in a more abstract sense, so that we get a sense of the range of ways that people think about sustainability in practice – what they call "sustainability" will enhance, or inhibit, their ability to embrace new directions and to innovate.

Conceptions of Organizational Sustainability

Over the past decade we have been observing and documenting ways in which practicing managers and executives talk and think about sustainability in relation to their organizations. We have conducted two large formal research studies capturing qualitative descriptions of sustainability by managers. These were not check-box surveys of what firms were and were not doing, but rather in-depth conversations with managers as they sought to make sense of some of the ideas surrounding business and sustainability. We have personally conducted, recorded, and sifted through thousands of transcript pages from interviews with over 200 managers in dozens of organizations across a wide range of industry sectors: electricity production, environmental services, forestry, oil and gas, primary manufacturing (aluminum, steel, and chemical production), mining, information and communication technologies, tourism, national government, and nature conservation. All of the organizations that participated in our research had previously and publicly expressed intent towards sustainability or sustainable development, to a greater or lesser degree, using various terminologies. Our aim was to try to capture and represent general ways that managers think about sustainability: the piecemeal descriptions of managerial thought and organizational initiatives, the kinds of themes that emerged, and the qualitative nature of how those themes are discussed and debated. We have also conducted our own "sustainability conversations" with hundreds of other managers in executive learning events[4] and classroom settings in the dozens of MBA, executive MBA, and undergraduate courses we have led independently, and sometimes together, over the past decade. Here we will share a framework we have developed to try to characterize the general nature of such conversations – the mindsets that people hold as they talk with, and sometimes past, each other as they try to make sense of "sustainability" in business.

Conversations are wonderfully messy, often undirected and internally inconsistent, and not nearly as neatly compartmentalized as the themes appear in our framework. It is often through conversation that people try to work out what they think – as novelist E.M. Forster wrote: "How can I tell what I think till I see what I say?" We noticed through the course of our research and in the discussions with executive learn-·ers that managers and executives are sometimes frustrated in trying to communicate on sustainability ideas with their colleagues – especially when challenged with the need for absolute clarity and definition. In the pressure of a busy day, there is seldom time for the deep reflection and dialogue necessary to delve into meanings we create on sustainability, and the implications of one view versus another. We constructed this "four conceptions" framework to facilitate sustainability conversations among managers and executives, and we have used it to that end. It helps to bring some order to the conversation and encourages participants engaged in dialogue to stretch each other into new areas of thinking. People are able to identify their own conceptions, to point to them on a chart, and to see their own views contrasted with other ways of thinking, talking, and acting on sustainability ideas in business. They stop talking past each other and begin to talk to each other, then with each other. They move from dissonance, to discussion, to dialogue.

These four conceptions serve as *frames* for thinking and talking about sustainability. Frames are interpretive mechanisms that help us to organize our experience and guide action by condensing and simplifying the world we observe so that we can deal with it.[5] While we have drawn this framework of conceptions in a static way, what goes on inside of it is highly dynamic: *framing* as an activity is the social process by which meanings and interpretations are constructed, along with the actions that issue from them.

The root of the word "dialogue" is from the Greek *dialogos*, where *dia* means passing through, and *logos* denotes meaning – "dialogue" is the flow of meaning between and among individuals in a group, out of which may emerge new understandings.[6] As a result of our research and the topics explored in our executive teaching, we believe that talk is the first form of action, it is how people create the meaning that drives the actions they take; and we believe that "sustainability" is first and foremost a process of meaning-creation among human actors – people trying to sort out what is important, how they should live, and what they think about the systems in which they operate. We will provide an overview of our four conceptions of sustainability framework, and then conclude with ideas on how these conceptions form the frames for managerial sense-making and action-taking. We follow in chapter 7 with consideration of the "social dynamics" of sustainability – how talk turns to action for change.

Conceptions of Sustainability – Key Dimensions: "Reductive to Integrative" and "Actual to Possible"

In "grounded" research, the raw data of in-depth conversational interviews are collected and coded, then analyzed for content and gathered into themes. Those themes can then be constructed into conceptual maps so that they can be organized and explained. The explanation, however, works better in reverse: starting with the high-level concepts, down to subthemes, and then to the illustrative words of the interview subjects. This is how we will present our ideas here.

Our guiding research question was: How do practicing managers in sustainability-focused organizations describe and make use of that concept? There are two primary dimensions, each a continuum, along which we have organized meanings of sustainability expressed by managers. We have called those dimensions "Reductive to Integrative" and "Actual to Possible." Crossing those dimensions yields a 2x2 matrix depicting four conceptions of sustainability that became evident through our research (see Figure 6.1) and which was reinforced through our practice as teachers. We will outline the nature of the key dimensions and then follow with a description of each of the four conceptions.

Reductive to Integrative

It is increasingly common to hear reference to "the triple-bottom line" in business organizations – simultaneous attention paid to progress on financial, environmental, and social performance metrics. Also commonplace is reference to "stakeholders," most often meaning

Figure 6.1. Four Conceptions of Organizational Sustainability

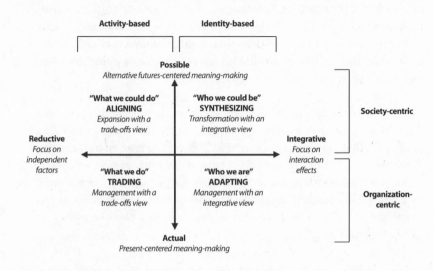

employees, customers, investors, communities, suppliers, and governments, though as we saw in chapter 5, there are often many more stakeholders in an expanded view of those who might impact or be impacted by the achievement of an organization's goals. What we find most interesting in the course of our many sustainability conversations is that different people offered varying descriptions of the *nature of the relationship* among the three facets of the triple-bottom line, or between the organization and its stakeholders. For example, while many made reference to the need for "balance," or even "trade-offs," others spoke primarily in terms of "integration" or "interdependencies" – of the mutually reinforcing effects of value creation on multiple fronts. Rarely is it argued that trade-offs are *never* required; running an organization is always in part an exercise in allocating scarce resources. But some managerial conversations focus mainly on the integration of stakeholder aims, and on the possibilities for mutual, simultaneous value creation, while others tend to stay stuck on trade-offs.

We use the term "reductive" to capture ideas that characterize factors as independent and focus on trade-offs; for example, that stakeholder needs are constraints that need to be managed; the prime locus of concern is the financial performance of the organization; the triple-bottom line is a zero-sum equation, where value gained in one domain (e.g., environmental protection) means value lost in another (e.g., profit for investors); cost-and-risk reduction is the main "sustaining" objective. Concerns over business or organizational sustainability are stated in colloquial terms – that is, to sustain the business as a going concern. In the words of one manufacturing executive:

> Well, true sustainability is ... it starts with a business perspective and then I think it cascades into: all right, *how* do I want to do business, in the context of "What's my social responsibility?" But if you start saying I'm going to save the environment and I don't have to make any money, well you're not sustainable. You're going to be done. So I attach the word sustainability to "my business must be sustainable." From a pure business perspective my view of sustainability means I'm going to make money for hundreds of years.

The notion of trade-offs is in the foreground in a reductive view: "saving the environment" is secondary to making money – we can preserve nature, as long as there is some cash left over. A senior manager at a coal-burning power generation plant talked of the cyclical nature of the trade-offs that society is willing to accept among different dimensions of the triple-bottom line. The clear implication is that society must choose between environmental preservation and economic prosperity, since they work in opposite directions:

> Environment though, if you look at it, follows the economic cycle. When you are at the peak of the economic cycle, people are willing to make that environment-economy trade-off. Society as a whole is willing to pay for things that they recognize might give them a problem the rest of the time, but the environment advances on the agenda at the peak of the economic cycle. If you hit the trough again, environment vanishes from the radar screen, and jobs and the strength of the economy become the overriding factors.

Conversely, an "integrative" view embodies synergistic, win-win thinking, with a focus on positive interaction effects among stakeholder groups, or among the three dimensions of the triple-bottom line. Such a view holds potential for mutual value creation, and there is primary consideration of the role of the organization in society.[7] To illustrate, this chemicals company executive directly challenged the focus on trading-off among stakeholder needs and instead emphasized the need to focus on "interdependencies":

> The old thinking was that if you make money you can do this positive social and environmental stuff, and that's true to a point – but I think the true philosophy of sustainability is the interdependence. It's not about charity; it's about the fact that if you do the right things in the community, the community will do the right things for you. If you do the right things for the environment, you'll have a stronger business so that you can make more money. It's not about a condescending view – I don't know if that's subtle or if people don't get it, but it's very important. It's about interdependence rather than balance. It's about mutual dependence or interdependence rather than charity. It's fundamental.

Contrary to the trade-off views above, where positive environmental and social performance needs to be traded off or balanced with economic performance, here the emphasis is on "and" rather than "either/or." Another manufacturing executive described sustainability as "an integrated business issue," and not just an environmental constraint:

> ...one of the problems in my mind is that for a lot of people who haven't spent time trying to understand the sustainability framework [forms a triangle with his hands], when they hear the term sustainability, they equate it to environment: "It's an environment thing; it's one of these Greenpeace things, you know, the sustainable earth." They see it as being an environmental issue as opposed to necessarily an integrated business issue. For me, a sustainability framework starts to create this view on the interdependency and how these things mutually drive each other.
>
> *Interviewer: When you say "the sustainability framework" you make a triangle with your hands ...*
>
> Yes, I'm talking about the triple bottom line. In my mind, the concept before was that the only thing that mattered was your financial performance. If you had good financial performance, then you could afford to do these nice things – plant a few trees, throw a party for your employees, make

them feel good, do whatever, but it was really all about financial performance. As opposed to saying, "Some of these things actually drive financial performance."

Through a reductive view, the task of managing is mainly seen as allocating resources and trading off interests, while attempting to capture some residual value. An integrative view sees the role of the manager as finding synergies among stakeholder needs, creating value where none existed before.

Actual to Possible

A second broad distinction we often observe is in the way that managers talked about alternative possibilities for their organizations or their industrial sectors. Do they think broadly about possible futures, or are their ideas of the future unduly constrained by what exists currently? In what is their thinking anchored? Here "actual" refers to "what is," in the mind and the language of the leader. It describes meaning creation and modes of expression centered in the perceived realities of the present state: current political structures, relationships, markets, operations, products/services, capabilities, and cultural traditions. That is not to say that responses we have categorized as *actual* do not consider the future, only that expressions of the future are framed in the present: the future is seen mainly as an extrapolation of present conditions. Sustainability is seen as constrained by current activities:

> I've seen examples of these "sustainable" [signals with finger quotes] business models in developing economies. Say I'm going to sell them clean water. Their medical costs drop, people stop dying. There are people that have said, "Gee, you know, if I could find a way – I don't have to charge them very much money to make money, to make a profit – to provide clean drinking water to these people." That's more around the true triple-bottom line. Do I think that we'll go that way? No ... it's pretty hard to drive a truckload of steel out in the middle of a field and say "any takers?"

This senior executive sees the company defined by its primary current product – flat rolled steel – and imagines the future as simply more of the same.

We have used the term *possible* for ideas of the future that were expressed without worrying about constraints imposed by the current situation. Sustainability is described by some, not as a continuation of the status quo, but as an idea that opens up a range of possibilities of alternative futures: new relationships, political structures, new strategies, products, geographic markets, or organizational capabilities. Expressions under *possible* depictions of sustainability are more divergent than convergent in nature. Another manager in the same steel company related his own personal transition, from being mentally constrained by the present to considering a role for the company uninhibited by current conditions:

> That is where my head was at originally, thinking okay, that is probably a stretch for us. But now, when I look at this stuff, I'm saying, "You know, why couldn't we?" Over a twenty year time frame, you can build whatever core competencies you want. If food, water, and energy are going to be the things that are really important to the planet twenty years from now, and people are going to be looking to companies to help us out of the bind that we are getting ourselves into, why couldn't we play a big role in there, either as a front-running supplier, or supporting some of the key players that are energy companies and helping them solve energy problems? Why not?

At first pass, this seems counterintuitive: how can "sustaining" be about change? For integrative thinkers, the idea of sustainability goes beyond the colloquial meaning of "to keep something going." Or at least they interpret that idea on a much bigger level, and take the thing we are trying to keep going as, not the current business and its product lines, but life and human development on this planet. Many described emergent global forces, collected under the banner of sustainability, as critical business drivers, as in the words of this CEO:

> There are substantial global issues and those global issues will result in changes to the way that governments work, to the way that the business ultimately works ... I think our society is about to change dramatically – it's already changing. So, from that perspective, how are we going to respond as a company?

The labels *actual* and *possible* are different from "today" and "tomorrow" – here they describe the place in which our thinking is anchored, whether we are thinking about the present or the future. If we are thinking about tomorrow but are anchored in the current *actual*, we will cut off new ideas. If we anchor in what is *possible*, today's constraints can fall away – "why not?"

Four Conceptions of Organizational Sustainability

Crossing these two dimensions we have a 2x2 matrix delineating four diverse and distinguishable conceptions of organizational sustainability. We have labeled these conceptions trading, aligning, adapting, and synthesizing, and we believe they aptly capture general ways of thinking and talking about sustainability in organizations that we have encountered in our research.

Each conception offers a coherent, internally consistent way of expressing an idea of sustainability described with reference to common features. As with any constructed typology, things may not always be this tidy in real life. People can range across different ways of talking about sustainability from one conversation to the next – or even one sentence to the next in the same conversation. What this picture does is help to sort out our ideas about sustainability – what it is, what we value, how we see stakeholders, what is the role of the manager or leader. So in describing how any one given manager thinks about sustainability, this picture may not be entirely "true," but it is useful, in that it describes four general types of thinking about these issues along a spectrum. Where a given organization sits on this picture will depend on the nature of the rich mix of conversations going on daily within its walls and with the full range of stakeholder interactions. How the organizationally dominant conception contrasts with the individual mindsets in the company is something that we will explore more deeply in chapter 7.

Organizing Features of the Four Conceptions

We describe each of our four conceptions using the following eight questions: (1) What is the fundamental *motivator* at play? (2) What is the primary organizational sustainability *objective* (i.e., what is "sustained" under each conception)? (3) What is the perceived *usefulness* of a sustainability framework for those organizations embracing one? (4) What is the role of *organizational values* under each conception? (5) What is the logic or *rationale* for organizing thinking this way? (6) What is the strategic role for *organizational capabilities*? (7) What is the primary role of *leaders* in the organization? And, finally, (8) What is the role of *dialogue* in helping to realize the sustainability objectives? The next section briefly outlines each conception following these questions, and a summary is presented in Table 6.1.

A Trading Approach to Sustainability: Management with a "Trade-offs" View

The *trading* conception of sustainability is focused on "what we do" – activity in the short term aimed at meeting the operating plan and maximizing organizational (usually financial) value subject to constraints imposed by stakeholders. Under this conception, the interpretation of the term "sustainability" is closest to its colloquial definition of "to keep our organization going," and less societal level values-laden than described under other conceptions. The usefulness of a sustainability framework is that it broadens the concept of the business to include stakeholders as legitimate actors and provides a negotiating frame to manage the trade-offs that are seen as unavoidable. "What is sustained" are local stakeholder relationships, which protect the license to operate the current business. Some managers in our research characterized stakeholder groups as entities whose interests were to be traded off – the various needs of stakeholders were depicted as discrete, mutually exclusive:

> I think at the end of the day we have a certain responsibility to look beyond just making money, so there will be times when you will do activities that cost you money. If you're sitting there talking to shareholder[s] and they're asking you, "How come my dividend's not bigger?" – our answer should be, "I operate my business in a way that is acceptable within the social fabric of Canada, and given that context here's what I can afford to give you as a dividend."

Clearly in the forefront of this description is a view that the aim of a sustainable business is to optimize investor (financial) wealth that is subject to constraints imposed by other stakeholders. The three facets of the triple-bottom line under a trading view are things that have to be managed carefully because, in the words of one executive, "any one of those, if you mismanage it, can bite you in the ass real fast." The experience of BP investors following the Gulf of Mexico disaster in 2010 is one highly salient example of stakeholder anger destroying shareholder value – in this case angry stakeholders included the President of the United States. At the extreme, sustainability-framed initiatives are window dressing or an exercise in bureaucratic compliance. As a manager in government put it:

> I don't think this department really cares about whether I may achieve or not achieve sustainable development. On this side of the house, we want very much for a project to succeed because it is a sustainable development initiative. But it is not their primary agenda – it is an agenda to ensure that a department gets good marks with the Auditor General.

The role of values in a trading conception is to serve a negotiating frame to sort out the perceived trade-offs and reduce organizational risk; values assume more of a background than a foreground role. That is not to say that values are not important, or that these organizations are unethical in any way, simply that financial values are deemed overriding and that societal-level values were not put forward as key to directing the business of the organization. Concern for stakeholders is argued for on grounds more instrumental than moral, and values are criteria for negotiating trade-offs among them.

In a trading conception, the key logic frame is economic optimization. Technical capabilities are important to build operational excellence, and community relations skills are important for maintaining the license to operate. The role of leaders is to manage the organization capably and to dedicate effort and energy towards stakeholder consent or appeasement. Dialogue with stakeholder groups is aimed at maintaining (or regaining, if it has been lost) the implicit or explicit license to operate from stakeholders. For example, one senior manager described his organization's effort to win back support from local communities surrounding a large nuclear generating station after years of corporate arrogance and insensitivity to stakeholder needs:

> I was involved in the neighborhood program where we went out with little videos and so on, and we went through all the people, going door to door

and saying, "We live in your community, if there is anything you would like to know, here are some numbers"... and we became a lot more open to the community. And that was a change from the old belief, which was "We are the experts, trust us. You know – sleep safe." And we changed because we understood that just saying "we're the experts," well, frankly, just naming yourself as an expert isn't of any value, really. And the community was saying, "Yeah, you're the experts, but we've got questions and concerns, maybe you ought to listen."

An Aligning Approach to Sustainability: Expansion with a "Trade-offs" View

The *aligning* conception of sustainability is focused on "what we could do" – activity focused on alternative futures, with the aim of maximizing organizational value subject to "globally-local" (or what one manager termed "glocal") constraints imposed by organizational stakeholders. Organizational goals are aligned with stakeholder needs, and the focus is on organizational value capture. Again here, the interpretation of the term "sustainability" is mainly "to keep the business going."

What is sustained in an aligning view is organizational growth and a globally-local license to operate. The usefulness of a sustainability framework is that it stretches thinking to include broad global forces in the future context, and it helps to mitigate risk. For example, mining giant Rio Tinto focuses on maintaining a "social license to operate" – support from local communities and governments surrounding its operations – in order to reduce political and economic risk and to keep returns flowing. In developing a sensitive site in Madagascar, Rio Tinto secured access by implementing biodiversity protection policies, training local Aboriginal peoples in higher-skilled jobs, and reducing greenhouse gas and energy use.[8] However, trade-offs still dominate in an aligning view. Critics of mining activities, including critics of Rio Tinto's Madagascar operations, charge that such sustainability policies merely serve to buy forgiveness from locals and that environmental and social costs are incurred for financial (company) and/or economic (government) gain. Constraints imposed by stakeholders can be managed with tactical manoeuvring to ensure the license to operate is maintained. One coal power executive described it as deliberate "social engineering" at the site's community level:

Table 6.1. Four Conceptions of Organizational Sustainability along Thematic Dimensions

Features		Four Conceptions of Organizational Sustainability			
Value Creation Mode		Trading	Aligning	Adapting	Synthesizing
Activity/Identity motivator		What we do	What we could do	Who we are	Who we could be
Sustainability Intent	Sustainability objective	Maximize organizational value subject to local stakeholder constraints	Maximize organizational value subject to "globally local" stakeholder constraints	Simultaneous value creation for all organizational stakeholders	Leverage inclusive stakeholder view to create value for the organization and broad global society
	What is sustained?	Competitive operations License to operate Local stakeholder relationships	Organizational growth License to operate "Globally local" stakeholder relationships	Stakeholder value Industry advantage Core values and Organizational self-image	Corporate brand Core values and Global human welfare
	Usefulness of a sustainability (triple bottom line) framework	As a negotiating frame: Mitigate risk by negotiating trade-offs	As a negotiating frame: Mitigate risk, exploit growth opportunities by negotiating trade-offs in new markets	As an integrating frame: Build sustainable competitive advantage and organizational identity by leveraging interdependencies	As an integrating frame: Provoke organizational reorientation by broadening conceptions of context and capabilities
Sustainability Alignment	Role of values	Criteria for negotiating trade-offs	Contextually relative criteria for negotiating trade-offs	Ground for integrating stakeholder aims	Compass for setting organizational direction
	Key logic	Business/Economic: Finding efficiencies	Political: Accessing new markets	Organizational: Seeking industry advantage	Societal: Seeking integrated value
	Strategic capabilities view	Focus on technical capabilities and community relations	Geographically localized relationship building	Focus on building advantage in current industry through culturally embedded resources	Abstract derivation of capabilities base – position versus macroview of global opportunities
	Primary role of leaders	Capable management Stakeholder appeasement	Risk management Opportunity analysis	Stakeholder engagement Values integration	Building organizational identity and commitment
	Role of dialogue	Understand stakeholder wants/needs Communicate organizational actions	Establish entry Negotiate value capture	Attune to interdependent view Search for stakeholder win-win	Broaden strategic reference frame Enrol stakeholders in new direction

Maintaining the public franchise is important. And how are we doing? At a site community level, excellent, I think what we're doing is textbook stuff. At the appropriate time it would be worth a couple of chapters in a few public affairs or social engineering textbooks, because it absolutely works, we know it works, we're very good at doing it. There aren't many companies that do it as well as we do, at a site community level. It's very strategic and very, very, very well received. We get positive media every time we're out there. We get positive media, and people know we're there.

Here values are contextually relative, adaptable to local operating conditions, and serve as criteria for negotiating trade-offs. The key activity is expropriating (i.e., capturing) value in new markets, and a frame of political logic figures prominently in playing off the local and national, for example, governmental stakeholder constituencies. Key capabilities are focused on local relationship building and public relations to support the operating franchise. The primary role of leaders is identifying opportunities and managing risk, and the principal role of dialogue is to win entry into new markets and geographies, and to negotiate the distribution and capture of value created.

An Adapting Approach to Sustainability: Management with an Integrative View

An *adapting* conception of sustainability is centered on "who we are." Respondents voicing elements of this conception were focused on building strategic advantage for the organization in a way that was strongly rooted in societal level values, and on mutual value creation with stakeholders. What is sustained is simultaneous value creation on multiple stakeholder fronts, or on all three dimensions of the triple-bottom line. We call this integrative view "adapting," because organizational leaders are focused on opening up to and integrating with stakeholders and environmental forces with the objective of mutual value creation. This view is rooted in the actual present, and so what is also sustained is the organizational self-image, the "idea" of the organization itself. One senior manager, in articulating his view of sustainability, felt that the idea of the company was more powerful and pervasive than any commitment to a particular strategy:

... ultimately this company is an idea, not a legal creation. It's an idea held in a bunch of people's heads, and the idea of the company is one where always the needs of shareholders and employees and customers were explicitly talked about in the same breath, and then the overlay of the community became ingrained in the place. There was an understanding that if our customers liked what we did, and investors liked what we did, there would be profit-sharing to go around, and better job security, and there was also this notion that we treat each other right, and we do the right thing in the community. This has become much more pervasive than the current strategy ... that idea of the company is fundamental and held by many.

The usefulness of a sustainability framework under an adaptive conception is that it provides an integrative frame for building mutually reinforcing effects that can contribute to the firm's competitive advantage. For example, after Nike was successfully targeted by activists in the late 1990s for its labor practices, chairman Phil Knight expressed a renewed focus on responsible management in *Nike's 2004 Corporate Responsibility Report*,[9] including audits of all offshore production facilities, their labor practices, and environmental standards. Nike's new integrative thinking has evolved into such initiatives as the Global Alliance to improve workers lives in developing countries, microfinance projects through the Nike Foundation, and zero-waste targets for shoe production. From outside companies in these kinds of situations, we can view these as reputation-enhancement projects, meant to protect the brand; however, from inside a company, these are often identity-driven changes to restore a sense of self after a public rebuke.[10] A sustainability framework offers a meeting table for disparate parts of the business to come together and seek out complementary points of leverage, a point put forward by one executive this way:

Do we know how to leverage it completely yet? I don't think so, but have we gotten some insights into it? Yes, I think so – why are we successful, and some of our competitors are in totally different situations? Do you understand it only intellectually, or do you also understand it in here [taps chest], what it means? ... So, I think having a sustainability framework has helped the senior management team, gives us a place to take all of our diverse thinking and at least put it in a consistent framework and start to have discussions ... we've all got different views and different perspectives and different biases that we bring to this framework. But it provides a place, a table for you to meet, and bring these things together ...

Enduring societal-level values provide the ground for integrating stakeholder aims, and the key logic frame is organizational, that is, the way that the organization is perceived as an organically integral part of its business and socio-political environments. The view of capabilities expressed under an adaptive conception is that, beyond technical skills to run the business, managers in particular should develop a capacity for integrative thinking to think of the business as a system of complementary parts working together. The two previous quotes also highlight the view that such a capacity can become culturally embedded in an organization – a part of the fabric of the culture, and not simply something laid out in the strategic plan. The primary role for leadership here is to build integration by engaging (*versus* simply appeasing) key stakeholders in the business, which includes acting as a "translator" from one form of organizational discourse to another (e.g., helping employees translate customer needs, as well as shareholder and community expectations, into meaningful performance specifications), and bringing together more closely the idea of "values" and "value creation" where both are the subject of dialogic processes. Dialogue is a critical means to attune the organization to an interdependent view of stakeholder needs, rather than seeing them as zero-sum trade-offs, and organizational values form the ground for integration.

A Synthesizing Approach to Sustainability: Transformation with an Integrative View

A *synthesizing* conception seeks a synthesis of global forces and objectives – economic value creation, the eradication of social injustice and suffering, and environmental rehabilitation and conservation together with the financial objectives of the business and its investors. Stakeholder needs, rather than constraints, are viewed as opportunities, and the "philosophical" approach to stakeholders is held as a source of competitive advantage. As one CEO of a large science and manufacturing company said:

... what we believe is ultimate sustainability is to say, "With that core philosophy of having respect for a broader stakeholder view beyond shareholders, can you in fact build off that to create a business value in and of itself?" ... It is not: "we will create shareholder value constrained by the environment and the broad stakeholder group." We will in fact use our approach to the broader stakeholder group and the environment to in fact stimulate the creation of shareholder value that would not have come otherwise.

The sustainability objective here is to leverage an inclusive stakeholder view to create value broadly for society – to sense out what the critical global issues are and then bring the organization's capacity to bear to help solve those problems, while at the same time creating financial value for the company and its investors. One executive described his company's forays into Asia in those terms:

> ... we were talking about getting nutrition to people in the world, and what are the barriers to that? Why does that have to go to India? Because there thousands of people die every year because people adulterate the oil that they use to cook their food in. They're trying to make a buck, so they cut it with motor oil, and God knows what, and people die as a result of it, and there is no good reason for that. So there was a lot of consciousness brought to [the question] "What are the issues and how can we address them, and then do it at a profit?"

The usefulness of a sustainability framework under a synthesizing conception is a strategically provocative frame that encourages a reorientation of the organization to new growth opportunities. For example, the core model of Better Place described in chapter 2 integrates environmental concerns with human need for transportation, but it is reconsidering what is possible in terms of our culture on how we use and pay for it. Better Place starts with the idea that oil is finite and will only get more expensive, and that climate concerns mean that electric cars, driven by clean power, will be a big part of the mix going forward.[11] Integrative possible thinking has allowed it to conceive a business model where drivers lease kilometres, like air-time minutes on a cell phone, and Better Place supplies the infrastructure – the cars, the charging stations, and the connections to green power. This big-picture, integrative perspective was described by one senior manager at a science company that was in the midst of a strategic reorientation exercise:

What "sustainability" has done is started to have people think about what businesses we should be in. Should we be in plastics and synthetic material, when you look at the growth of that business and you look at the energy demands of that business? So I would say that is what it has done, it has taken us to asking very fundamental questions.

What is sustained in a synthesizing conception is the organization as a corporate identity, rooted in a set of cohering values. This conception is also the most outward looking, and so what is sustained (or improved) is global human welfare as well as the organization; within this concept the social issues form the context for problem-centered business development for financial sustainability. Naturally, this is simpler to do in those businesses that have built consumer brands on this kind of awareness (e.g., The Body Shop, Ben and Jerry's, or Patagonia) or that began as "social mission" businesses (e.g., cooperatives like Desjardins or Migros). It is harder to do in larger and more established businesses where investors retain their hunger for competitive returns (e.g., in oil and gas or chemicals manufacture). Ultimately, organizational values serve as the compass for setting strategic direction for all organizations. In chapter 5 we discussed the *complex responsive processes* view, in which strategy is the emergence of organizational identity – what we do reflects who we are, and vice versa. And new strategies may be formed at the nexus of organizational values and of a vision for global sustainability, even where those values remain primarily financial – provided money can be still be made from the products and industries of the future. One senior manager put it this way:

How it all relates to sustainability – we will tend to make investments in the kinds of business that reflect our idea of ourselves. The company is just a construct at the end of the day, and incorporates a bunch of values. I think we will tend to make investments that reflect our values and our sense of what this company needs to be and will relate to … it won't betray any particular group of stakeholders, so we will not rape and pillage the environment or do this at a huge social cost, and we'll try to do something that has the opportunity to contribute on all fronts, for which we will be admired. That's a really big factor – people want to do things for which they will be admired, and we'll do something that we think is consistent with being around for another century or more.

The key logic frame is societal – social welfare and the establishment of the socially responsible markets of the future is the lead reference point. Core organizational capabilities are considered abstractly to allow for strategic reorientation, and there is likely a shift in attention towards the knowledge-intensive aspects of the business. For example, one organization in our study held long-standing capabilities in chemical science and was widely considered part of the chemicals industry. By considering its core capabilities more broadly as simply "science," the company was able to make some shifts towards biotechnology in the acquisition of new businesses, turning its hiring focus towards recruiting biologists rather than chemists while still maintaining its core identity.

The role of leadership in a synthesizing conception is to initiate movement in a new direction and to build and sustain organizational commitment in that direction, while at the same time working to preserve coherence around the organizational identity. The objective for some is to create new market imperatives formed around sustainability drivers:

> We are looking at creating – we call them "market transformation projects" – and we are looking at it that way because we are literally trying to change the market. We want to shift practice; we want to shift the thrust, the demand towards green technology and sustainable products.

Maintaining commitment to new, unproven directions is not easy: one CEO described the nature of his ongoing conversations inside the company with his executive team around the world:

> We're having a lot of dialogue, but we're losing money in emerging markets right now. It's costing us. My president in America [who reports to me] says, "Why the hell are we doing that stuff in emerging markets? Why are we bleeding to death? It'll never make money!" [laughs] ... that's what he says! So I keep saying, "Well, it's the right thing to do. We're going to lose some money for a while, so you make some more here!" This is a real life dialogue, you know. So, you have to be bold.

Another senior leader described the need to sustain leadership commitment to new directions and to build commitment with those within the organization and with stakeholders. Success depends on how the efforts are framed for dialogue among participants and on explicitly challenging existing beliefs about what "growth" means:

> I had a number of NGO activist groups tell us it was an oxymoron, we could not grow sustainably. Well, it depends on what you're growing; we're not talking about growing stuff, we're talking about growing value, whether that's shareholder value or societal value, that's what we want to be growing. So, that has worked much better for the businesses, to be able to link in and say, "Okay, now we see the connection, we need to grow, and we need to think about what it is that we need to grow sustainably?" It's created conversations, which was what we ultimately wanted. Let's start the conversations.

Our four-conceptions model is a descriptive framework, in that we only attempt to describe ideas on sustainability most often put forward by executives and managers working in organizations with that stated aim. None of the conceptions is "wrong" – they are merely collective descriptions of what people take sustainability to mean. Each conception, however, offers strengths and limitations for movement towards more sustainable practice. We will explore some of those enablers and inhibitors for change in chapter 7.

Conceptions of Sustainability as Provocative Frames for Sustainability Conversations

As working managers attempt to reconcile the goals and actions of their organizations with the main principles of sustainable human development – inclusive, connected, equitable, prudent, and secure – it is no wonder they "can't get it in their heads all at once." Sustainability is a big idea, a contestable global concept that provokes thinking and dialogue on what it means in practice. Across our four conceptions, some managers think of sustainability as making money while being sensitive to stakeholders; or expanding to capture global opportunities while doing so; or really integrating with care the needs of stakeholders around the current business, according to deeply held values; or seeking to create new value while addressing global human welfare, including addressing issues such as poverty and environmental degradation; or some combination of all of the above. Each conception has an associated way of thinking about stakeholders, values, leadership, and dialogue, and each of these contributes to our ongoing meaning-making on sustainability.

Too often we hear, "We just need to agree on one definition of sustainability, and then measure and manage it!" That is like saying, "We need to come to one definition of art (or justice, or democracy)." We believe that the primary value of "sustainability" as a concept in management is that it asks us to first make sense of it and then question what we value. We reject the quest for a unitary, static definition and suggest that "sustainability" is *first a process of meaning creation through conversation*. These four conceptions serve as *frames* for thinking and talking about sustainability, and *framing* as an activity is the social process by which meanings and interpretations are constructed, along with the actions that issue from them. It is through conversation that framing happens – how people sort out what they believe and think, and what they do. To highlight that critical point, we offer a view in Table 6.2 of the four conceptions as they focus on the role of conversation. We define authentic *sustainability conversations* as a combination of *generative dialogue* and *strategic conversation*. Sustainability conversations are necessary to create movement towards more sustainable practice.

LEADERSHIP SKILL BUILDING:
Process Questions, Skills, and Skill-Building Exercises

PROCESS QUESTIONS CHAPTER 6: Fostering Sustainability Conversations

Leaders can use these process questions to think about fostering productive sustainability conversations:

- How can we create space for sustainability-focused conversations in structured and informal encounters, especially among senior organizational leaders?
- How can we help to build a sense of identity in what sustainability means to individuals, recognizing that sustainability is not just about "what we do" but also about "who we are"?
- How can we resist rapid closure in conversations on sustainability in order to invite "possible"-focused themes as well as "actual"-focused themes?
- How can we bring consideration of global sustainability issues into our leadership development initiatives?

Table 6.2. Four Conceptions of Organizational Sustainability and a Role for Generative Dialogue and Strategic Conversation

Features		Four Conceptions of Organizational Sustainability			
	Value Creation Mode	Trading	Aligning	Adapting	Synthesizing
	Activity/Identity motivator	What we do	What we could do	Who we are	Who we could be
Sustainability Intent	Sustainability objective	Maximize organizational value subject to local stakeholder constraints	Maximize organizational value subject to "globally local" stakeholder constraints	Simultaneous value creation for all organizational stakeholders	Leverage inclusive stakeholder view to create value for organization and broad global society
	What is sustained?	Competitive operations License to operate Local stakeholder relationships	Organizational growth License to operate "Globally local" stakeholder relationships	Stakeholder value Industry advantage Core values and Organizational self-image	Corporate brand Core values and Global human welfare
	Usefulness of a sustainability (triple-bottom line) framework	As a negotiating frame: Mitigate risk by negotiating trade-offs	As a negotiating frame: Mitigate risk, exploit growth opportunities by negotiating trade-offs in new markets	As an integrating frame: Build sustainable competitive advantage and organizational identity by leveraging interdependencies	As an integrating frame: Provoke organizational reorientation by broadening conceptions of context and capabilities
Sustainability Conversations	Role of generative dialogue among managers	Generating shared understanding of the relationship between the business and its stakeholders	Generating shared view of values application in different contexts	Generating shared view of positive reinforcing effects of stakeholder value creation	Generating shared view of the business context and organizational capabilities
	Role of strategic conversations	Defining negotiation frames to engender stakeholder feelings of inclusion and support	Exploring grounds for entering new markets and assessing potential for value capture	Building socially complex strategic routines and resources	Building sustainability-focused strategic thinking through the organization

LEADERSHIP SKILLS CHAPTER 6: Unearthing Underlying Assumptions through Generative Dialogue

In chapter 2 we examined the components of critical thinking: assessing *claims*, weighing *evidence* offered in support of those claims, and inferring the *underlying assumptions* that link the claim to the evidence. These are essential skills in leading *generative dialogue* in organizations. *Generative dialogue* occurs when participants actively engage with the aim of unearthing and conversing on assumptions held by group members, in order that shared assumptions can be discovered or formed.[12] By exploring underlying assumptions, managers can generate common frames of thinking, shared meaning, and a collective world view – or, at the very least, can understand the operating frames of their colleagues and have a more informed dialogue on strategic actions. It is through generative dialogue that managers can explore "what we believe" and "who we are." *Generative dialogue* is a precursor to *strategic conversation*. Once generative dialogue opens up the strategic imagination, strategic dialogue serves to creatively (versus analytically, i.e., evaluating and eliminating) explore possibilities, and to find creative solutions to messy problems.[13] When generative dialogue and strategic conversation are centered on sustainability challenges, these are *sustainability conversations* – provocations for new ways of thinking and acting as we relate societal challenges to our organizational contexts.

Building Leadership Skills – Learning Team Dialogue: What Are Your Conceptions of Sustainability?
Using the four conceptions as a ground for generative dialogue, choose an organization with which you are familiar and reflect on the questions that follow. Write down your first thoughts, then apply the critical thinking framework from chapter 2. What are your claims? What evidence can you offer? What assumptions are you making that link your claims to your evidence? Share you reflections with your learning team, and consider the similarities and differences.

- How do we think of stakeholders in relation to the operations of our organization?
- What is our primary organizational sustainability objective?
- What is "sustained" in our view of sustainability?
- What if we think of our operations in terms of the triple-bottom line: what does that mean?
- What role do organizational and societal level values play in our stakeholder interactions and strategy setting?
- What is the strategic role for capabilities in our organization, and which organizational capabilities are most valued?

- What is the primary role of leaders in our organization in pursuing sustainability? How does that fit with our model of leadership, both espoused and in practice?
- How could we deliberately employ dialogue to build momentum toward realizing our sustainability objectives?

In chapter 7 we examine more closely the social dynamics that emerge when people feel some tension between their own conception of sustainability and the dominant one in their organization. We apply a *complex responsive process* view, described in chapter 5, to try to understand better how to have inclusive sustainability conversations that enable, rather than inhibit, positive organizational change.

CHAPTER 7

Wicked Problems and Complex Processes:
The Social Dynamics of Sustainability

We do our business, and hopefully it's for environmental good, but we do impact the environment negatively. In order to be sustainable, one would have to be vigilant at reducing the negative impacts on the environment.

We are looking at creating, we call them market transformation projects and we are looking at it that way because we are literally trying to change the market. We want to shift practice; we want to shift the thrust, the demand towards green technology, sustainable products.

– Senior Managers from a Regional Conservation Authority

In the last chapter we considered the difficulties managers face when attempting to introduce a sustainability mindset into their organizations, and how multiple conceptions of sustainability emerge in their efforts to make sense of a societal-focused global ideal in an organizational context. The complexity of sustainability issues becomes most pronounced when practitioners strive to take an integrative approach to social, economic, and environmental challenges while still maintaining financial performance. Issues of sustainability have been described as *wicked problems*, characterized by broad disagreement on both the problem and the solution, and where stakeholders work in various directions to frame the situation they are faced with and the optimal response. The quotes above come from two senior managers in the same organization, one that has publicly committed to a sustainability vision. The first takes the view of sustainability as a trade-off between business and the environment. The second addresses how the organization might serve as a catalyst for change and transformation so that economic, social, and environmental goals can be reconciled with financial performance. Can you imagine what might transpire in a meeting between these two managers? Would there be conflict? Would they talk past each other? Would organizational sustainability be advanced or hindered by their different understandings of what this contested concept means in their own firm? These two quotes are representative of the multiplicity of meanings of sustainability described in the previous chapter, and the challenges that these different views pose for an organization that is attempting to define exactly what the problem is and to generate potential solutions for a range of stakeholders. We will now consider how this diversity of interpretations creates tensions within an organization: whether this tension is embraced as something positive that can help to expand the organization's thinking with regard to the issue, or whether it is negatively viewed as "noise" that must be eliminated, to avoid any distraction from the present course of action. How it is perceived will impact the organization's potential for innovation and change.

Social Dynamics of Sustainability: Individuals and Their Organizational Context

In chapter 6 we identified four conceptions of sustainability that capture generalized ways of thinking and talking about sustainability in organizations that we have observed in our research and executive teaching, and we identified various features that make up the *content* of the sustainability conversations taking place within those organizations. Here we will explore more fully the *process* of how these sustainability conversations play out in organizations and what the implications of these conversations are for organizational change. Considering sustainability challenges as wicked – that is, systemic and multifaceted – problems, we suggest that in order to fully understand the implications of sustainability for societal level change, it is essential to explore the quality of the social processes both *within* and *between* organizations, which we do in this chapter and in chapter 8, respectively. Here we will explore the diverse set of conversational themes that emerge in relationship between individuals and their organizational context as a result of the adoption of a sustainability vision and mindset by actors within the organization. We describe this internal or *intra-organizational* process as the *social dynamics of sustainability*, or the range of interactions that take place between individuals and the dominant operating ideas in their respective organizations. These social dynamics can be felt negatively or positively by the individual, depending on the degree of alignment between individual and context. If positive on the whole, then change is enabled; if negative, change is inhibited. By developing the appropriate set of management capabilities, these dynamics can move from being a hindrance towards being a source of energy and innovation for an organization; one that will allow it to have a significant impact on sustainability issues as well as enhanced organizational prospects. Organizations that develop these capabilities and associated social dynamics may contribute to advancing sustainability as a *social movement*, along with their own goals, rather than limiting themselves to the more narrow focus of making their own business more sustainable. In this chapter, we describe some social dynamics and resulting tensions that we have observed, using our *four conceptions of sustainability* framework from chapter 6, and we will outline leadership capabilities that can help to turn those tensions from negative to constructive. In chapter 8, we will consider how multi-sectoral collaboration extends these sustainability conversations beyond the organization to the societal level and how it is an essential external or *interorganizational* social process that fosters societal learning required to address the complex global problems of sustainability.

BOX 7.1
MINI-CASE: THE WICKED PROBLEM OF CLIMATE CHANGE[1]

Why is climate change considered a "wicked problem"? The cause of the problem is diffused across a range of stakeholders, none of whom can be definitively identified. There is little agreement as to how to resolve the issue and often the solutions proposed may cause more harm than good. For example, the alternative fuel generated by corn-based ethanol as a potential solution to greenhouse gas emissions is arguably a very inefficient source of energy. Depending on how stakeholders perceive the issue, various solutions may be entertained. NGOs, individual citizens, governments, or energy companies each frame the problem in very different, and often incommensurable, ways. For example, the United

States Climate Action Partnership (USCAP) is a group of businesses and environmental organizations that has come together to put pressure on the federal government to create a policy framework on climate change and establish legislation that would demand significant reductions in greenhouse gas emissions by organization. At the same time, the industry-backed Energy Citizens group and the U.S. Chamber of Commerce have actively opposed such legislative developments. In designing a policy framework, what would be the optimal approach? Cap and trade? Carbon tax? Benefits and challenges for each of these proposed solutions can be argued from multiple perspectives. What are the political implications of each of these decisions? What are the resource implications? If climate change hits the poorest people in the world the hardest, what are the obligations of those who are benefiting from the current industrial system?

Is there a social process that might help to resolve this complex problem?

The Social Dimensions of Wicked Problems

Climate change, global poverty, health care management, biodiversity loss – these challenges have all been described as wicked problems, where the problem-solving process is complex because the social context, especially with regard to resource and political implications, is constantly changing. Wicked problems often emerge when organizations are facing ongoing change or challenges they have never previously encountered. Sustainability issues have recently surfaced on the radar of many firms, and they present new and difficult situations that neither they nor other industry competitors have grappled with before. Often in such conditions of uncertainty, we take refuge in technological optimism or in the belief that technology improvements will solve our problems; technology is something that we can easily understand and manipulate and thus it provides an illusion of control over complex problems: nuclear power or carbon capture and storage as "solutions" to climate change would be good examples of techno-optimism; genetic modification of crops as a "solution" to malnourishment in the developing world would be another. Unfortunately, they may not be socially or politically acceptable, they may have negative and unintended side effects, and they may not even work.

These examples represent an extension of the "technocentric" view we described in the previous chapter. In order to move to a "sustain-centric" or "sustainability mindset" perspective, we must be acknowledge that the social complexity of wicked problems is as significant as the technical challenges, and as such, solving these problems is primarily a *social process* – something we do not have a good understanding of how to do. This social process is influenced greatly by the organization's view of stakeholders. Each of the four conceptions offers a different perspective on who matters and why, which influences the way that stakeholders are involved, or not, in the organization's decision-making processes. In fact, wicked problems are to a great extent considered a problem of *interaction* between stakeholders.[2] An example of this can be found in the stakeholders' struggles over water resources in the "Campaign to Hold Coke Accountable" in India. A negative interaction of stakeholders arose because of the view that Coca-Cola was destroying communities in India through water shortages, pollution of groundwater and soil, and exposure to toxic waste and pesticides. At the same time many community members embraced Coca-Cola for what it has done to provide employment for the communities. Contradictions and complexity abound, which raises the question, What social process, both within and between organizations, might help to resolve these interactions in a positive manner?

Complex Responsive Processes as a Way to Approach Wicked Problems

Although we have described how sustainability as a management imperative is growing in popularity, and a clear "business case" (in particular industries and marketplaces at particular points in time) has been established for many forward-thinking firms, we suggest that the mainstream approach to sustainability is limited in its potential because it is based on a generalized or conventional systemic view of organizations. In chapter 3 we discussed how this perspective is useful for promoting single- and double-loop learning: getting better at what we currently do (for example, increasing efficiency in the "pollution prevention pays" style of 3M) and challenging whether we are doing the right things (for example, enhancing effectiveness in the "sustainable growth" mode of DuPont). Double-loop learning will allow us to challenge the governing assumptions that guide our actions and behaviors in order to improve business practices, but it stops short of supporting us in challenging governing values and norms that are the basis for these assumptions.[3]

The sustainability mindset is ultimately transformational; it requires a fundamental challenge to how we think about value creation and our norms of behavior. This perspective may shift the kind of markets we serve, the products we choose to design, and, indeed, the very nature of the business we are in; it is how oil and gas companies may one day genuinely move "beyond petroleum" into marine renewable energy rather than simply another play for increasingly inaccessible and risk-laden resources in the Arctic and elsewhere. It is how automotive firms may in due course transcend selling cars and instead begin to lease the service of mobility in co-owned vehicles that double up as micro hydrogen power plants.

The systemic view of organizations is very good at generating incremental improvements to current operations in the form of eco-efficiency or corporate social responsibility initiatives, but it is less successful in fundamentally challenging existing business models in a way that will allow us to respond more effectively to the complex challenge of wicked problems. Because a systemic view of organizations limits us to single- and double-loop modes of learning, it often leads to treating sustainability primarily as a business strategy, albeit an enlightened one, with a relatively narrow view of the business case for sustainability. The opportunities for value creation that emerge from this systemic perspective are limited to more traditional measures such as ROI and brand value that are offered by initiatives linked to cost and risk reduction, and reputation and legitimacy enhancement in the eyes of stakeholders. An example of this approach to value creation can be seen in the iconic Canadian coffee chain Tim Hortons, which has embraced a goal to reduce packaging across its supply chain and manufacturing operations as well as to reduce energy and water consumption at new locations. The company is also exploring energy-saving features and green-building certification for various restaurant locations, is focusing on achieving an increase in fuel efficiency for its distribution fleet, and is working with municipalities to ensure that its paper cup is compatible with recycling and composting programs. These efforts are firmly rooted in the *trading* and *aligning* conceptions that we described in the "sustainability conversations" framework in chapter 6.

While these initiatives may be important as part of an enlightened "corporate greening" strategy, how might we extend the conversations to keep that momentum going, beyond eco-efficiency and the enhanced legitimacy that this offers, towards greater innovation in sustainability?

A Focus on Social Process

We will consider in the following pages how a complex responsive processes (CRP) view of organizations, described in chapter 5, allows for a broader conceptualization of the business case for sustainability by enabling us to move away from a focus on the *system* to a focus on the *process*. Insights from the CRP view help us to advance our understanding of robust social processes in organizations, that is, processes that promote healthy conversations, something we will explore in more detail here. The opportunities for value creation are expanded in this view, with potential gains to an organization not only of strategic competitive advantage but also the potential to generate broader societal and ecological value. Linking this to our conceptions of sustainability framework means that conversational themes would expand to the *adapting* and *synthesizing* quadrants. E.I. DuPont's recent, and not uncontroversial, foray into biotechnology is an example of an organization that is engaging in these kinds of sustainability conversations. The organization divested its nylon business, a core part of its operations for decades, in order to extract themselves from cyclical factors such as the commodity price of oil and engage in ventures that would enhance economic value addition while simultaneously reducing the company's ecological footprint. DuPont subsequently acquired the seed company Pioneer Hi-Bred, making extensive investments into biotechnology research and development in order to strategically reinvent its business and align it with principles of sustainability. The company also set up a high level Biotechnology Advisory Group of stakeholders to help it debate the issues of global sustainability raised by genetic modification and other technologies. In taking this approach, DuPont was simultaneously aspiring to meet the world's demand for food and fuel, reduce the company's impact on the planet, and create shareholder value. Will it be successful in its efforts over the long term? How do the conversations that take place in the organization support its aspirations? What leadership capabilities does DuPont need to develop in order to succeed with this initiative? Wicked problems demand that we embrace the paradox and uncertainty[4] that are sure to arise in situations such as the one described above. Such ambiguity is part and parcel of an organization striving to adopt a sustainability mindset. It is our suggestion here that a CRP view of sustainability will refocus management attention on how to build social processes that will encourage the emergence of innovation and entrepreneurialism that sustainability requires.

Sustaining the Organization or Sustaining Society? Incremental and Transformational Approaches to Sustainability

Over the past decade, "business cases" for sustainability have made significant inroads, both in the management literature and in a wide range of sectors and individual organizations. In fact, the conventional motivation for engaging in more sustainable business practices has moved away from what managers can do for society or the environment, considered in more philanthropic terms, towards a serious focus on the implications of sustainability issues for the future competitive advantage of organizations.[5] We explored in chapter 6 how there has been significant uptake in sustainability as a relevant frame for managers in mainstream business. However, despite this advance from fringe concept to a more established area of managerial thought and practice, it is unclear that any significant social or environmental transformation has accompanied this evolution. Continued failure of international organizations and national governments to secure a comprehensive commitment to action on climate change is just one example of such failure of governance systems, despite the active engagement of a number of global corporations in climate change summits.[6] Global environmental and social issues continue to proliferate and the debate on exactly what the issues are and what should be done about them is often still a very contentious one. The environmental and social challenges facing BP, and which faced Monsanto before it, are examples of the dangers of disconnected thinking between avowed mission and strategy and actual performance. The limitations of a conventional business case, narrowly defined, leads us to ask, Is there a better way to unleash the potential of organizations in this domain, to scale up sustainability from its current status as a business strategy or reputation-management tool with limited scope and impact to that of a social movement, bolstered by organizations that are fully committed to a sustainability vision?

Real Transformation Requires a Societal Focus First

The most commonly held understanding of sustainable development, the Brundtland definition, introduced in chapter 1, has a mandate of intergenerational justice embedded in the idea of meeting our needs without selling short the possibilities for future generations to flourish. Through our research and teaching, we have observed that many managers struggle with these and other societal level concepts of sustainability, as they create significant challenges for introducing such a global concept into the day-to-day work of the organization. As a result of the complications of attempting to adopt a sustainability mindset within an organization, the solutions offered both in management theory and those directed towards practitioners are most often intended to reduce complexity, with practitioners offered the "silver bullet" of how to make a business more sustainable, or how to mobilize a traditional, generic business case for sustainability.[7] Some academics and consultants point to the importance of driving towards convergence on one definition of sustainability in order to make progress that can be measured, however incrementally. While these approaches are useful for what they illuminate about initiatives firmly centered in an organization's current reality, such as eco-efficiency and reputation and legitimacy, they are problematic for encouraging novelty and innovation towards societal level transformation, as they keep the locus of sustainability on *sustaining the organization as it is* rather than focused on the broader societal level ideal. In fact, the phrase "business sustainability" is often used as a substitute for "sustainable development," but the ampersand in "business & sustainability" signifies an important difference in the assumptions and values underlying this approach that should not be overlooked. "Business sustainability" advocates most often seek to improve the status quo in incremental ways, supported by a systemic view of organizations rather than attempting to provide insight into social processes that support the emergence of innovation. Efforts to motivate a rational and linear business case for sustainability, while usefully intended to motivate organizations to treat this as a serious business issue, more often than not are where the conversations begin and end, as evidenced by the majority of organizational initiatives that are focused internally on today's issues.[8] From this perspective we are seen as just one green purchase away from achieving sustainability, while the limits or challenges of the conventional model of doing business remain fundamentally unquestioned. It may be argued that such attempts to simplify sustainability in order to increase its palatability to mainstream business effectively overlook the richness of the organization's context and the attendant social complexity; because of this we miss opportunities to create more value for a wider range of stakeholders in an integrated manner, and to push beyond the status quo into the realm of transformation.[9]

Bridging from Societal to Organizational

Sustainability is intrinsically a challenge to the status quo, and therefore is inherently about change and transformation. All theoretical and practical work in a sustainable development frame begins with the assertion that that current conditions, practices, and assumptions are *un*sustainable, and that change is required: change that is either a technocentric, incremental evolution of the current system, at a minimum, or more preferably, a radical, transformational change to fundamental values underpinning the commercial system.[10] Consideration of sustainability in management therefore necessarily includes consideration of change and how change happens in a complex environment.

The question, then, is How do we enable organizational change towards sustainability in a way that positively impacts societal level initiatives, allowing organizations to function as social movement actors – that is, as actively engaged corporate citizens – while at the same time engaging managers at the organizational level? In order to answer this question, we will draw from insights in our own research in the area of "sustainability conversations." In the next section we will consider the social dynamics of sustainability that emerge when leaders struggle to make sense of this construct within their own organizations. A process view of complexity sees the interaction of small differences (or "microdiversity") as a key driver of change and evolution. By attending to *dominant* (i.e., organizationally legitimate) and *shadow* (i.e., organizationally illegitimate or subversive) themes in the organization's sustainability conversations, it is possible to engage a wide range of individuals in an understanding of what sustainability means to them in their daily work. Doing so can unleash the potential energy of many minds working in different ways towards a sustainability vision.

BOX 7.2
MINI-CASE: TATA COMPANIES AS SOCIAL MOVEMENT ACTORS[11]

For 140 years, Tata companies have functioned as social movement actors in India, encouraging labor welfare reforms that extended beyond their legal responsibilities as an organization. These reforms were not only more progressive than the national legislation but also exceeded what many Western companies were doing at the time. Examples of this are the eight-hour working day which was instituted in 1912, maternity benefits that were introduced in 1928, and a retirement gratuity that was established in 1937. Tata companies were recognized for their commitment to advance social welfare initiatives within their communities. This included a broad scope of activities that ranged from the development of national institutes for science and technology to providing emergency help for crisis situations.

What social processes gave rise to these conversations?

Sustainability Conversations and Change: Dominant and Shadow Themes

In our work of examining the meaning-constructions of practicing managers, our analysis repeatedly led us to consider the role of organizational conversation in meaning-construction and change. The implications of conversation for organizational life are profound. Juanita Brown and David Isaacs[12] point to the very practical outcomes of decision making that leaders can shape by the nature of the conversations they engage in with internal and external stakeholders. They suggest that when people care about the questions they are working on and when their conversations are truly alive, participants will naturally organize themselves to do whatever has to be done. Self-organization that arises from engaging conversations leads to the view that conversation *is* action.

From a CRP perspective on change, the role of conversation in meaning-construction figures prominently.[13] A complexity perspective offers a process-based view of social meaning construction, in which conversation is the primary ordering force of both social meaning and individual mind: "Conversations, stories and narratives are complex responsive processes of symbols interacting with each other to produce emergent themes of meaning that organize the experience of those engaged in the conversational activity."[14] At the end of the chapter we will consider further how this CRP view provides radical insights for organizations concerning the sustainability-focused meaning-constructions of individuals in their organizational context, and the implications for practicing managers who are working to promote healthy processes that support sustainability.

The complex responsive processes view is a relevant frame for considering wicked problems because complexity is integral to these issues: they can't be "managed" like traditional business problems and so the implications for management competencies are profound. As discussed in chapter 5, within a conventional systemic view of organizations attention is on the behavior of the macro system, and the idea of microdiversity is not meaningfully considered. This is a significant potential shortcoming since microdiversity is the key driver of innovation and adaptation in complexity thinking in the natural sciences.[15] As we have noted, innovation and change are intrinsic to sustainability, and so it is entirely consistent that the insights that have emerged from our research have been enriched by a focus on this microdiversity. In our work, this is found in the conversational themes around sustainability that take place in organizations. The focus on microdiversity also addresses our observation that incremental approaches to sustainability may not translate to change at the societal level.

In the multiple research projects we have conducted we found that, first, there are a range of sustainability conversational themes that can be interpreted as legitimate and shadow themes in different organizations; and second, that a set of *social dynamics of sustainability* emerges from the interaction of these themes. We found that a complex process view of sustainability allows us to consider how organizations might best engage a multiplicity of themes in order to positively impact sustainability at the societal level.

A CRP view focuses on how processes of communication self-organize into dominant and shadow themes that give meaning to organizational life, and how those themes and patterns change in unpredictable ways. Conversations reflect and create power dynamics in relationships, and so change can only occur when there is a shift in the conversational themes that are viewed as legitimate. The logical extension of this is the idea that when people speak to each other differently, their organization will change, so from a CRP view facilitating different conversations becomes an essential part of facilitating change. *Legitimate themes* comprise what people feel they are able to speak about openly and freely while *shadow themes* represent conversations in which people feel they are able to give less acceptable accounts of themselves and their actions as well as others and their actions. The social dynamics of sustainability are created in sustainability conversations when these shadow themes challenge legitimate or dominant themes in the organization; whether these dynamics are positive or negative in any given organization depends partly on the leadership signals and the quality of the managerial capabilities in that organization.

Interaction of Individuals and Contexts: The Social Dynamics of Sustainability

In chapter 6, we characterized sustainability as a *process of meaning creation through conversation,* and we presented four conceptions of organizational sustainability and their features as conversational themes and subthemes organizing the meaning-creation process. Through the course of our research, it has not been unusual to encounter multiple conceptions at play within a single organization; however, for each organization there appear to be conversational themes that are more frequently evident in the viewpoints of respondents. These we have called the "dominant conversational themes" in an organization: if it were possible to map the nature of all of the sustainability-focused conversations among managers in real time, there would be a clustering with a locus in one conception or another.

What we also observe is that our conversational interviews with individuals tend to center in one region or another of the map depending on the viewpoint of the respondent – and that these conversational themes can range across conceptions. A given individual creating meaning around the concept of sustainability can pull the discussion towards certain themes. The same process takes place in every conversation in every organization every day in similar ways.

In considering internal conversations at the individual level, we are in essence considering the ongoing construction of one's point-of-view – what is called the thinking process in cognitive terms – we are considering meaning-creation, taking the view that individuals create meaning through ongoing internal and socially interactive conversations. Under a process perspective, our personal world view is formed through the ongoing interactions with the world around us, and through our continual inner conversations, or "self-talk," as we process what we encounter. In turn, the interacting sum of all of our individual world views shape the social world around us – as in the pragmatic saying at the opening of chapter 1: "The mind and the world jointly make up the mind and the world." This process view is more dynamic, more situated in the time-based give-and-take of conversation and meaning-creation and evolution, than a more spatially oriented system view, where the focus is on "the organization" as a static entity. In a process view, the organization is something that we create and re-create everyday through conversation – it is a living thing, an ongoing social construction.

Tensions between Individual Mindsets and Dominant Organizational Themes

When individuals articulate their views on sustainability, they also discuss their interpretations of the organizational position, and many describe tensions they feel between their own views and the contextual meaning-environment in which they operate every day. For example, as illustrated in Figure 7.1, a person whose own mindset and individual conversational themes are situated in the *synthesizing* quadrant might feel certain tensions with the dominant conversational themes in the organization, and those tensions might differ depending, for example, on whether the dominant themes are in the *trading* or *adapting* quadrants.

Whether these tensions are ultimately conflictive or creative will depend on the ongoing social dynamics – the continuous action-

Figure 7.1. Shadow and Dominant Themes: Tensions between Individual and Context

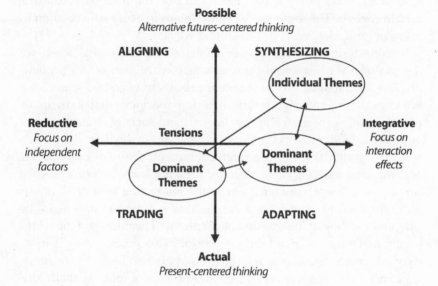

response-action-response process – resulting from that tension as individual conversation themes (or individual viewpoints) and dominant organizational themes continue to interact. These tensions will be made conflictive or creative depending on the nature of the responses by both individuals and the formal organization (its leaders and management processes). If individual conversational themes are not embraced or included in the mainstream current of conversations, negative (change inhibiting) social dynamics can result. Many managers describe exactly those situations: in which their own constructed meanings around sustainability are out of step with the dominant organizational themes. We believe that if conversational themes from all four of these conceptions of organizational sustainability are adequately embraced in the dominant conversational themes, then there is the potential to initiate positive (change enabling) "social dynamics for sustainability."

Figure 7.2 presents a situation where the dominant conversational theme in an organization is in the *trading* quadrant (or "reductive-actual" –

Figure 7.2. Four Conceptions: Nature of Conversations and the Potential for Tension

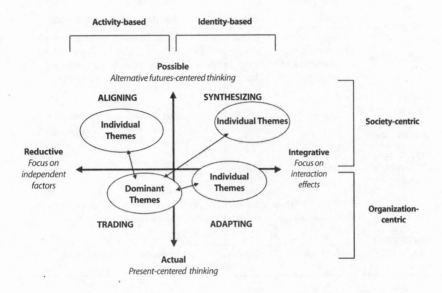

settling for trade-offs in managing day to day). Individuals whose sustainability-meanings are centered in conversational themes in any of the other three quadrants (*aligning, adapting,* or *synthesizing*), which are shadow themes in this organization, will feel tension with their context. These felt tensions are resolved by individuals through the social dynamics they enact, and they will differ in their qualitative nature depending on the relative location of individual themes and their respective contextually dominant conversational themes. In general, these tensions are activity-based in nature on the left side of the framework, and identity-based on the right side; and in the lower quadrants the tensions are organization-centric, and in the upper quadrants, society-centric.

Table 7.1 presents some examples reported by managers with respect to felt tensions when particular types of conversations are excluded from the dominant themes. For each conception where individual themes may be anchored, we have listed the nature of the conversational themes, the kind of tension that managers report (as one example – there are other descriptors possible), and the potentially negative

Table 7.1. The Social Dynamics of Sustainability

| | Activity-based | | Identity-based | |
	TRADING	ALIGNING	ADAPTING	SYNTHESIZING
Conversational themes	What we do: seeking closure on tangible organizational debates and activities	What we could do: exploring possibilities using tangible facts and defined activities	Who we are: seeking alignment between organizational values and actions	Who we could be: seeking alignment between organizational values and societal values
Felt tensions if these themes are not included in organizational conversational themes	Confusion	Impatience	Inauthenticity	Meaninglessness
Potentially negative (change inhibiting) social dynamics	Reservation	Frustration	Alienation	Rebellion
	If sustainability conversations are inclusive of all themes, then there is potential to redirect social dynamics (process of individual meaning-making in context) towards …			
Potentially positive (change-enabling) social dynamics	Connection	Opportunism	Commitment	Enthusiasm

(change-inhibiting) social dynamic that could be put into motion. If the conversational field were broadened to be inclusive of all themes, there is the potential to alter the trajectory of the social dynamics to a positive (change-enabling) direction. For example, in column four: if individual sustainability-conversational themes are situated on "who we could be" – suppose an individual holds an idealist, entrepreneurial idea of the sustainability-focused possibilities for the organization – and those themes are largely absent from the organizational themes (say they are focused on "what we do" – and talk of new possibilities is not admitted as legitimate, as depicted in Figure 7.2), then the felt tension in the individual could be one of *meaninglessness* – a lack of alignment between organizational and societal values as constructed by the individual. Managers who report this combination may resolve the tension through *rebellion* – either through creating their own societally focused sustainability meaning in their work, or by leaving the organization altogether. As one manager told us:

Our "sustainable development strategy" is a frustrating piece to me. You won't find me in there – it has no meaning for me. I find it's been kind of high-jacked by the people that worry about being audited, so they aim low. I find they don't look for the big picture, and I'm definitely a "big-picture" person. So I just do good work outside the formal system.

For organizations with genuine intent towards more closely aligning organizational sustainability with notions of global societal sustainability, such a loss is an enormously missed opportunity to build momentum for change. However, inclusion of a synthesizing view of value creation into the organization's dominant conversational themes can turn rebellion into enthusiasm, and this enthusiasm can be leveraged as a change enabler, as one manager reported:

We see it as our role to be part of the sustainability movement, to raise the consciousness of communities. We feel there is an educational role for us as stimulators of discussion, grapplers of problems. We raise issues and we communicate. So it's a great opportunity for us to take the sustainability discussion and integrate it into our programs to share it with a broader audience.

But what if the dominant conversational theme in an organization is about "who we could be," and shadow themes are centered on sustainability as "what we do"? This is described in column one of Table 7.1. When these shadow themes are absent from the dominant conversation, it creates *confusion* for some individuals:

I don't think any one person knows everything that's going on here. It's grown into this huge thing, so it's difficult to, it's a big boat to be steering, and I think there needs to be more of an understanding from everyone as to what we're doing. That way you get more cohesion as far as everyone's now going in the same direction.

This tension manifests in a negative social dynamic of *reservation* about the whole idea of sustainability:

I think it is a real dangerous track, to be honest with you, a totally dangerous track. I do not think it is traditional in what we do. If you do not do your base work well and you start going a different course, they are going to say, what is with those guys, what are they really doing, what do they really want to do? That is my big concern. Sure there are lots of issues and I am not necessarily, I am not ignorant of what the issues are but I do not think as an agency we should be spearheading it. I think we do our work better when we concentrate on our base work. My big concern is that you go that route, you lose track of your core stuff and you are a duck on a windy day, you are going to get shot. That is not a good thing. I think what you do is you sell what your agency is supposed to do and you make it make sense to people.

By contrast, in an organization where the sustainability conversations were more inclusive of this theme, there was more often a social dynamic of *connection* between individual and dominant themes:

We don't sell anything directly to consumers … so it's obviously a harder link. It's much easier for a business that's in the consumer market to be able to help people make that link, that's why you try to help people in the nylon business understand that ultimately nylon is making airbags and I think the business leaders are trying to make people understand that you are part of a whole value web, actually, in terms of creating this products and services that society needs.

The potential permutations are too numerous to depict in full, so we have summarized in Table 7.1 a sample of the social dynamics we have observed in our research that emerge when plotted across the four conceptions, to provide a snapshot of the multiplicity of social dynamics at play in any given organization at any given moment.

Moving down the first column: (1) if an individual's conversational themes were centered in a particular quadrant; (2) and themes in that quadrant were not included and accepted as legitimate in the organizational themes, and that individual reported feeling tensions; (3) those tensions could lead to negative social dynamics – that is, that individual behaving in a way that is counter to the sustainability objectives of the organization; (4) if organizational themes were broadened to be inclusive of all potential conceptions, and to admit those into the legitimized free-flow dialogue in the organizations, there would be the potential to engender more positive social dynamics and to raise the potential for positive change.

In the public documents of all of organizations we have researched in depth, sustainability is framed as an impetus for change, for doing business differently. From a complex responsive process view of organizations, the capacity to change rests on the ability to disrupt "stuck" patterns of conversation and meaning-making. Complexity theorist Ralph Stacey puts it this way:

> Organizational health has to do with the capacity to change, to produce new forms, and this depends crucially on free-flowing, flexible conversation ... Organizational illness, on the other hand, is an inability to change that occurs when conversational life follows stable attractors in which themes are simply repeated with only superficial change ... an organization's internal capacity to move spontaneously to a new form depends upon the degree of diversity in its conversational themes.[16]

From this we suggest that admitting diverse "shadow" conceptions of sustainability into legitimate organizational themes has the potential to fully engage the workforce, to increase the capacity for innovation, and to raise the level of organizational health.

LEADERSHIP SKILL BUILDING:
Process Questions, Skills, and Skill-Building Exercises

PROCESS QUESTIONS CHAPTER 7: A Complex Responsive Process View of Sustainability

There are four over-arching process questions that a CRP view requires to be posed in any transformative change process: (1) what is the quality of participation in the conversational life of the organization? (2) what is the quality of anxiety and how is it lived with? (3) what is the quality of diversity? and (4) what is the quality of unpredictability and paradox? As described in Table 7.2, each of these process questions has implications for management competencies and for developing healthy social processes that support sustainability.

LEADERSHIP SKILLS CHAPTER 7: Implications of the CRP View: Management Competencies for Healthy Sustainability Conversations

A key insight for leaders that comes from understanding the social dynamics of sustainability is that conversations play a significant role in maintaining the status quo

Table 7.2. Implications of a CRP view for Management Competencies and Healthy Sustainability Conversations

A Complex Responsive Processes View Refocusing Attention*	Implications for Management Competencies	Implications for Healthy Sustainability Conversations
Quality of participation in conversational life of the organization Attention to the thematic patterning of interaction: patterning of power relations, inclusion and exclusion, ideological themes emerging.	**Manager as process consultant** Observing and feeding back thematic patterns; unblocking stuck conversational themes. **Relevant competencies:** Social process consultation Emotional intelligence Critical thinking	Create space for sustainability focused conversations in structured and informal encounters, especially among senior organizational leaders. Recognize that individual themes may be centered with an identity-focus or an activity focus. Engage in sustainability conversations that will help to build a sense of identity in what sustainability means to individuals. In contexts enabling of change, sustainability is not just about "what we do" but also about "who we are."
Quality of anxiety and how it is lived with Attention to threatened identities as innovations arise; to feelings of incompetence in the face of uncertainty.	**Manager as holder of anxiety** Reflecting on the sources of anxiety in the living present; building trust and confidence in change and oneself. **Relevant competencies:** Reflective practice Comfort with ambiguity Counseling	Resist rapid closure in conversations on sustainability; invite "possible"-focused themes as well as "actual"-focused themes. More broadly focused, long-term activities encourage integrated meanings that are more enabling of change than more narrowly focused, short-term activities that encourage fragmented enactments.
Quality of diversity Attention to the importance of unofficial ideologies that undermine current power relations.	**Manager as moderator of challenge and conflict** Noticing the tension between legitimate themes and shadow themes, and how inclusion and exclusion occurs **Relevant competencies:** Critical thinking – surfacing assumptions Complexity thinking	Infuse the organization, through conversation or through structured development sessions, with frame-stretching information and questions on global sustainability. Engage in sustainability conversations that will promote the adoption of language and thinking about sustainability beyond the organizational level. Societal level enactments of sustainability are more enabling of change than exclusively organization or industry level enactments.
Quality of unpredictability and paradox Attention to how unpredictability is tolerated and how paradox is a source of generative tension.	**Manager as leader of emergent enquiry** Accepting that unpredictability is inseparable from creativity; holding paradox open and leading enquiry on it. **Relevant competencies:** Complexity thinking Design thinking	Seek to identify tensions arising among conceptions of sustainability, and leverage those tensions constructively.

*Column 1 adapted from Stacey (2003).

or encouraging change. To expand the field of conversation, leaders in sustainability-focused organizations can use the four key process questions identified above to explore the specific management competencies required to support healthy sustainability conversations.

Quality of Participation in Conversational Life: Managers as Facilitators of Sustainability Conversations

The CRP perspective directs attention towards the things such as the patterning of power relations, who and what gets included and excluded in organizations, ideological themes that arise, and challenges to the identity of managers and employees that can result in a general level of discomfort and anxiety. When sustainability is viewed as a social movement with radical implications for the fundamental day-to-day work of an organization, rather than a business strategy with tangential and incremental opportunities for shifting the business agenda, the tension between legitimate and shadow themes becomes more significant. As we described earlier, relationships are organized in conversations that form and are formed by the power relations between people. Organizations can only change when the themes that order conversations and power relations change, and organizational learning is critical for any change for these themes to occur.

In order to support this change, managers need to act as facilitators of sustainability conversations. Process consultation[17] involves attending to the patterns and assumptions that emerge in conversational exchanges and opening these up for feedback in the ongoing process. Coming from the tradition of organization development practitioners and psychotherapists, process consultation is now a core organizational competency for innovation.

In our experience, a competent manager is one who is sensitive to the themes that emerge in conversation and one who can observe and reflect back these thematic patterns, unblocking stuck conversational themes. Specific relevant competencies are social process consultation, emotional intelligence,[18] and critical thinking skills,[19] that is, the ability to identify dominant claims and surface basic assumptions – both reality assumptions about how we think the world works, and values assumptions about the way we think it ought.

Building on these management competencies, leaders for sustainability need to specifically work to encourage the following social processes in their organization in order to help develop healthy sustainability conversations:

- Create space for all four conceptions of sustainability-focused conversations in structured and informal encounters, especially among senior organizational leaders.
- Recognize that individual themes may be centered with an identity focus or an activity focus: engage in sustainability conversations that will help to build

a sense of identity in what sustainability means to individuals. In change-enabling contexts, sustainability is not just about "what we do" but also about "who we are."

Quality of Anxiety and How It Is Lived With: Managers as Holders of Anxiety

The CRP perspective focuses attention on the importance of free-flowing conversation in which people are able to search for new meaning. When individuals engage in new conversations, this reflects the new ways that they are making sense of their own identity. One inevitable outcome of this is anxiety, as new conversational themes serve to threaten both individual and collective identities. In our sustainability conversations framework, this can be seen in the synthesizing quadrant where the question of "who we could be" serves to challenge the very identity of the organization. When sustainability is embraced in all of its complexity, and when it is considered for its significance at the societal level, this can create a sense of disorientation for individuals in the organization. This results from the attendant innovative implications of this perspective, such as the reinvention of products and markets, rather than an exclusive focus on the incremental meanings that are "safer" and easier to make sense of within an organization's traditional approach to business, such as eco-efficiency. The uncertainty that comes with creativity can give rise to anxiety, even shame at feelings of incompetence. For this reason, the capacity for living with anxiety is critical to organizational change and innovation.

Innovation and competitive potential depends on managers who are capable of reflecting on the sources of anxiety in the living present and of building trust and confidence in change and in others. Again, in our experience, humility, reflective practice,[20] and comfort with ambiguity through mindfulness,[21] along with the skill to counsel and encourage others, are important management competencies.

Building on these management competencies, leaders for sustainability need to work to encourage social processes in their organization in order to help develop healthy sustainability conversations:

- Resist rapid closure in conversations on sustainability; invite "possibility"-focused themes as well as "actual"-focused themes. More broadly focused, long-term activities encourage integrated meanings that are more enabling of change than more narrowly focused, short-term activities that encourage fragmented enactments.

Quality of Diversity: Managers as Moderators of Challenge and Conflict

The possibility of what might emerge in organizations is enhanced by the ability of non-linear interactions to amplify small differences; in plain terms this means that small differences at the micro level can have big effects at the macro level (the so-called butterfly effect). From this perspective, innovation in organizations emerges in the amplification of the diversity between participants in their patterns of communication, even when that diversity is quite small. In trying to make sense of sustainability, often managers seek to reduce complexity and drive to a single definition of what sustainability means, often one that is defined at the organizational level. In fact, sustainability is very much about calling on and explaining the relevance of a diverse range of social and environmental drivers that form the strategic context for the firm. A CRP view, therefore, focuses attention on the importance of diversity in meaning (versus a culture of sameness) and on unofficial ideologies (witnessed in shadow themes) that may undermine existing power relations.

To borrow an idea from the social movement literature, the social dynamics of sustainability that result from tensions between conversational themes can be thought of as a process of "micromobilization" in organizations. Micromobilization can be understood as the social psychological processes by which individuals are transformed into agents who are able to challenge the status quo and the local tactics that individuals use in order to contribute to the goals of broader social movements.[22] Encouraging a diversity of conversational themes may allow an organization to act as a mobilizing force for social change. By engaging more employees in the conversation through the inclusion of a greater diversity of themes, the organization may more effectively perform as a social movement actor[23] positively impacting the relationship between organizational and societal level sustainability, rather than simply as a traditional business organization solely concerned with competitive advantage and shareholder value.

While competent managers are not encouraged to incite revolution and revolt, a critical skill lies in noticing, tolerating, and holding the tension between legitimate themes and shadow themes, and observing how inclusion and exclusion occurs – what is acceptable to discuss or not, and, more important, how that gets decided. Here again, critical thinking skills are essential for surfacing assumptions, and complexity thinking skills are necessary to hold apparent contradictions in creative tension.

Building on these management competencies, leaders for sustainability need to specifically work to encourage the following social processes in their organization to help develop healthy sustainability conversations:

- Infuse the organization, through conversation, or through structured development sessions, with frame-stretching information and questions on global sustainability.
- Engage in sustainability conversations that will promote the adoption of language and thinking about sustainability beyond the organizational level. Societal level enactments of sustainability are more enabling of change than exclusively organization or industry level enactments.
- Tolerate debate, ambiguity, and even opposition.

Quality of Unpredictability and Paradox: Managers and HR Practitioners as Leaders of Emergent Enquiry

A CRP perspective focuses attention on how unpredictability is tolerated and how paradox is a source of generative tension. An apparent paradox between two stated organizational aspirations can be an ongoing source of creative tension. For example, Walmart's mission to be globally dominant in consumer goods *and* be a leader in environmental and social sustainability is to many a paradoxical notion. Suncor's ambition to be a "sustainable energy company" while leading the development of the controversial Alberta oil sands is equally paradoxical. Left unresolved, these paradoxes have the potential to generate many exploratory conversations inside and outside the companies concerned.

Differing and contradictory conceptions of contestable concepts such as sustainability can be strong change motivators.[24] Unpredictability is an important part of the creativity that emerges from organizations, and therefore the focus should be on processes of emergent enquiry rather than managerial operations of planning and control in order to encourage innovation.

A critical role for managers is to accept the unpredictability of the creative state and to have the capacity to hold paradox open and lead enquiry on it. In the Walmart example, the inherent paradoxical tension between global consumerism and environmental and social sustainability has the potential to be an overarching driver for novel meanings, innovation, and change surrounding Walmart's core identity and business model. The role of the manager is to hold the paradox open and to bring emergent enquiry into everyday conversation. Complexity thinking skills are relevant here, as is a capacity for design thinking. As we explored in chapter 2, design thinking encourages us to engage stakeholders as designers in a conversational approach that thrives on instability and focuses on what is possible, allowing for the emergence of new ideas. Complexity thinking enables managers to creatively hold the tension between multiple stakeholder perspectives on multiple issues, encouraging new and emergent outcomes that optimize human development within ecological limits.

To take a conversational approach to design thinking means to engage internal and external stakeholders in bringing to the surface and generating paradoxical creative tension. Stakeholder engagement processes,[25] formal and informal, can help to generate paradoxical conceptions of identity and action by drawing attention to alternative perspectives and interests regarding the organization. DuPont's Biotechnology Advisory Panel and the sustainability reporting stakeholder panels of numerous other corporations are mechanisms for formalizing dialogue with stakeholders. Just as important, however, are the behaviors and mindsets of the middle managers who appear in many and diverse communities as representatives of the organization.

Building on these management competencies, leaders for sustainability need to specifically work to encourage the following social process in their organization in order to develop healthy sustainability conversations:

- Seek to identify tensions arising among conceptions of sustainability, and leverage those tensions constructively. For example, where a trading view dominates in an organization but some individuals create meanings that embody a synthesizing view, identifying strategic opportunities where the organization can stretch to encompass both perspectives would create more value for internal and external stakeholders.

SKILL BUILDING EXERCISE CHAPTER 7: Learning Team Dialogue: Engaging Employees by Expanding the Field of Conversation

- Using the "sustainability conversations" framework and reviewing the websites, sustainability reports, and external media commentary regarding an organization familiar to the group, make an assessment of the likely dominant sustainability conversational themes for each of these organizations – for example, try to determine:

  - How is the sustainability objective "framed"?
  - What is being "sustained," implicitly or explicitly?
  - How are organizational stakeholders conceived or described?
  - How does this relate to your own organizational experience?

- Using the four process questions offered by a CRP view of sustainability, identify four ideas for how the organization you have researched might expand its sustainability conversations by engaging shadow conversational themes that arise from other conceptions of sustainability in the organization.
- What new actions do you think the organization you have researched might take based on this new set of sustainability conversations taking place? That is, how would this reflect in its strategic direction, innovation in products, and markets?
- How might your own organization expand its sustainability conversations by applying the four process questions offered by a CRP view? What new actions might your organizations take based on these new conversational themes?

Conclusion

In this chapter we have explored the concept of sustainability as a wicked problem that can be addressed by taking a complex responsive processes (CRP) view of organizations, rather than the more common approach – incremental, piecemeal activity – that emerges from a conventional systemic view of organizations. We have considered the four conceptions framework presented in chapter 6 and noted that, while there are multiple conceptions of sustainability at play in organizations, there is often an observable, organizationally dominant conception. We have described the potential for tension, both creative and destructive, between the dominant conversational themes in the organization and the shadow themes of individual organizational members, and that tension surfaces as the social dynamics of sustainability which are manifest as either alienation or engagement of individual employees, variously described. Because of these different meanings, we have identified a key leadership role as "conversation starter" who must creatively manage the tension that occurs from multiple meanings constructed around sustainability through conversational processes. We have suggested "responding" capabilities of leaders and elements of conversation process that will help to support organizational health through encouraging the capacity to change and produce new forms through free-flowing conversation. By taking a complex responsive processes view of sustainability, we believe that it is possible to understand how the organization might function as a mobilizing force for societal level change.

PART FOUR: REINVENTING

From Stakeholder Management to Social Integration: Building Collaboratively Competitive Organizations

Admonishing people to improve their learning will do little good; we will have to design social structures that nourish it. Developing a learning society will require many years of criticism, social experimentation, failed experiences and a great deal of thinking and discussion.

– Lester W. Milbraith, Political Science Scholar[1]

Smart companies are recognizing that the most effective way to leverage change in our interdependent world is through common endeavour with others.

– Holliday, Watts, and Schmidheiny, *Walking the Talk*[2]

In chapter 8 we focus on "reinventing" the organization. We synthesize the learning from earlier chapters and draw on design thinking for insights on how to encourage organizational innovations that will advance sustainability outcomes.

The traditional business case for sustainability or corporate social responsibility[3] is built on a value proposition that is most often focused on *trading* off stakeholder interests in order to reduce costs and risks to the organization. Enlightened self-interest means that many organizations are now seeing the value in *adapting* to stakeholder interests in order to generate strategic competitive advantage or *aligning* with stakeholder values and demands in order to build the reputation and legitimacy – and, indeed, income – for their business. While both of these approaches represent progress compared with a strict focus on organizational level sustainability towards a broader stakeholder approach, we suggest that in order to truly reconstruct value we need to *synthesize* organization and societal level views of the concept. In order to do this, organizations must develop value propositions that are focused on relating stakeholder interests *and* the range of complex global issues we outlined in chapter 4, integrating various perspectives in a way that creates value in multiple dimensions. In this chapter we will consider how this can be done by considering business as a social actor and exploring how design thinking might encourage a practical approach to reconstructing value. In doing so, managers and leaders can develop the potential to transform their organizations and allow them to respond to the question laid out in Figure 1.3, How can we create new products and services to shift our current trajectory?

Here we take up the challenge posed at the end of chapter 5, and depicted in Figure 5.1: moving from a focus on organization-centered "stakeholder management" towards actions that encourage "social integration," in order to further the potential for a stakeholder approach to generate value, optimizing results for multiple interests and for society as a whole. Using our conceptions of a sustainability framework in chapters 6 and 7, we highlight the power and potential for building a synthesizing, "integrative-possible" conception of sustainability to enhance and stretch more traditional approaches. Moving from stakeholder management to social integration requires that we encourage "sustainability conversations" at the societal level and then bring that societal focus back into corporate strategy. Strategy is an act of learning – *social learning* at multiple levels, including the level of society broadly. Strategy here is framed as a "collaboratively competitive" concept, where the role of the leader extends to building multi-actor and multi-sectoral collaborations in order to explore new forms of value creation. In this chapter we employ concepts in social learning towards facilitating social integration, and we consider the capabilities necessary for the leader to catalyze and support societal learning in the process of reconstructing value. Continuing with our focus in part four on "reinventing," in chapter 9 we will challenge how we construct notions of success and progress at the societal level in order to further advance the potential for synergies to be created between various organizational stakeholders and social actors.

What Is Social Learning?

Social learning refers to a process of iterative reflection that takes place when we share our experiences and ideas with others and reflect on our insights so that new learning emerges.[4] Social learning theory is generally concerned with the *process of learning* and is consistent with our earlier focus on "rethinking" considering that (1) people can learn by observation; (2) perception and interpretation are important to the learning process, and (3) underlying beliefs impact individual learning.[5] In management training and development programs such as communication skills, coaching, and leadership skills development and decision making, learning is often focused on developing individual traits and capabilities and is based on psychological theories of human behavior. These programs are often geared towards improving the performance of the organization, where performance is usually about enhancing efficiencies within the status quo rather than challenging underlying assumptions and questioning the effectiveness of these pursuits.

Rather than situating learning at the level of the individual, social learning advances the idea that learning is embedded in relationships,[6] and that communities construct meaning through social processes.[7] The "communities of practice" approach has become popular in organizations that are seeking to engage in double-loop learning. Communities of practice are groups of people who come together around common interests and expertise and expand their knowledge by interacting on an ongoing basis.[8] They represent a shift in learning away from the individual acquisition of practical skills and knowledge towards a collaborative effort that impacts practice.[9] Communities of practice challenge traditional boundaries of organizations through a focus on a socially oriented approach to learning and knowing.[10] This applied learning perspective incorporates multiple levels of learning and describes learning as a dynamic inter-level process rooted in a relationship between individuals, teams, interdepartmental groups, and organizations. In this approach, learning is about the organization's relationship to its external context, and so can expand to take into account the strategic positioning of the organization and the importance of multiple stakeholders in that process.[11]

Loblaw Companies Limited is a major Canadian grocery and retail company led by a sustainability-oriented executive chairman, Galen G. Weston. Under Weston's leadership, Loblaw has become an example of an organization that has implicitly recognized an inter-level process of learning and the strategic relationship to multiple stakeholders in developing its "sustainable seafood commitment." Following well-established programs at Unilever, various European supermarket chains, and Walmart (Asda in the United Kingdom), the initiative is intended to help the organization realize its vision of "healthy oceans, stable communities, and sustainable business." Loblaw is working to develop a sustainable procurement practice that is committed to responsible sourcing in every seafood category and categories that contain seafood and is committed to sourcing all seafood, including all canned, frozen, fresh, wild, and aquaculture seafood from sustainable sources by 2013. In order to do this, the company is taking a multi-level and multi-sectoral approach to collaborating with stakeholders. The company has identified a diverse group of external stakeholders that includes the WWF (World Wide Fund for Nature), the Marine Stewardship Council (MSC), the Aquaculture Stewardship Council (ASC), SeaChoice, the David Suzuki Foundation, the Ecology Action Centre, the Living Oceans Society, Greenpeace, brand vendors and distributors, and relevant government agencies, for example Fisheries and Oceans Canada (DFO) and the Fishery Council of Canada. Together with other key stakeholders, including independent marine science advisors who share the organization's vision, and Loblaw staff, franchisees, stores, distribution centers and support centers, the company has gathered around it numerous sources of multi-level engagement and learning.[12]

Innovation as a Process of Social Learning

In chapter 3 we considered the idea of levels of learning and how reconstructing organizational value propositions requires a move from weak to strong sustainability through incorporating multiple levels of learning in organizational initiatives. From this perspective, it is appropriate to view sustainability as a process of social learning or a collaborative reframing of what business the organization is involved in that includes multiple interest groups and stakeholders. Social learning involves ongoing critical reflection and embodies single-, double- and triple-loop learning[13] that is fundamental to reconstructing value.

Many organizations talk about innovation and creativity but few develop systems and processes that actually allow and encourage transformational ideas to emerge. One reason for this is that it is often deemed strategically unwise to step too far outside the mainstream of any particular sector. Institutional theory[14] speaks to the "inertia" that exists in many organizations, especially as they get larger and more established and develop a formula for their success. Established organizations are often modeled on what other organizations are already doing in their sector so that their activities are considered "legitimate" in their particular industry. Incumbent mainstream organizations typically avoid entrepreneurial reinvention even when it is demonstrably sensible for them to experiment. Harvard strategy professor Clayton Christensen described this as the "innovator's dilemma."[15]

Another driver of risk aversion is the need to protect corporate reputation and brands. Significant commercial advantage is generated by an organization's brand value and so often the protection of these brands results in a risk-mitigation approach to sustainability. An example of this is the Coca-Cola Company that regularly leads the global brand value league with a calculated value of more than USD$71 billion in 2011.[16] In 2011 the company created a global Office of Sustainability and appointed its first chief sustainability officer (CSO) in an effort to better integrate various sustainability initiatives in the areas of water, climate protection, packaging, and recycling. This is taking place in an effort to ensure that the company meets its 2020 Vision sustainability goals but more importantly to improve the image of an organization that is frequently under attack from civil society groups. The Coca-Cola Office of Sustainability is responsible for creating and overseeing the corporation's integrated global sustainability strategy and for tracking all global partnerships and key sustainability projects.[17] Despite these managerial coordination efforts, the difficulty of a large organization significantly transforming its business model and moving away from an iconic product that has brought them such great success for such a long time is an obvious challenge. Given the ongoing nutritional, dental health, and environmental controversies surrounding the company, it is almost inevitable that the company's sustainability stance will be to defend and protect "what is" – that is, a fabulously valuable brand.

Joseph Schumpeter's assertion in the mid-twentieth century that the central preoccupation of capitalism is not how it administers existing structures but how it works to creatively destroy them[18] generates problems for non-entrepreneurial corporate managers and leaders. Such individuals are invariably rewarded for how much they can work to increase gains for their investors in the existing system. Because the system is primarily focused on the market of expectations or the share price of the company,[19] there is an additional imperative that reinforces the status quo. At most, there may be room for single-loop learning, or enhancing the efficiency of current operations. This explains why so many companies, including Coca-Cola, predicate their sustainability efforts firmly on eco-efficiency and reputation and legitimacy initiatives rather than pursuing more fundamental approaches to innovation and transformation.

Viewing innovation in sustainability-focused organizations as a social process[20] allows us to think about how we might open up sustainability conversations and consider new possibilities for the organization to create value, for itself and for a wider range of stakeholders. By engaging in a multi-stakeholder process of societal level learning, we suggest that it is possible for leaders to undertake innovation that is truly geared towards creating products and services of value that meet human needs, and which acknowledge global ideals such as social justice and ecological limits to growth. In order to accomplish this, the role that managers and leaders need to fulfill will be both as social *intrapreneurs* and *social entrepreneurs*. A social intrapreneur is a corporate changemaker who works *inside* a large organization and challenges the status quo in order to innovate and create market-based solutions to social and environmental issues.[21] A social entrepreneur on the other hand identifies a social or environmental issue and then creates a new business venture – a social enterprise – that will address the issue. While the purpose of these organizations is to further social or environmental goals, in the private sector they have to also maintain profitability, and in the non-profit sector they need to tend to their financial imperatives, in order to continue to exist.[22]

Learning at Multiple Levels Simultaneously

The levels of learning considered in chapter 3 focus our attention on the idea that excellence in leadership requires the ability to stimulate single-, double-, and triple-loop learning in organizations in order to promote innovation and change. This is not an evolutionary view of learning, that is, we need to move away from single- and towards triple-loop learning if we are to encourage a sustainability mindset to emerge. Rather, leaders need to encourage all forms of learning to continuously take place in different parts of the organization at different times to create both short-term and long-term value for stakeholders. Triple-loop learning enables a fundamentally different approach to individual, organizational, and even societal level change. In this style of learning, leaders are not enhancing processes or reflecting on their activities with a goal of simple continuous improvement; instead, a deep-seated level, they are redirecting the trajectory of the organization. Without single-loop learning it would be difficult for established sustainability initiatives to make measured progress towards objectives and goals. Conversely, if a focus on increasing efficiency in established projects is the only preoccupation of leaders in the organization, then moving towards a longer-term vision of sustainability aligned with societal and ecological imperatives would be virtually impossible.

Leaders as Provocateurs and Meaning-Makers in Learning

Leaders who are prepared to think the unthinkable are effectively questioning the direction that has been laid out for them by the history, leadership, identity, culture, and strategies of the organization. By fundamentally challenging organizational behaviors and assumptions, leaders can develop their organization's awareness of potentially radically changing circumstances and enable the organization to respond in a proactive manner to "wicked problems" that are complex and continuously shifting. This kind of thinking may be contrasted with the idea of "maintenance learning" that rewards "good soldiers" and requires moulding to the status quo, or "shock learning" that inhibits change by encouraging the belief that employees are not in control of complex events and so must depend on organizations and strong leaders to protect them. Both maintenance learning and shock learning are in clear opposition to "innovative learning," which happens less often but which emphasizes the autonomy of the individual to understand and work within the organizational context in a positive way in order to make change happen.[23]

The development of design thinking capabilities can support innovative learning and result in creative solutions to global problems. An example of this can be found in Sustainable Health Enterprises (SHE), which was founded by the American entrepreneur Elizabeth Scharpf in response to social problems in developing countries. SHE's first initiative is designed to address the issue of millions of girls and women in developing countries who miss up to fifty days of school/work per year because they do not have access to affordable sanitary pads when they menstruate. Ensuring that girls and women are able to participate in the education system and the workforce is essential to the current and long-term well-being of communities. The organization is helping women to set up new businesses to produce inexpensive, quality, eco-friendly sanitary pads from locally sourced raw materials, starting with banana fibers in Rwanda. Businesses are launched by partnering with existing local women's networks, providing access to microfinance loans for women who are sharing start-up costs, and training the local women in business skills and in health and hygiene.[24] This kind of design thinking that leads to sustainable innovation acknowledges the constraints of limits to growth while foregrounding human development. It is exactly what organizations need to embrace in order to identify desirable, feasible, and viable concepts specific to their own business context that will create value on multiple fronts. Innovative learning is critical to reconstructing value, and conceiving of learning as a triple-loop social process offers both a challenge and an opportunity for organizations to develop the capabilities required of leaders in order to support this approach.

The Tragedy of the Commons and Societal Learning

If managers and leaders do not engage in double- and triple-loop learning in order to reconstruct value, they risk experiencing a "tragedy of the commons." This phrase describes a dilemma in which multiple individuals acting independently in their own self-interest can ultimately destroy a shared limited resource even when it is clear that it is not in anyone's long-term interest for this to happen.[25] The tragedy of the commons can be characterized by four kinds of traps: (1) social traps where some people may fall prey to the temptation to profit at the expense of other people; (2) temporal traps where individuals choose short-term benefits at the immediate expense of their own future selves; (3) spatial traps where people in a certain location may benefit while those who are in a different location suffer; and (4) political traps where parochial thinking dominates when what is required is collective global action. The "tyranny of small decisions"[26] that precedes tragedies of the commons describes how a series of small, individually rational decisions can negatively impact the potential for future decision making. Well intentioned small decisions may limit the possibility of engaging in a desired course of action because they do not allow for higher level integrative thinking on complex issues of sustainability.

The collapse of commercial fisheries for Atlantic cod in Eastern Canada is a good example of this phenomenon. A ban was placed on the fishing industry in 1992 when the abundance of six of seven fish stocks was too low to support continued commercial exploitation. There were three key events that led to the development of this scenario: (1) population abundance being overestimated; (2) overcapacity in the fishing fleet; and (3) the higher mortality of young fish. None of this was recognized due to statistical bias and overreliance on commercial catch per unit data which were not representative of the true abundance of the fish. As the populations declined, fishing mortality and the discarding of juveniles increased, reducing the number of fish entering into the fishery until populations were reduced to the point of commercial extinction.[27] What were the assumptions made that led to the series of disastrous decisions that occurred? Using the idea of "traps" that individuals can fall into is helpful to interpret what took place in this case. Social, temporal, and spatial traps meant that it was a short-term benefit for those companies geographically located in the area to continue to fish at unsustainable levels, despite the presence of evidence that, interpreted differently, may have suggested a collapse was imminent. Large companies benefited in the short term and moved on to focusing on fishing in different regions when the cod fishery collapsed; in contrast, local employees and communities, while thriving when times were good, were ultimately devastated when the collapse took place. Political traps meant that while earlier government intervention could have made a difference, there were local constituency interests to satisfy and a financial impact of this industry on the national GDP that encouraged a particular bias in the interpretation of data that were available. It is even possible that key data that would have impacted this interpretation was actively suppressed by certain vested interests, specifically the illegal large scale discarding and non-reporting of small fish as the population declined and fishing mortality increased.[28] It is easy then to see how climate, water, energy, food, and other commonly held resources could each fall prey to this same phenomenon without a healthy participatory stakeholder process of triple-loop learning to challenge the trajectory.

As we discussed in chapter 3, triple-loop learning embodies the perspective of learning as a social process, participatory and relational; we do not learn how to challenge our underlying assumptions and reinvent our thinking as individuals reflecting in isolation, but as social creatures in conversation with one another. Social learning can take place in teams, departments, organizations, or, at a more macro level, in society. "Societal learning" represents a shift in world views that leads to the development of new perspectives, goals, and behaviors of social systems that are larger than individual organizations.[29] Societal learning emerged from traditions of thought that considered what elements make a society successful, what change processes will lead societies to improve, and what learning and leadership capabilities are essential for this shift in perspective to take place in a manner that minimizes conflict and optimizes value creation.[30] There are numerous examples where societies have failed to learn and have collapsed – the Roman Empire, the Vikings of Greenland, the North American Anasazi, and the list continues.[31] This phenomenon is so common that archaeologists have a term for it: a "dieback," a situation that arises when a society exceeds the carrying capacity of the environment and its population steeply declines, usually as the result of conflict.[32] Archaeologist Stephen LeBlanc makes the point that as awareness of these patterns and the sophistication of modern technology increases, so does our ability to avoid conflict and collapse in the future. Skills in critical and complexity thinking are essential to unearthing the underlying assumptions that give rise to these patterns and to understanding the interrelationships between various elements of situations so that strategic and design thinking skills can allow us to optimize decisions about how to make sense of and use information.

A contemporary example of the opportunities and challenges of engaging in a process of social learning can be seen in the relatively quick and effective response in the 1980s to the recognition that the stratospheric ozone layer was getting thinner. This layer of the air acts like a shield, protecting life on earth from the damaging ultraviolet rays of the sun. A broad coalition of governments, scientific researchers, civil society groups, and others came together to address this problem and implemented innovative and effective approaches to phase out these ozone-depleting substances. The Vienna Convention for the Protection of the Ozone Layer was developed in 1985 and outlines states' responsibilities for protecting human health and the environment against the negative effects of ozone depletion. This framework led to the negotiation of the Montreal Protocol in 1987, which has since been ratified by 197 states and was described by Kofi Anon as "perhaps the single most successful international environment agreement to date." There are numerous "wins" that can be highlighted in the development of this protocol, namely, a solution identified through truly global participation; 98 per cent elimination of ozone depleting substances; healing of the ozone layer with full recovery expected by 2050; support offered to developing countries in the process; a 98 per cent rate of compliance; numerous health benefits; and a positive impact of the reduction of CFC's on climate change.[33] However, there is much work that remains to be done. Despite this success, as a result of banning CFCs there has been an increasing adoption of HFCs as a substitute. The problem with this is that HFCs are potent greenhouse gases that live an extremely long time in the environment; an unintended side effect of the Montreal Protocol that has positively impacted ozone is that it has negatively impacted climate. Taking an integrative perspective on the complexity of global issues of sustainability enables us to consider how the emergent outcomes of action to resolve one issue have exacerbated another. While the reduction of CFCs has had a positive impact on both ozone and climate, the continued adoption of HFCs threatens to negate that progress if it is not addressed in a timely manner.

This reveals the essence of social learning to reconstruct value: in order to work it must be viewed as an ongoing process of conversation with multiple stakeholders. This is true across the spectrum of levels, from international agreements such as the Montreal Protocol to local arrangements to address specific community issues. Expanding the scope of the Montreal Protocol to include phasing out HFCs is technologically feasible as there are chemical and technological substitutes available,[34] but this will only happen if this agreement is viewed as a process of ongoing interaction. Ultimately, this conversation with stakeholders will allow us to continuously engage in the process of reflective practice to reconstruct value, iterating between the thinking skills and the questions prompted by each of these. In doing so we can move from the solutions created in design thinking to new insights generated through critical thinking, continuously reconsidering the underlying assumptions that give rise to the societal problems we face. We will reflect on this more fully in the next chapter when we consider how we define progress and success at the societal level and how the activities we engage in promote or detract from this. Sherwood Roland, a scientist who received the Nobel Prize for Chemistry for his pioneering work in ozone depletion, spoke to this process of societal engagement that scientists need to partake in when he said in his acceptance speech: "What is the use of having developed a science well enough to make predictions if, in the end, all we are willing to do is stand around and wait for them to come true?"[35] Complex global issues of sustainability require leaders who are able to critically reflect on information and data and who can creatively engage in the redesign of our systems through an ongoing conversation with stakeholders in light of current and emergent insights.

Societal Learning: Social Learning among Societal Actors

The idea of "societal learning" is particularly relevant for reconstructing value in that it describes a useful mechanism for developing novel relationships, strategies, and organizational structures to accomplish new goals. In chapter 1 we explored the idea that sustainability is fundamentally about change. Societal learning, with its focus on how micro level changes in relationships, strategies and structures lead to macro-level transformation of goals, is particularly helpful to envisioning a process of innovation to address sustainability issues.[36] By moving away from thinking about learning as an individual-centered, psychological phenomenon towards a relational process of social learning, we are able consider how societal learning and change might take place. Sustainability conversations that are situated in a multi-sectoral context and focus on developing new ways of talking and thinking about organizational strategies and structures in relationship with one another are a potential leverage point to enable broader level societal learning.

BOX 8.1

MINI-CASE: SOCIETAL LEARNING AND INNOVATION IN THE
CANADIAN BOREAL FOREST AGREEMENT[37]

In May 2010, twenty-one member companies of the Forest Products
Association of Canada (FPAC), and nine leading environmental organizations, signed the world's largest conservation agreement – the
Canadian Boreal Forest Agreement – that applies to 72 million hectares
of public forests licensed to FPAC members. While outcomes of this
agreement still remain to be seen, this development holds the potential
to catalyze societal learning among the signatory environmental organizations, the FPAC, the association's companies and the provincial
governments, First Nations, and local communities across the country
that members of the agreement are now working with to seek their
leadership and full participation in advancing the goals of the agreement. The agreement is intended to stimulate innovative practices, specifically committing to:

- The development and implementation of world-leading forest management and harvesting practices.
- The completion of joint proposals for networks of protected areas and
  the recovery of species at risk including woodland caribou.
- A full life-cycle approach to forest carbon management.
- Support for the economic future of forest communities and
  for the recognition of conservation achievements in the global
  marketplace.[38]

The goal of the agreement is for parties to work together to conserve
significant areas of Canada's vast boreal forest, protect threatened woodland caribou, and provide a competitive market edge for participating
companies. "The importance of this agreement cannot be overstated,"
said Avrim Lazar, president and CEO of FPAC. "FPAC member companies and their ENGO counterparts have turned the old paradigm on its
head. Together we have identified a more intelligent, productive way to
manage economic and environmental challenges in the boreal that will
reassure global buyers of our products' sustainability."[39] Traditionally,
members of FPAC and these environmental organizations had been involved in an adversarial relationship, but this has shifted with this new
commitment to a common goal. "This is our best chance to save woodland caribou, permanently protect vast areas of the boreal forest and put

in place sustainable forestry practices," said Richard Brooks, spokesperson for participating environmental organizations and Forest Campaign Coordinator of Greenpeace Canada. "Concerns from the public and the marketplace about wilderness conservation and species loss have been critical drivers in arriving at this agreement."[40]

The societal learning transformation involves a triple-loop, third-order change in values, behaviors, beliefs, and structures. In the next chapter we will reflect more deeply on these societal learning questions when we consider how an embedded, sustainable, and transformational approach to reconstructing value ultimately requires us to challenge our notions of progress and success at the individual, organizational, and societal level. Innovation in how we organize ourselves is at the heart of societal learning and is critical to enabling more sustainable organizational practices. The generative dialogue enabled by leaders, whose relational and critical thinking capabilities allow them to function as meaning makers, creates possibilities for new relationships to be forged between people in different sectors; relationships that were not formed previously because they were blocked by underlying assumptions and traditional views and ways of working together, now become functional, demonstrating again the iterative nature of this model of reconstructing value – reinventing and rethinking are inextricably linked.

BOX 8.2
MINI-CASE: SOCIETAL LEARNING AND CHANGE AT SABCOHA[41]

HIV/AIDS has a significant impact on business, through costs incurred by organizations, the contraction of markets, and a decrease in societal well-being that compromises the foundation for a healthy economy. This epidemic is a critical issue for companies doing business in South Africa, in particular for labor and capital intensive industries and those with high labor mobility, as anywhere from 10 to 40 per cent of the workforce may be infected with HIV/AIDS. Companies in the sectors most affected – mining, transport, energy, and manufacturing – have become world leaders in their response to HIV/AIDS in the workplace. Much of this activity has been made possible through the multi-sectoral collaborations catalyzed by the South African Business Coalition on HIV/AIDS (SABCOHA). CEO of the coalition Brad Mears states that "some of the most comprehensive and successful HIV/AIDS workplace programmes are being developed in the [South African] private sector,"[42] and companies such as SAB, Anglo American, and Volkswagen have demonstrated leadership in program development that is now being replicated in other countries. Mears describes how employers are increasingly initiating community-wide programs as HIV/AIDS is both in the workplace and the broader community. Leading businesses such as Eskom and Volkswagen are working in partnership with SABCOHA to pilot "supply chain" workplace programs, offering services such as voluntary testing and counseling, provision of antiretrovirals, and broader health and wellness services to employees who don't have access to these resources in the smaller supplier companies. SABCOHA's partnership with the International Executive Services Council, a U.S.-based non-profit organization, delivers "BizAIDS" training, preparing hundreds of small business entrepreneurs every year to deal with HIV/AIDS and related emergencies. Mears describes how "in the corporate sector there is considerable capacity, infrastructure and technical skill that business is able to share with government and other sectors regarding HIV/AIDS programs and activities. There is also a great deal of capacity to complement what government is already doing, especially in the area of systems and data management, sharing of expertise and increasing capacity – particularly in the areas of medical aids and general practitioners."[43] This participatory and collaborative approach to addressing HIV/AIDS is enabling progress to be made with regard to this complex issue.

Multi-Sectoral Collaboration: Stimulating Societal Learning through Adaptive Co-Management

Given how important triple-loop learning is for reconstructing value and stimulating societal learning and change, how can managers and leaders more effectively engage in the participatory process that is required for this innovative thinking to occur? Societal learning requires a process of collaboration that engages organizations in multi-stakeholder and multi-sectoral learning partnerships and ultimately leads to a challenging of governing norms and values in the system. By raising the question, How do we decide what is right? governance models can be questioned and reinvented so that new ideas representing multiple stakeholder perspectives can shape the trajectory of various organizational activities.

Governance and sustainability is an underexplored topic in the business and sustainability field and the term governance has multiple interpretations. Here we are referring to a broader interpretation of the idea, or "those ways by which we agree to be reliable personally, organizationally and politically ... via laws, norms, rituals, shared beliefs, roles, etc. These are incorporated within institutions such as those responsible for education, early socialization, religion, the market and government."[44] In relation to reconstructing value, it is useful to consider how ideas around adaptive co-management might help to inform our design thinking processes and enable us to engage stakeholders in decision making and learning in a way that positively addresses the uncertainty created by the complexity of social-ecological systems. While there are many different descriptions of adaptive co-management, the distinctive feature of this approach is a participatory process of iteratively learning-by-doing that allows for a sharing of rights and responsibilities with stakeholders. It is an approach to governance that acknowledges conditions of change, uncertainty, and complexity. By drawing this into management thinking, we can design an innovative approach for organizations to relate to their stakeholders that incorporates multi-stakeholder collaboration and learning by doing in order to stimulate triple-loop learning.[45]

Adaptive co-management is characterized by the following: (1) a common focus created between stakeholders and their different interests through the development of a shared vision, goal and/or problem definition; (2) stakeholders who are positioned at multiple levels engaging in a high degree of dialogue, interaction, and collaboration; (3) responsibility for actions and decision making shared across multiple levels; (4) different stakeholders at multiple levels with various degrees of autonomy; (5) a commitment to the generation and sharing of knowledge from a wide range of stakeholders; and (6) an orientation towards learning that is flexible and continuously negotiated, acknowledging the fundamental condition of uncertainty

Adaptive co-management is essentially a view of governance as a process of social learning that focuses the attention of managers and leaders on the design thinking capabilities of learning from experience, specifically how learning by doing responds to social and ecological feedback and provides management flexibility.[46] In order to achieve this there is a need for collaboration, joint decision making, and multi-stakeholder involvement to stimulate self-organized processes of learning.[47]

Design Thinking and Societal Learning

In chapter 2 we explored how design thinking held potential for enabling the reinvention of business and allowed managers and leaders to ask and respond to the question, How can we create new products and services to shift our current trajectory? Developing design thinking capabilities in leaders can assist with moving the focus away from solely engaging in business ventures with near-term viability, which results in enhanced efficiency, towards creating new opportunities that are more forward looking. A strategic approach to sustainability suggests that future economic opportunities will be generated by firms that have the ability to develop disruptive technologies that meet societal and environmental needs, such as renewable energy, information technology, and other clean technology initiatives.[48] Leaders need to develop the capacity demonstrated by design thinkers of embracing uncertainty and experimenting within different contexts to generate this breakthrough potential to reconstruct value propositions for their organizations, or for developing new social enterprises that create social and environmental as well as economic benefits. SELCO Solar India[49] is an example of a social enterprise that has a mission to "enhance the quality of life of underserved households and livelihoods through sustainable energy solutions and services." The venture was established in 1995 by challenging two "myths" regarding sustainable technology in a developing country context, namely, that poor people cannot afford or maintain sustainable technologies and that social ventures are inconsistent with commercial goals. SELCO creates products based on end-user needs and offers service and financing options that make it possible for customers to afford their systems. One of their numerous projects to date is a solar lighting initiative at Neelbagh School located in Karnataka, a state in South West India. This free residential school for underprivileged children, whose families are primarily migrant construction workers and poor farmers, was connected to grid power at a cost of about Rs 3,000 each month and with a diesel generator for backup power. They suffered from an inconsistent flow of the power supply that had adverse economic, social, and environmental impacts. The power disruptions were expensive for the school (costing approximately Rs 53,000 each year), classes were disturbed when the backup generator was running, and the noise and low brightness of lights compromised the learning environment for students. Due to the costs, the students were forced to change their approach to studying and to work exclusively during daylight hours. Sustainable technology in the form of a solar powered LED light system installed at the school in February 2010 had positive benefits for the environment and eliminated the need for grid power lighting and backup generator use. This resulted in an economic savings of Rs 4,000 a month and Rs 5,000 maintenance costs per year on the backup generators, as well as a 30 per cent reduction in electricity bills. Social benefits included the development of better quality lighting, eliminating the disruption of school activities due to energy supply issues, and providing students with the opportunity to study anytime and anywhere.

Collaboratively Competitive Organizations

A conversational or evolutionary approach to design – one that consistent with the societal learning approach rather than one that is dominated by the designer – helps to open up the design process through engaging multiple stakeholders in a participatory manner as designers, leading to greater opportunity for emergent and transformational outcomes.[50] This can be seen where companies and NGOs enter into co-creation business models, or the development of an integrated business model where the firm becomes a central avenue for the NGO to deliver value and the NGO enhances the company's capacity to deliver value. This innovative business model creates key opportunities for creating value such as delivering low-price products to low-income consumers or niche products to consumers in developed markets; developing hybrid business models that engage corporations, small businesses, NGOs and entrepreneurs in the developing world;[51] and building the legitimacy of the business and expanding the potential impact of the NGO.[52] The development of innovative products has been connected to the high number of creative ideas generated through multi-sectoral cooperation.[53]

Because of this, many companies are beginning to see the benefits of being "collaboratively competitive" on a range of issues that are of mutual benefit to them. For example, Guayakí, Numi Organic Tea, and Traditional Medicinals are companies that have a lot in common: they are focused on natural foods, health, and wellness; they are based in California and are committed to standards of organic production, fair trade, local sourcing, and sustainable business practices; and they are B Corporations (see the mini-case in Box 8.3) The companies share best practices and attribute a good deal of their success to their collaborative interactions, which include sharing buyer contacts, best practices, and emerging market opportunities. They have held events together, and Traditional Medicinals has co-packed products for the other two organizations.[54]

BOX 8.3
MINI-CASE: B CORPS: A NEW FORM OF GOVERNANCE[55]

Benefit Corporations are a new type of corporation built on the idea that business can solve social and environmental problems. Since 2010 a number of states in the U.S. have passed Benefit Corporation legislation that requires an organization by law to create general benefit for society as well as for their shareholders. These corporations must also publically report on their social and environmental performance and do so using third-party standards that meet the requirements of being credible, independent, and transparent. Benefit Corporations and Certified B Corporations are often both called "B Corps" where the first is a legal status administered by the state and the latter is a certification conferred by the non-profit B Lab, and many Benefit Corporations will also become Certified B Corporations. The vision of both is to ensure that economic, social, and environmental goals will be simultaneously advanced by business, to a higher level of transparency and accountability than traditional businesses. The Benefit Corporation addresses two key problems that currently impede progress towards sustainability: namely, that current corporate law makes it difficult for businesses to take employee, community, and environmental interests into consideration when making decisions; and a lack of transparent standards makes it difficult to differentiate between "good companies" and "good marketing." The comprehensive performance standards allow consumers to identify and support businesses that align with their values, investors to drive capital to higher impact investments, and governments and multinational corporations to implement sustainable procurement policies. While Benefit Corporations do not have to engage in multi-sectoral collaboration towards triple-loop learning, there is greater potential for this given the innovative legal structures and performance standards, and how these organizations are designed to create value for stakeholders.

A balance of cooperation and competition in a society can reap the benefits and mitigate the potential negative impacts of both. Competition produces positive benefits when it offers alternatives in the market place, eliminates producers who are not efficient (or who produce goods that are not useful to society), and helps organizations strive to be better at what they do. It also has the potential for many destructive impacts socially and environmentally that we have witnessed over the past several decades, in particular as capitalism increasingly focuses on growing consumerism rather than reconstructing value. Cooperation means that things might be accomplished together that individually would not be possible to achieve, and all organizations depend on internal cooperation in order to perform at a high level.[56] In fact, the leadership capabilities required for innovation driven by competitiveness and those required for collaborative innovation towards sustainable business management significantly overlap and are manifest through similar structures and processes of relationship building, integrative thinking, inventiveness, and learning,[57] all hallmarks of entrepreneurial behavior. The idea of developing collaboratively competitive organizations holds the potential to unleash the innovative thinking required to reconstruct value.

BOX 8.4

MINI-CASE: COLLABORATIVELY COMPETITIVE ORGANIZATIONS: THE
SUSTAINABLE APPAREL COALITION[58]

Over thirty apparel companies, retailers, manufacturers, NGOs, academics, and the U.S. Environmental Protection Agency have engaged in the
Sustainable Apparel Coalition, an initiative that emerged from an initial
collaboration between Patagonia and Walmart on the Outdoor Industry
Association's Eco Index and Walmart's supplier sustainability assessment program. The coalition's Sustainable Apparel Index is being developed as an industry-wide tool for evaluating the environmental impacts
of any kind of apparel. "We started wondering what kind of strategy we
could develop to take the work that the OIA was creating and broaden it
out, to get it in place beyond the outdoor industry," said Rick Ridgeway,
chair of the coalition and vice-president of environmental initiatives
at Patagonia. "We realized to really leverage it we'd be smart to invite
Walmart to join us in extending an invitation to a very large circle of
companies in the apparel and footwear sector to adopt a uniform sustainability index."[59]

This collaboration creates competitive benefits for companies that are
participating in the initiative, namely, (1) lowering supply chain costs
and impacts; (2) driving efficiencies with vendors through use of the
same tool; and (3) managing risks, improving reputations, and getting
ahead of potential regulations by making these changes proactively.

The coalition's intent is to reduce the environmental and social impacts
of clothing and footwear, and thus to promote promising innovations
and identify ways to improve practices throughout the supply chain.

Members of the coalition so far are Adidas, Arvind Mills, C&A, Duke
University, Environmental Defense Fund, Esprit, Esquel, Gap, H&M,
HanesBrands, Intradeco, JC Penney, Kohl's, Lenzing, Levi Strauss & Co.,
LF USA, Marks & Spencer, Mountain Equipment Co-op, New Balance,
Nike, Nordstrom, Otto Group, Outdoor Industry Association, Patagonia,
Pentland Brands, REI, TAL Apparel, Target, Timberland, U.S. Environ-
mental Protection Agency, Verité, VF Corp, and Walmart.

LEADERSHIP SKILL BUILDING:
Process Questions, Skills, and Skill-Building Exercises

PROCESS QUESTIONS CHAPTER 8: Developing Collaborative Capacity in Sustainability-Focused Organizations

In order to develop the collaborative capacity required to reconstruct value and stimulate societal learning, leaders can engage the following process questions drawn from principles of adaptive co-management[60] in their day-to-day operations. Thinking about an organization that you know well, consider these following questions:

1   How inclusive of diverse interests and representative of multiple scales (i.e., individual, organizational, community, global) are the stakeholders the organization engages with – for example, on new product and service issues?

2   Is information exchanged that leads to a shared understanding or agreement between stakeholders – for example, on future strategy issues?

3   Are decisions achieved through dialogue by involving diverse inputs or knowledge systems – for example, on issues of capital investment?

4   Are stakeholders jointly committed to undertaking and sharing the consequences of their actions – for example, on questions of mergers, acquisitions, and closures?

5   Is knowledge gained by learning from actions and making modifications – for example, in experimenting in new markets?

LEADERSHIP SKILLS CHAPTER 8: Building the Capabilities to Develop Collaborative Capacity in Sustainability-Focused Organizations

In order to engage in these process questions identified above, leaders need to build the capabilities required to successfully catalyze organizational and societal level learning. Cross-sector collaborations are strengthened by the recognition that no one sector can solve an important sustainability issue. Major problems facing society can only be meaningfully addressed if many organizations – including governments, businesses, non-profit organizations, foundations, higher education institutions, and community groups – collaborate effectively in generating solutions. The challenge of integrative public leadership has been defined as bringing together diverse groups in organizations in semi-permanent ways, across sector boundaries, in order to address complex public problems and strive towards the common good.[61] To effectively support societal learning and change, it is helpful to consider Waddell's[62] six societal learning leadership concepts that highlight the capabilities required of leaders. They are:

1   *Action Framework – Societal Systems Building.* Societal learning leaders need to understand their actions and strategies in the context of system relationships.
2   *Power Source – Appreciating Differences.* Understanding and acknowledging diversity and differences by leaders is essential for effective action. By understanding differences, it will be possible to create synergies between different sectors
3   *Key Operating Dynamic – Coproduction.* Coproduction leads to mutual gain between sectors when organizational leaders identify and commit to their goals and discover how to achieve them through collaboration. Coproduction requires a model of shared leadership, sharing power with leaders as co-directors.
4   *Spirit of Relationship – Collaborating:* Leaders emphasize participation and consensus. There is a focus on learning to support continual capacity development and quality improvement rather than a predetermined structure of how collaborators should work together. The belief here is that an appropriate structure will emerge if the spirit of the relationship is committed.
5   *Lubricating Forces – Dialogue and Learning.* Mental models and unexamined assumptions can create challenges for societal learning. Leaders need to spark a process of dialogue with the following four capacities in order to identify creative opportunities:
    •   Voicing – speaking the truth of one's perspective
    •   Listening – without resistance
    •   Respecting – awareness of the impossibility of fully understanding others' positions
    •   Suspending – suspension of assumptions, judgment, and certainty
6   *Hard Work – "Emerging the Future."* An attitude of exploration and a visionary approach from leaders is essential to societal learning.

BUILDING LEADERSHIP SKILLS CHAPTER 8: Learning Team Dialogue: Building Collaboratively Competitive Organizations in the Pharmaceutical Industry

The pharmaceutical industry has been criticized for being overly focused on commercial profit. Activists, non-profits, and specialized foundations accuse "Big Pharma" companies of not being truly innovative and of taking advantage of the latitude they are given by many governments that prioritize intellectual property rights over the basic right of access to health.[63] The sector is facing a number of key sustainability issues, including (1) structural challenges: such as changing healthcare systems and the rise of generic competition; (2) internal challenges: such as the cost and length of R&D combined with declining R&D productivity; and (3) reputational challenges: such as the question of whether "Big Pharma" companies have patient interests at heart. In the minds of politicians and the public, there is a need to reconcile pharmaceutical profits with public health and to balance investments in the development of lifestyle over life-saving drugs, both in developed and developing countries. Despite these major challenges that reveal how there are fundamental problems with the business models of global pharmaceutical companies, there is no apparent vision in this sector for how to recreate a generative and positive relationship with society. While there are pockets of excellence at various companies, they generally work within the status quo rather than encouraging transformational change.[64]

Considering this, identify an organization within the pharmaceutical sector and engage in a learning team dialogue focused on the following three questions:

1   Using the principles of adaptive co-management, define a process of engagement that could guide multi-sectoral collaboration between the company you have chosen and other organizations towards innovation in products, services, and markets. What kinds of collaborative innovations might you envision taking place as a result of these interactions?

2   What other social actors would you involve as part of a more fundamental reassessment of the pharmaceutical industry and its role in society at a global level and how would you establish the conditions for successful dialogue with these actors, including those who are antagonistic and critical of the industry?

3   Drawing on the six capabilities for societal learning, identify the key capabilities this organization would need to acquire and/or develop in order to achieve success with this collaboratively competitive strategy.

Conclusion

In this chapter we have challenged the traditional business case for sustainability by introducing the idea of stakeholder integration as a way to move beyond the incremental learning and change encouraged by a more instrumental stakeholder management approach. We suggest that in order to reconstruct value we need to engage in a process of triple-loop learning that will allow us to synthesize organizational and societal level views of sustainability. By taking a view of business as a social actor and drawing on the design thinking approach introduced earlier, we describe how engaging in a participatory process of social learning with internal and external stakeholders will provide greater opportunities for societal learning and change. From this perspective, strategy can be thought of as a "collaboratively competitive" concept that relies upon leaders and managers developing the capabilities required to encourage multi-stakeholder and multi-sectoral collaboration in order to build organizations that develop an authentic sustainability mindset which is both embedded and transformational. We will further explore the notion of societal learning and change in chapter 9 when we consider how redefining our ideas about success and progress are essential to reconstructing value.

CHAPTER 9

Reconstructing Value:
Leadership in Reinventing Notions of Success

Anyone who believes that exponential growth can go on forever in a finite world is either a madman or an economist.

– Kenneth Boulding, Economist

Most of our assumptions have outlived their uselessness.

– Marshall McLuhan, Media Theorist

What if You "Owned" the Whole Problem?

In chapter 8 we examined the concept of social learning: progressive learning that happens in relationships across sectors of society and subsectors in industry. Social learning helps to cultivate a more constructive, holistic, and sustainable perspective by bringing together disparate and sometimes opposed actors in society: business, civil society, and government sectors especially, along with various political affiliations and ideologies, mixed social strata, nations, and cultures. Through a process of social learning we can seek to understand, empathize, and learn from one another, co-creating a more sustainable future, in full recognition of the truism that we are all on this ride together. As Marshall McLuhan said, "On spaceship earth there are no passengers, only crew."

In chapter 9 we consider the full context for human activity within the biosphere (the earth's land, oceans, and atmosphere), and we offer some societal level principles and design criteria for reconstructing our ideas of value.

Developing a *Biosphere Consciousness*

Aspirations towards a sustainable world require that we bring a raised sense of consciousness, a perspective that encompasses the whole human project on earth: its capacity for joy and meaning and its significant challenges, all playing out in complex ecological interdependence with the natural world. This is what social commentator and author Jeremy Rifkin calls a "biosphere consciousness."[1] He describes the historical progression of human cooperation and identity-creation, from local tribes to broader religious ties to the founding of nation states. As energy sources and communication capabilities improved, and peoples' worlds expanded and became more interdependent, they connected with broader networks of like-minded others for the sake of collaboration and survival – often reinforced by choosing a common enemy or threat. Building empathy and common cause with others has always been an essential driver of human progress. The common threats now come in the form of the mounting sustainability challenges of our time, and to meet those challenges Rifkin suggests our ultimate hope lies in building global empathy: discovering a sense of shared identity as humans on a collective journey, bound by our mutual dependence on one another and on the life-sustaining conditions within earth's biosphere – building a biosphere consciousness.

A Thought Experiment

So let us take our discussion on social learning a step further with a thought experiment in biosphere consciousness: What if you were not merely one of the players in the learning process – what if you owned responsibility for the whole thing? What if somebody handed you the design brief to put the world on a more sustainable path? What would you do?

   You might look down on your planet with its rapidly expanding population of 7 billion people and see an uneven distribution of resources and riches, vast wealth alongside abject poverty. You might seek to understand the various logics of the systems of production, consumption and governance. You would calculate the sustainability of the material throughput system, the rate of consumption over the rate of replenishment and renewal. You might assess the ability of people to feed and water themselves now and in the future, to provide themselves with shelter from the elements, and to find enough energy to operate their societies. You would study the effects of their activities on the environment that gives them sustenance – the oceans, soil, air, and climate that support life.

You might even try to determine whether the lives that most people were leading were lives of purpose, meaning, dignity, and fulfillment. Then you might contemplate and perhaps begin to worry, as several indicators would be showing cause for alarm: the fossilized energy on which the system increasingly depends is diminishing; depletion of soil and acidification of oceans is putting the food supply in peril; population is growing and there are enormous disparities in equity and living standards; water security is not good and projected to worsen over the next couple of decades; a changing climate is threatening to upset the fragile balance of the earth's ecosystems, and you can see that human activity is contributing to that. You would see all of these issues as interconnected and mutually interdependent. You would see a design challenge of significant proportions. Then, as chief design architect, what would you do?

We suggest there are two obvious options. One is to stand back, let the human drama play out in its current configuration, and see what happens – leave people to focus on personal security, to do their best for themselves and their families, and let the fittest survive. The other option is to work towards solutions to put the world on a different path: perhaps draft some principles to guide things based on good science, cascade those into policy frameworks for governance and action, and then engage as many people as possible in a vision of shared prosperity, and in action for bringing that about. As chief design architect in our thought experiment, the choice is easy: the first option would be dereliction of duty; the second would be fulfilling your job description. But what about the reality for us as individual citizens here on earth? We believe the choice is easy there, too: because if you are not working to improve things, then you are likely complicit in making them worse by unconsciously participating in the systems of logic from which the problems arise. There is no neutral ground, no escape, and no life boat. No passengers, only crew.

Unfortunately, for most CEOs of business organizations, whatever their personal convictions, they are not expected by investors to take a biospheric level view unless it aligns very closely with the creation of shareholder value. This is an almost impossible call for CEOs of oil and gas or minerals firms which are by their very nature extractive and non-sustainable in the ecological sense. Consequently, those industries rarely show biospheric leadership. However, there are a growing number of mainstream companies in agriculture and renewable energy whose entire raison d'être depends on an economic world view that accepts biophysical limits. Firms like Whole Foods (organic produce) and Vestas (wind turbines) clearly make more money the closer the world comes to accepting the dangers of unsustainable food and energy sources. Unilever has long embraced the importance of only harvesting from sustainable fisheries as defined by the Marine Stewardship Council, and Tembec has achieved 100 per cent compliance with Forest Stewardship Council standards. Both of these companies, therefore, explicitly acknowledge the biospheric logic of avoiding the unsustainable harvesting of natural resources.

In some cases a biospheric perspective has been internalized sufficiently to change entire corporate strategies. InterfaceFLOR is one iconic story – a company led by a charismatic leader, the late Ray Anderson, who decided on a "mid-course correction" in order to become a restorative company. But one of the more interesting and dramatic corporate reinventions that occurred in the late twentieth century was the conversion of DuPont, the chemical company, into DuPont the biotechnology and materials company, committed to food, energy, and personal security and safety. In chapter 7 we described the shift in the business portfolio of the company – but what can we infer about the level of consciousness brought to bear in redirecting the corporate strategy in such a transformational manner? In the 1990s, under the visionary leadership of Ed Woolard, the company started to move away from its dependence on commodity-based products, divesting its oil and gas and nylon businesses, and instead repositioned itself on a path to "sustainable growth" through innovation and knowledge-based industries. CEO Chad Holliday (1999–2009) further consolidated this strategy, finding time along the way to chair the influential World Business Council for Sustainable Development. It is at least arguable that because of its embrace of the concept of "sustainable growth" and its understanding of the company's ultimate reliance on nature, that this is one company that is working towards an understanding of its role as an economic and social actor within a biospheric perspective. DuPont's vision is "to be the world's most dynamic science company, creating sustainable solutions essential to a better, safer and healthier life for people everywhere."[2]

In this chapter we explore the implications of pursuing sustainable business strategies in key industries by focusing on a few key principles – an *embedded view* of environment, society, and economy; a *sustainability mindset* that supports human development while respecting natural limits; and an ethic of *transformation* that engages people in generative dialogue to question and reform the assumptions underpinning our ways of operating. Before developing these three principles for reconstructing sustainable value, we should take a moment to first consider the question of value itself, and how that often plays out in our political processes. Our aim is to point to the ideologically driven political traps we can fall into so that we can move past them towards building a biospheric social consciousness.

Questions of Value

What Do We Find Valuable? What Is Good, Right, and Important? What Kind of Life Is Worth Living?

Questions like these have been at the heart of moral philosophy for centuries, so when we talk about reconstructing value, we are doing so within the shadow of a long tradition of inquiry and debate. We cannot adequately review all of the major lines of philosophical thought in this book, but we should give consideration to a couple of significant distinctions. Issues in sustainability are often highly politically charged, and questions of value are acted out daily in the modern politics of our time, usually according to "left" and "right" political leanings: a major oil pipeline is proposed, or climate negotiations commence, or subsidies to renewable energy are provided, and people and groups begin lining up on the "left" (typically characterized as collective-thinking, social justice oriented, and *usually* in line with an environmental perspective or "ecocentric" view) and the "right" (more individualistic, free-market thinking, often in line with a more technocentric view and *occasionally* an environmental conservation slant). Sides are then taken on ideological grounds. We have avoided discussion of political ideology in this book, with the view that left/right characterizations quickly become caricatures, and are largely unhelpful. There is, however, an unavoidable tension between the core ideas running through modern liberal democracy, and the requirement for a collective sense of responsibility and collective action in matters of sustainability. If one cares about ideas in sustainability (and we assume readers of this book do), then one is likely to care about a few associated values: respect and preservation of nature for its own sake, or at the very least out of an enlightened self-interest in continued human prosperity; social justice in our time so that all people have an opportunity for a decent life; and equity between generations, so our children and grandchildren are not disadvantaged by the problems we have created. Preservation, equity, justice – these are all ideas that require us to think beyond ourselves to some degree. Yet Western liberal democracy is founded on the central notion of freedom for the individual to pursue a good life, and autonomy in choosing what defines a good life for oneself. How do we reconcile talk of biosphere consciousness and "we are all in this together" with "it is a free world and I can do what I want"?

Basic Ideas in Political Liberalism: Moving Past "Left" and "Right"

Liberalism in political theory is different from our common usage in politics, where "liberal" is used to differentiate from "conservative" (or Democrat/Republican in the United States).[3] In political theory, modern liberalism is contrasted with classical ideas dating at least to the Ancient Greeks. In classical thought, the goal was to design the perfect state governing people, and one of the roles of the state was to define for people what was good (morally correct) and right (just and equitable). The will of the people came second to the aim of creating an ideally functioning state, and a key goal of the state was to develop rational, moral citizens.

In the modern liberalism that underpins most Western political systems, the focus is shifted to the freedom and happiness of individuals, and the role of the state is to allow that to flourish, rather than to define and direct it. People are assumed to have natural human rights, and there is a limit to interference from the state.[4] There is an assumption that individual freedom to pursue a good life is primary – it is central to the U.S. Declaration of Independence: "unalienable rights" including "Life, Liberty and the pursuit of Happiness." The political "left" and "right" both embrace the idea of personal liberty and freedom, but mainly differ on the role of the state in setting conditions for individual happiness. As put by philosopher Robert Talisse:

> Generally speaking, Democrats maintain that part of what it is to protect the rights and liberties of individuals is to help maintain the social and economic conditions necessary for the effective exercise of individual rights. Democrats hence tend to support government programs designed to redistribute social goods such as wealth, education, and healthcare. Republicans, by contrast, tend to believe that the free market is a sufficient means to social justice. Republicans hence support policies that promote competition among providers of goods; in this sense, they maintain that the state should intervene as little as possible in distributive issues.[5]

The differences are more about means than ends. What has evolved more recently – in the past fifty years or so – is the growing awareness and acceptance of natural limits to human development. As populations have grown and resources have been depleted, the constraints on our design challenge have shifted. We will need ideas from both the "right" and the "left" to see our way forward: competition *and* cooperation; the use of market mechanisms *and* judicious regulation of the commons where necessary; a focus on economic prosperity *and* the prudence and empathy to see that the least well off are not neglected; confidence in technological advance *and* a recognition of natural limits. Falling back into shortcuts in thinking directed by ideological rigidity is putting the solution ahead of the problem. We highlight these differences so that we can identify and examine our assumptions and biases as we work to build a biosphere consciousness.

Three Principles for Reconstructing Value

At the center of our reconstructing value model throughout this book are three principles: an *embedded view* of the environment, society, and

Table 9.1. Three Principles for Reconstructing Value and System Design Criteria

Reconstructing value	
Principles	**Social system design criteria**
An embedded perspective: Society is embedded within and depends upon the ecological biosphere; economy is embedded within and serves society.	Construct well-rounded policy metrics aimed at improving well-being for individuals and communities. Build business strategy and civil society activism towards advancing measures of human progress.
A sustainability mindset: Focusing on equitable human development now and in the future, within the regenerative limits of the biosphere.	Set limits on resource extraction and use based on the best available science, and ensure a fair distribution of benefits and burdens. Decouple prosperity from material consumption.
System transformation: Broad engagement in reordering the assumptions that guide our policy decisions.	Engage stakeholders meaningfully in co-constructing policy frameworks (public and corporate policy) that are stable and fair across geography and time.

economy; a *sustainability mindset* that supports human development while respecting natural limits; and an ethic of *transformation* that engages people in generative dialogue to question and reform the assumptions underpinning our ways of operating. Table 9.1 summarizes our three principles and outlines the design criteria that will allow us to translate these into policy directions for business, government, and civil society.

An Embedded Perspective

Society Is Embedded Within and Depends upon the Ecological Biosphere; Economy Is Embedded Within and Serves Society

As we described in chapter 1, an embedded perspective admits that environment, society, and economy are hierarchically nested systems – that is, society exists wholly within and is dependent on the earth's biosphere, and the economy is a human creation existing within and serving society. In a truly representative picture, the three circles would be concentric, with environment on the outside, society inside that, and economy in the middle – this would be the ecological reality of the physical relationships ("a. How thing really are" in Figure 9.1). It is common to see them drawn as three

Figure 9.1. Three Pictures of the Environment, Society, Economy Relationship

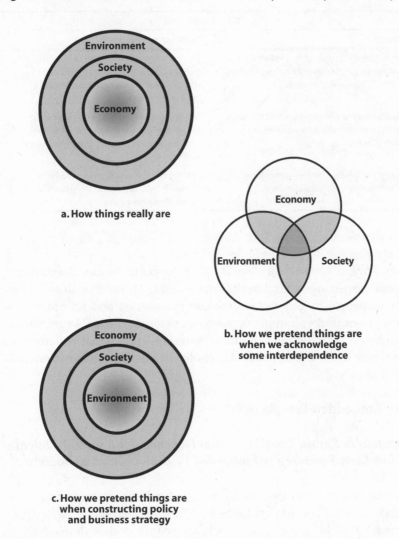

a. How things really are

b. How we pretend things are
when we acknowledge
some interdependence

c. How we pretend things are
when constructing policy
and business strategy

interlocking circles in corporate reports in communications when companies want to demonstrate that they are concerned with the social and environmental impacts of their operations ("b. How we pretend..." Figure 9.1). This implies that there are areas of the economy that exist outside of human society and parts of society that thrive outside of the natural environment, which does not make sense. Even more common in practice, however, is the case where the implied relationship is inverted in the ways that we think and talk about them ("c. How we pretend ..." Figure 9.1). We attend to the health of the economy above all, because its functioning affects our livelihoods and quality of life: society exists within the economy. The environment is typically seen as a place within society where we find resources to use as inputs to commercial production and as a place to send our waste at the end of the pipe. Oil companies and mining companies are typically in this space; often attempting to minimize or mitigate social and environmental costs and impacts, but always prioritizing the need for economic growth.

This inverted logic entirely ignores natural limits to economic and societal growth. Under this logic, pursuit of economic growth is paramount and is the key policy driver for shaping the economy, and that is a sustainability problem for three reasons. First, economic growth is invariably measured in term of gross domestic product (GDP), with the assumption that what is good for GDP is good for society, and that is not always the case. Second, the logic of the growth imperative in public policy metrics such as GDP is mirrored in the corporate level growth imperative in earnings and share price, which too often leads to managerial behaviors that are suboptimal for the organization and society,[6] and leave many human needs unmet. Third, there is a strong correlation between gross domestic product and material throughput, and so our definition of prosperity depends on continuing to burn through more and more stuff and on inflicting environmental harm as a by-product. It is for this reason that the share price of extractive industry companies is so dependent on assets that have been identified and booked for future exploitation.

Beyond GDP

Gross domestic product is a measure of economic activity in a nation's economy, typically measured in terms of the total market value of recognized goods and services (housework or care for your elders does not count) produced in a period, normally in annual terms. Growing GDP is the primary policy goal of governments in developed countries – but not all things captured by GDP are necessarily good for society: for example, if cancer rates rise, or if the number of traffic jams increase, that is good for GDP, as medical services and gasoline sales contribute positively to GDP. But clearly our lives are not improved by contracting disease or by the frustration, lost time, and increased air pollution that comes with traffic congestion. Conversely, there are many things that contribute to our quality of life that are not considered in GDP, such as an educated, engaged populace, or a fair work–life balance. Critiques of GDP as an indicator of social progress are long-standing, and in 2008, Nicholas Sarkozy, then president of the French Republic and the European Union, established the Commission on the Measurement of Economic Performance and Social Progress to examine the problem and recommend alternatives. The twenty-five-member commission was headed Joseph Stiglitz and advised by Amartya Sen, both Nobel Prize economists, and coordinated by Jean-Paul Fitoussi. Its aim was to identify the limits of GDP as an indicator of economic performance and social progress, including measurement problems, and to make recommendations towards the production of more relevant and feasible indicators of social progress. The commission identified the essential problems with using GDP as an indicator of social progress, which were published in a report as follows:[7]

- There is a widely reported gap between statistical metrics (such as economic growth, inflation, unemployment) and perceptions of people relating to well-being.
- Some important aspects of well-being are not captured in measures of production such as GDP, and some items that are captured are not positive for society.
- An aggregate measure like GDP is often expressed as GDP per capita – an average measure of economic activity that glosses over income disparity that may exist.
- A focus on a single metric can lead to market distortions to artificially keep that number growing – the creation of more complex debt instruments, for example, that inflated a borrowing/consumption bubble and "mirage" growth, as was the case from 2004 to 2007, largely leading to the market crash of 2007–2008.

The report's findings are organized under two main messages: we need to find better measures of economic performance in a complex economy, and we need to look beyond measures of economic production towards those capturing human well-being more broadly. There are twelve major recommendations under those themes, some directed at improving measures of current well-being, and some directed at ensuring that well-being is sustainable over time. The report was addressed to several audiences: political leaders; policymakers working on assessing and advancing social progress; academics and developers of statistics; civil society organizations seeking to influence policy and public opinion; and the media and the public at large seeking better decision-making processes and more active democratic participation. Clearly, the analysis and recommendations are meant to feed and encourage social learning among sectors of society – to help construct a shared, embedded perspective where social progress is optimized and served by economic activity.

Measuring Well-Being

While the Stiglitz-Sen-Fitoussi report clearly articulated the task in redefining social progress, several national and international efforts at defining metrics for well-being beyond GDP have been developing as well. The Organization for Economic Cooperation and Development (OECD) works to advance economic progress for its thirty-four market-based, democratic member countries, and in an effort to address the problems with the single metric of GDP, the OECD has launched the *Better Life Initiative* and the associated *Better Life Index*. The *Index* contains twenty-one measures under eleven indicators in two major categories – quality of life and material living conditions.[8] Figure 9.2 shows the framework of the eleven indicators and the relation to GDP. The traditional measure of GDP capture none of the quality of life metrics and only some of the material living conditions, while also including what the OECD calls "regrettables": the oil spills, train wrecks, illnesses, and environmental degradation that feed economic activity but that do not make our lives better.

The *Better Life Index* draws directly from the Stigliz-Sen-Fitoussi study, including consideration of the sustainability of well-being through the preservation of four types of capital: natural, economic, human, and

Figure 9.2. OECD Better Life Index

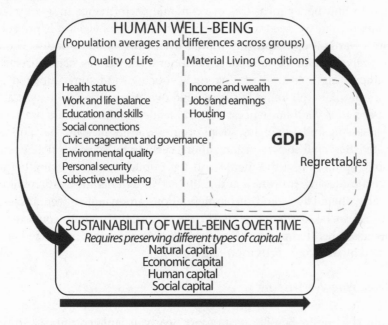

Source: Adapted from OECD, *Better Life Initiative: Compendium of OECD Well-Being Indicators* (Paris: OECD, 2011), http://www.oecd.org/std/47917288.pdf

social – and assessment as to whether stocks of those are sustaining or depleting. The OECD also hosts the Global Project on Measuring the Progress of Societies, a "network of networks" dedicated to advancing and sharing initiatives in measuring social progress. *WikiProgress* is the global online platform for the project, an interactive portal for connecting national and regional initiatives (see www.wikiprogress.org). One such example, the Canadian Index of Wellbeing (CIW),[9] was launched in 2009. It defines well-being as:

The presence of the highest possible quality of life in its full breadth of expression, focused on but not necessarily exclusive to: good living standards, robust health, a sustainable environment, vital communities, an educated populace, balanced time use, high levels of civic participation, and access to and participation in dynamic arts, culture & recreation.[10]

The CIW includes measures in those eight domains, and then bundles them together into a single composite metric. Figure 9.3 shows the CIW aggregate metric as compared to GDP: there has been a growing divergence between the two since 1994, indicating that GDP alone does not reflect overall well-being.

An Embedded View: Design Criteria

An embedded view focuses on social progress served by economic activity, in full acknowledgment of the limits to growth imposed by the natural environment. A well-functioning economy is a means to an end – human social progress and environmental flourishing – rather than the end itself. Reconstructing value from an embedded perspective means building comprehensive policy metrics aimed at improving well-being for individuals and communities, and shaping public policy, business strategy, and civil society action towards advancing social and environmental progress metrics. Such metrics become the objective value function in running organizations and governments, aided by active social learning across sectors. Embracing an embedded perspective is a necessary (but not sufficient) condition for reconstructing sustainable value. To do that, we also need to adopt a sustainability mindset.

A Sustainability Mindset

Focusing on Equitable Human Development Now and in the Future, Within the Regenerative Limits of the Biosphere

Table 1.2 in chapter 1 outlines the main tenets of a sustainability mindset. Two themes apparent in that list are (1) to be sustainable we need to learn to live within the carrying capacity of the planet, which will require informed restraint and cooperation; and (2) *sustainability* means concern for human development and well-being now and in the future, so it includes values of social justice and equity. These two themes are entirely consistent with the Brundtland definition: "development that meets the needs of the present, without compromising the ability of future generations to meet their own needs." The need to live within our resource means is clear ("without compromising the ability"); and

Figure 9.3. Well-Being and GDP

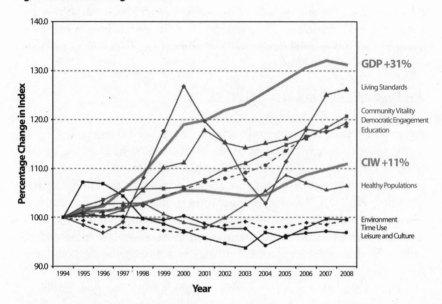

Source: Adapted from "Trends in the Canadian Index of Wellbeing Within Eight Domains and Compared with GDP, 1994–2008" in CIW, *How Are Canadians Really Doing: Highlights: The Canadian Index of Wellbeing 1.0* (Waterloo, ON: CIW, 2011), 3.

an ethic of social justice runs through both halves of the Brundtland definition: equitable care and concern for all those living today, and intergenerational justice for the young and those not yet born.

Staying Within Regenerative Limits

In chapter 4 we outlined many of the resource challenges we face in the areas of food production, energy supply, water security, and climate change, all driven by an increasing world population and higher levels of relative affluence. Human development depends greatly on the extraction and use of raw materials from the earth: minerals, industrial ores, and fossil fuels, and renewable but depletable biological resources: forestry, agriculture, and fisheries. The throughput of these materials (how much we pull out and use up in a year) is closely correlated with economic development measured in GDP – the more material we extract or harvest, the greater is the national income and our standard of living. On the disposal end of the linear take-make-waste cycle, higher GDP is also correlated with negative environmental impacts like air, land, and water pollution. That linkage means that in aspiring towards economic growth we are also actively conspiring to increase the metabolic burn rate of extracted material and the volume and rate of environmental degradation. In order to break that link, we need to work towards *decoupling* economic growth from natural resources and impacts – or to deeply reconsider the growth imperative.

Decoupling Prosperity from Material Throughput

In discussions of sustainability, to *decouple* means to separate economic growth from resource extraction and negative environmental impacts. The former is often called *resource decoupling* and the latter is *impact decoupling*, and each has its own set of measures and challenges.[11] Two other key distinctions are *relative* and *absolute* decoupling. Relative decoupling is a measure of resource productivity in relation to economic growth: using less material or creating less environmental impact for a given amount of wealth creation. Resource extraction and impacts are still rising, but at a slower rate than economic growth. Absolute decoupling means that the rates of resource use and impacts are falling while economic growth is rising. From 1900 to 2005 there was evidence of relative decoupling when GDP was compared to material use (fossil fuels, minerals, metals, and biomass). Economic growth rose at a greater rate than material extraction, meaning global resource efficiency improved – more wealth per ton of stuff used. However, the absolute amount of material extracted and used by humans multiplied eightfold, from 7.5 billion tons per year to 60 billion tons, a worrisome trend (see Figure 9.4). On a per-person global average, resource use has more than doubled, from 4.6 to 10.3 tons/person/year.[12] Most of this material is non-renewable, with the exception of biomass (crops, plants, trees, fish, etc.) which is constrained by soil nutrients, freshwater supply, and regeneration potential, and is susceptible to overharvesting – unless, of course, all companies in the world embrace stewardship standards rather than just the small percentage of enlightened firms. Resource consumption is highly uneven across the world. Developing countries

Figure 9.4. Global Material Extraction

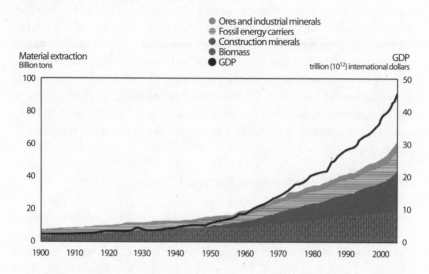

Source: Adapted from UNEP, *Decoupling Natural Resource Use and Environmental Impacts from Economic Growth,* Fischer-Kowalski et al. (Nairobi, Kenya: UNEP, 2011), www.unep.org

have per capita "metabolic rates" clustered around 5 tons/person/year, and most developed countries are in the 15–30 ton range – and rising middle classes in developing countries are aspiring to move closer to living standards in developed ones, with a lot more people. Resource use, environmental impacts, and social justice are increasingly becoming inseparable concerns.

Decoupling and Social Justice

"Contraction and convergence" is a framework applied to combine problems of resource use and negative impacts with principles of global equity and justice. "Contraction" refers to the need to cap and then reduce in absolute terms the rate and amount of material extracted (e.g., lumber, minerals) or negative impacts produced (e.g., tons of greenhouse gases). "Convergence" means striving for global equity by having developed countries contract more, while developing countries are allowed to catch up. This model is a tough sell to developed countries especially, but is proposed as the only way to simultaneously stay within environmental limits and enact equitable levels of development globally – the two main goals under a sustainability mindset.

The International Resource Panel (IRP) of the United Nations Environment Programme (UNEP) constructed three scenarios to help describe the urgency of decoupling resource use and negative impacts from economic growth, along with the implications of social justice via contraction and convergence.[13] The three scenarios illustrate options for 2050 with a 2000 baseline, using UN median population projections, and assuming that all countries will converge to similar per capita levels of resource use. The IRP allows that its scenarios are unrealistic on two counts: there is little evidence of convergence happening globally, and there are no physical constraints built in, which is unlikely to be the case. In that regard, the scenarios illustrate the implications of ignoring constraints, as is typical of mainstream growth models. Historically, when consumption rates bumped up against supply constraints, conflict ensued. Box 9.1 shows a summary of the IRP's three scenarios.

BOX 9.1

OPTIONS FOR 2050: THREE SCENARIOS FOR DECOUPLING

SCENARIO 1

Business as usual: Freeze (industrial countries) and catch up (developing world)

- Relative decoupling in the developed world allows metabolic rates to stay stable at year 2000 levels, about 16 tonnes/capita/year.
- For convergence to equal living standards, metabolic rates in developing countries would multiply three- to fivefold.

What is required for compliance

Developed countries continue to focus on relative decoupling.

Result

Global material throughput would be 140 billion tonnes per year, more than triple the 2000 base year.

SCENARIO 2

Moderate contraction and convergence

Reduction by a factor of 2 (industrial countries) and catching up (developing countries)

- Developed countries commit to absolute reductions in resource use, and reduce metabolic rates by a factor of 2, from 16 tonnes to 8 tonnes/capita/year.
- Developing countries increase metabolic rates moderately to 8 tonnes/capita/year.

What is required for compliance

Substantial structural change with new patterns of production and consumption.

Result

Global material throughput of 70 billion tonnes per year, 40 per cent more than year 2000, at roughly the same metabolic rate as year 2000 of 8 tonnes/capita/year.

SCENARIO 3

Tough contraction and convergence

Freeze global resource consumption at the 2000 level, and converge (industrial and developing countries)

- Far-reaching absolute resource use reductions by a factor of 3–5 in developed countries, to 6 tonnes/captia/year.
- Developing countries achieve 10–20 per cent average reduction in metabolic rates from 2000.

What is required for compliance

Unprecedented levels of innovation; commitment to a radically altered lifestyle.

Result

Global material throughput of 50 billion tonnes per year, same as year 2000, at a global metabolic rate of 6 tonnes/capita/year.

Source: UNEP, Decoupling Natural Resource Use and Environmental Impacts from Economic Growth, Fischer-Kowalski et al. (Nairobi, Kenya: UNEP, 2011).

Scenario 1 is likely unrealistic due to physical resource constraints, and Scenario 3 would be politically very difficult to achieve. Under Scenario 2, with aggressive innovation in decoupling and significant changes to cultural patterns of consumption, all people would be able to live reasonably comfortable lives with a good measure of well-being. The IRP concludes that what is threatened is not necessarily global well-being but the resource-intensive modes of consumption that are common today. Economist Tim Jackson has called absolute decoupling a "myth," since there is no evidence that it has ever occurred.[14] He calls instead for a radical restructuring of market economies away from the economic growth imperative altogether.

Social Justice as Fairness

In recalling our discussion on political liberalism and sustainability, we can look briefly to political philosopher John Rawls and his conception of "justice as fairness." In his landmark 1971 book *A Theory of Justice*, he articulated a vision of distributive justice in two simple principles, known as the *liberty* principle and the *difference* principle.[15] The liberty principle is to ensure individual freedoms, and the difference principle is to allow for differences among people, but still to strive for overall fairness. The objective was to propose design specifications for a society that is free and fair, while still allowing for differences among people and the ability to prosper if you work for it. To paraphrase Rawls' two principles:

1. All have equal liberty to such a degree that it does not encroach on the liberty of others.
2. Social and economic inequalities should be arranged so that:
    a) the overall arrangement must be the best one for the least well off,
    b) there must be opportunity for everyone to improve her or his lot in life.

Thus, our liberty to drink cheap coffee should not undermine the ability of a coffee farmer in Costa Rica or Ethiopia to generate a reasonable livelihood and a decent standard of living. Rawls also stipulated that in order to design a fair system, we must assume we are standing behind "a veil of ignorance," so that we do not know our place in the system we are constructing – our social standing, geographic home, our financial inheritance, our endowment of abilities or intelligence. Only then would we design fairness into the plan without self-interest. This approach is relevant to our thought experiment in biosphere consciousness and a sustainability mindset – what system would you design if you did not know who you were or where you lived or what you consumed?

A Sustainability Mindset: Design Criteria

A sustainability mindset focuses on equitable human development now and in the future, within the regenerative limits of the biosphere. Building on our description of the embedded view, sustainability requires us to set precautionary limits and standards for resource extraction and emissions based on the best available science, to decouple prosperity from material consumption, and to ensure a fair distribution of benefits and burdens. The extent to which we can make that happen will depend on broad and deep engagement in reordering the assumptions that underpin our ideas of value.

System Transformation

Broad Engagement in Reordering the Assumptions that Guide Our Policy Decisions

In chapter 8 we described processes of societal learning and change, building on our discussion of stakeholder perspectives in chapter 5. Here we have proposed a "full ownership" thought experiment as a way to lift out of the fray of stakeholder interactions and to build a big picture view – a biosphere consciousness. Our chapter 9 principles of *embeddedness*, a *sustainability mindset*, and *transformation* serve as design criteria (as objectives *and* constraints) for processes of societal learning outlined in the previous chapter. They allow us to move beyond ideas of corporate value and value communities towards building the integral commons, as described in chapter 5.

Embracing embeddedness means focusing on well-being beyond economic growth; adopting a sustainability mindset means staying within ecological limits while striving for a measure of social justice. Our third principle of *system transformation* means seeking broad engagement in proactively and collaboratively reshaping the assumptions that guide our public policy and strategic business decisions. Reconstructing value – fundamentally reordering our ideas of what is valuable and worth preserving and nurturing – can happen proactively and deliberately, or reactively and chaotically. But it will happen: simply looking at the three scenarios for resource and impact decoupling tells us that it will, along with the significant list of global issues we explored in chapter 4. We have natural limits on one end (where resources become more and more difficult to locate and extract, and therefore much more expensive to secure), and political limits on the other (where we ask the "haves" to sacrifice what they possess for the sake of the "have nots" in the name of fairness), and neither looks very easy nor appealing. The middle choice holds significant challenges as well: radical innovation in resource productivity, structural and cultural shifts in production and consumption patterns, and a high level of international cooperation, to begin. The UNEP report states that:

> ... the single clear policy implication of Scenario 2 is that any Government that gets ahead of the game by facilitating investments now in innovations for decoupling in the future will clearly reap the benefits when pressures mount for others to change rapidly by depending on technology transfers from elsewhere.[16]

In other words, change will come, and it is still in our hands to decide how it will happen.

System Transformation: Design Criteria

Recognition of embeddedness and pursuit of a sustainable way of operating requires that we examine the ways we measure and allocate value, and the ways that we govern ourselves. It requires that we engage in sustainability conversations about what matters, and about what kind of society we hope to create; that we engage stakeholders meaningfully in co-constructing policy frameworks (for public policy and corporate strategy) that are stable and fair across geography and time. One outcome of these multi-sectoral conversations can be "sustainability quality assurance systems" such as Marine Stewardship and Forest Stewardship Council standards, Fair Trade labels, organic food and other supply chain certifications. They do not, however, require all companies to comply, still less enthuse about such standards. Other multi-sectoral conversations take place in the form of advisory councils that help to influence organizational decision making through members' ongoing interactions and dialogue, such as DuPont's Advisory Committee on Agricultural Innovation and Productivity that was established to help the company identify "sustainable, science-based solutions that work for both the planet and the global farming community."[17] Regardless of the various ways in which these conversations are structured, when conversations are meaningful they require analysis of social values, with a bias towards social action, framed around a few simple questions: Where are we going? Is the destination desirable? Who gains and who loses? What should be done?[18] It is not enough for politicians and business and civil society leaders to claim to be bound by the rules of the game, because we humans made up the rules and the game, and we can remake them as we deem necessary for our own good. Leadership for sustainability means engaging deeply in reconstructing value towards embeddedness, a sustainability mindset, and system transformation.

LEADERSHIP SKILL BUILDING:
Process Questions, Skills, and Skill-Building Exercises

PROCESS QUESTIONS CHAPTER 9: Building an Embedded Perspective, a Sustainability Mindset, and Capacity for Transformation

In order to develop these three principles for reconstructing value, leaders can engage the following process questions. Thinking about an organization that you know well:

Embeddedness
1   How would our mission, strategy, core value proposition, and products/ services rate on contribution to measures of well-being?
2   Can we do a better job of bringing measures and certified standards of social, economic, and ecological value creation and well-being into our strategic planning and goals?
3   When we look at the forces in the complex of global human challenges (energy, food, water, climate, poverty, population, cities), is our business model on the right side of those issues? Are we pointed in a direction to make

things better or worse? Are there significant threats and opportunities that we are missing?

Sustainability Mindset

4   What portion of our success depends on ever-increasing levels of material and energy throughput?

5   How can we work to decouple our prosperity from material intensity and impacts?

6   What significant (*versus* incremental) material efficiencies can we develop and implement?

7   How can we shift our portfolio of products/services to high value/less resource and impact intensive?

8   What place does concern for social justice have in our mission, strategic planning, and goals – for example, with respect to human rights protection in our supply chains?

System Transformation

9   How do we work to build an embedded, sustainable perspective among our organization's stakeholders?

10   What efforts are we engaged in at the public-policy level that will encourage transformation to an embedded, sustainability-focused policy regime – for example, in the development of sustainability standards?

LEADERSHIP SKILLS CHAPTER 9: Putting It All Together

The primary leadership capability for reconstructing value is *transforming leadership*, which we described in chapter 1. Transforming leaders are those who help others to raise their perspective above their daily tasks to see their work as contributing to the larger human social project of creating conditions for flourishing. They bring together disparate, even seemingly opposed perspectives, and help to connect action to context – in the case of sustainability, connecting our actions to the global sustainability issues we have described throughout this book. Transforming leaders help engage multiple stakeholders and direct our conversations and actions towards altering our unsustainable assumptions and actions, and towards living better lives in the face of constraints confronting us.

SKILL-BUILDING EXERCISE CHAPTER 9: Culminating Assignment: Strategic Sustainability Reinvention: Reconstructing Value in a For-Profit Company

The goal of this learning project is to reinvent ideas of value creation in a for-profit organization, informed by complex global sustainability issues, and drawing on many of the concepts described in the preceding chapters. The outcome of the project should be a new business venture idea. It could be a modification of the existing products or services offered by the organization, or an idea for an entirely new spin-off organization or joint venture with another company.

The idea for the project should emerge from an imagined "sustainability conversation" between your focal organization and a civil society organization that is active in a relevant industry. As part of the task you will imagine a "learning partnership" between the for-profit firm and the civil society organization, in which each can learn from the others' perspective regarding the goals, opportunities, challenges, and potential threats in that sector. The conversations should be informed by the global sustainability issues we examined in chapter 4 – population growth, water scarcity, food insecurity, energy supply constraints, and climate change.

For example, you may have a big agriculture company enter into a learning partnership with a non-governmental organization focused on solutions for hunger or poverty. Or an energy company partnered with a community group working on reducing dependence on the electrical grid. Or perhaps an automotive company and a research institute working on building sustainable cities – what possibilities might arise? The idea must be some kind of new business venture that will help to advance human development, while contributing to resource/impact decoupling and staying within natural limits – it should not be merely a philanthropic donations exercise in the name of corporate social responsibility.

The objective is to reinvent business in a way that embraces an *embedded* perspective, adopts a *sustainability mindset*, and is *transformational* – it shifts our assumptions at the personal, organizational, and societal level.

Elements of a Student Assignment (this can be done as an individual assignment or group project):

1   *Issue identification*. Identify a global sustainability issue that is of interest to you – population/poverty, water, food, energy, climate, or sustainable cites. Draw on the overviews in chapter 4 and the additional resources in appendix 1.

2   *Identification of a company and their conceptions of sustainability*. Identify a for-profit company in that sector. By examining the company's public documents (website, annual reports, publications, news items), determine whether it has working definition of sustainability. Examine the language and activities recounted in the company's communications – interpret how the leadership in the organization is thinking and talking about sustainability issues. Assess the language and activities against the four conceptions of sustainability framework in chapter 6. Does their thinking appear to be *reductive* (focused on trade-offs, or social responsibility side-projects apart from the core business) or is it *integrative* (seeking win-win-win on the triple-bottom line, or moving sustainability issues to the core mission of the business)? Aided by the descriptors in Table 6.1, locate the company's *conceptions of sustainability* on the 2x2 grid in Figure 6.1. Note: This step is important for two reasons. One, getting a sense of the current "sustainability mindset" of the organization allows you to

see where there is room for strategic stretch and new opportunities. Two, it helps you to know where to begin your "pitch" to the company's senior executives – if your idea is too far from their current mindset, they will not be able to recognize themselves in your proposal. Strategic stretch is fine – you just may need to do more to raise the executives' level of literacy in the issues and opportunities to prepare them for your idea.

3   *Sector analysis.* Conduct a PESTLE analysis on your sector (the major political, economic, social, technological, legal, and environmental factors affecting the industry), outlining some of the major forces at work. You can start with a basic PEST model (see http://www.netmba.com/strategy/pest/) and add consideration of the top few legal and environmental sustainability issues/challenges facing the sector by drawing on some of the resources provided in appendix 1.

4   *Values, beliefs, and assumptions.* In your sector, what values, beliefs or assumptions do you see as foundationally important to shifting the trajectory towards more sustainable practice? You might organize these at various levels – individual, societal/cultural, and organizational. How would a "triple-loop learning" shift in basic assumptions (see chapter 8) open new opportunities for that sector? For example, if your idea is in the area of personal transportation, what are the current dominant assumptions (of individuals, governments, or companies) about commuting, travel, car ownership, or public transport? Identifying current assumptions can help with stakeholder engagement and successful implementation of your proposal. Draft some design questions to help generate ideas (e.g., questions starting with "What if ...?" "How might we ...?").

5   *Create a learning partnership with a civil society organization.* Identify a potential civil society organization (CSO) or non-governmental organization (NGO) to enter into a learning partnership with your chosen organization. The mission of the CSO/NGO should be relevant to issues you have identified in parts 1 and 3. Why do you think this would be a productive partnership? How might the partnership help to shift the sustainability conversations in the company? (See Wiser Earth at http://www.wiser.org/ for a database of CSO/NGOs, which is searchable by issue or by region.)

6   *Hold a design brainstorm of opportunities.* Using the *reconstructing value* design criteria from Table 9.1, your analysis in parts 2–5, and your knowledge of global sustainability issues, hold a brainstorm session on new opportunities. Some factors in the global issues will serve as design objectives (e.g., bring water to the rural poor) and others as constraints (e.g., economic or physical water scarcity). In design thinking, constraints are what drive creativity. In a group project you could even role play this as in the roundtable exercise – assign group members a role and perspective to bring to the conversation: business, government, or a civil society perspective relevant to the issue (add in an engineer, a visual artist and a cultural anthropologist if you have any around). To

raise the level of value creation, look to Table 5.1 in chapter 5: Conduct a "social learning" brainstorm dialogue to build a range of possible ideas.

7   *Recommendations.* From those possibilities, identify one or two new business opportunities (new products/services/markets) that you would recommend the company pursue. Rather than pitching just the potential return on investment, assess your idea against the factors in the OECD's *Better Life Index* described in chapter 9. How does your project help to advance human well-being? This will help you and your client organization to see the embeddedness of the social value of the project.

Note: This is an exercise in *integrative* thinking – putting all of the parts together. Your report should flow logically and coherently from analysis to strategic recommendations through to the projected impact; if you divide the labor into parts and paste it together, it will show!

Guidelines for the Structure of the Report
Total: 12 pages (double spaced) + Appendices (18 page limit)
Executive Summary: 1 page

Part A: Issue identification, company identification, description of conceptions of sustainability – what kind of *sustainability conversations* are evident in the company's communications? 2 ½ pages (include brief intro paragraph)

Part B: Sectoral analysis – summary of the PESTLE analysis, with the fuller work included as an appendix: key points and implications. 1½ pages

Part C: Underlying values, assumptions, beliefs – current and possible: In the sector: about PESTLE forces, and at various levels: individual, organizational, societal/cultural ; identify critical design questions. 2 pages

Part D: Create a learning partnership with a CSO/NGO: Why this organization? What new conversations might occur? 1½ pages

Part E: A design brainstorm of opportunities. Identify the key design criteria for your project and the key constraints. List and briefly describe your best three ideas. 1½ pages

Part F: Summary of Recommendations: Describe your recommended new venture idea, and the business model (i.e., how it will be profitable). Describe the benefits it will bring using the OECD *Better Life Index*. 2 pages

Appendices: 18 page limit for a total of 30 in whole report
Presentation: 20–30 minute *interactive* presentation + Q&A. Make us care about your idea!

Afterword
Leadership for Sustainability

As we have seen throughout this book, *sustainability* is a big idea. At the highest level, it is a broad, contestable concept that asks us to think about how we can create conditions for humanity and other life to flourish on earth, while respecting the earth's ability to absorb our impacts so that others can follow after us and continue to thrive. It includes attending to environmental care, securing our food and water, rethinking our energy systems, realizing social justice now and towards the future, and considering what makes life meaningful and worth living. That is a lot for one word to carry!

The ideas here are shaped by our belief that the sustainability challenges are large, there are no easy answers, and that we need to talk to one another, engaging as many as possible in the conversation, to figure out where to go from here. To assist in that journey, we wrote this book with three central aims: to lay out the number, scope, and complexity of the challenges we face, written for the lay manager to comprehend; to outline a collective "societal learning" process that is required for transforming our unsustainable assumptions and actions; and to offer a list of questions and a range of leadership skills that are needed to address this complexity. Ultimately, we suggest that we need to engage in a process of reflective practice and societal learning to help reconstruct our collective ideas of value. Along the way we have built a model that has some key principles at the core to serve as our collective design criteria: an *embedded view* of the environment, society, and economy that focuses on well-being beyond economic growth; a *sustainability mindset* that supports human development and with a measure of social justice, while respecting natural limits; and an ethic of *transformation* that proactively and collaboratively engages people in dialogue to reshape the assumptions that guide our public policy and strategic business decisions. We can work towards those principles, driven by good questions, through a process of 4R's of reconstructing value: rethinking, relating, responding, and reinventing.

We hope that the structure, the material, and the learning process of this book have been helpful as a guide towards thinking and acting on these issues in your management education, in your work, and in your life. The modes of thinking and the levels of learning presented in chapters 2 and 3 can help to raise our collective capability for addressing the challenges we face. In chapter 4 we described some of those challenges in more depth, and in chapter 5 we considered the importance of stakeholder engagement and the levels at which that can occur. Chapters 6 and 7 described the "conceptions of sustainability" we have observed among managers as they try to translate these big ideas into their daily work, and the "social dynamics" that can result as organizations attempt to change. In chapter 8 we delved more deeply into ideas from social learning, and in chapter 9 we outlined the design parameters at the core of our model: an embedded perspective, a sustainability mindset, and a transformational approach. The exercises distributed throughout can help to bring these concepts to life in real human dialogue and action, and the culminating exercise in chapter 9 serves to integrate the learning across all of the chapters. Of course, these are but a few ideas – the possibilities for constructing productive learning dialogues are unlimited. To confirm this, simply pick up a newspaper on any given day and you will find an abundance of stories that are relevant to many of the process questions at the end of each chapter. Questions of sustainability are increasingly the central questions of humanity in a world of growing population and diminishing resources.

Leadership for sustainability means bringing global issues into the conversational life of your family, your social interactions, and your work life, no matter your role or positional power, and asking how we can live better. Leadership for sustainability is *transforming* leadership – a social process for mutual transformation, for adapting our assumptions, rules, and governance systems with a pragmatic focus on improving the conditions for human and other life to flourish – to put the world on a sustainable path.

We began by saying that you have a problem to solve, and if not you, then who? Leadership for sustainability depends on you, on every one of us, and this book is for the leader in us all.

Appendix: Further Resources for Exploring Global Sustainability Issues

Population

UN Population Division: *http://www.un.org/esa/population/unpop.htm*
The UN Population Division is responsible for monitoring and appraising the broad range of areas in the field of population. Its work supports a number of intergovernmental bodies, helps to monitor implementation of the Millennium Development Goals, and provides access by governments to information on population trends and their interrelationships with social and economic development as an input to government policy and program formulation.

U.S. Census Bureau – International Programs: *http://www.census.gov/population/international/*
The U.S. Census Bureau conducts demographic and economic studies and strengthens statistical development around the world through technical assistance, training, and software products. For over sixty years, the Census Bureau has assisted in the collection, processing, analysis, dissemination, and use of statistics with counterpart governments in over 100 countries.

Population Reference Bureau: *http://www.prb.org*
The Population Reference Bureau informs people around the world about population, health, and the environment, and empowers them to use that information to advance the well-being of current and future generations.

Water

WiserEarth: *http://www.wiser.org*
WiserEarth is a social network for people and organizations doing work on sustainability issues. WISER stands for World Index of Social and Environmental Responsibility, and at the time of this writing, the website lists 10,725 organizations working on improving the world's water, including non-profit, for-profit, governmental, non-governmental, research institutes, foundations, village-based groups, student groups, and others.

UN Water: *http://www.unwater.org/*
UN Water strengthens coordination and coherence among UN entities dealing with issues related to all aspects of freshwater and sanitation. This includes surface and groundwater resources, the interface between freshwater and seawater and water-related disasters.

United Nations Environmental Programme: *http://www.unep.org*
The United Nations Environment Programme (UNEP) coordinates United Nations environmental activities, assisting developing countries in implementing environmentally sound policies and practices.

World Water Council: *http://worldwatercouncil.org*
An international multi-stakeholder platform to promote awareness, build political commitment, and trigger action on critical water issues at all levels.

Circle of Blue: *http://www.circleofblue.org/waternews/*
International network of leading journalists, scientists, and communications design experts that reports and presents the information necessary to respond to the global freshwater crisis.

Pacific Institute: *http://www.pacinst.org*
The Pacific Institute is a non-partisan research institute that works to advance environmental protection, economic development, and social equity.

World Business Council for Sustainable Development: *http://www.wbcsd.com*

A CEO-led, global association of some 200 companies that deals exclusively with business and sustainable development.

Waterkeeper Alliance: *http://www.waterkeeper.org*
A global movement of on-the-water advocates who patrol and protect over 100,000 miles of rivers, streams, and coastlines in North and South America, Europe, Australia, Asia, and Africa.

Water.org: *http://water.org*
A U.S.-based non-profit organization committed to providing safe drinking water and sanitation to people in developing countries.

World Resources Institute: *http://www.wri.org*
A global environmental think tank "that goes beyond research to put ideas into action," working with governments, companies, and civil society to build solutions to urgent environmental challenges.

WRI's Aqueduct Project: *http://insights.wri.org/aqueduct*
The project measures and maps water-related risks.

International Rivers: *http://www.internationalrivers.org*
International Rivers protects rivers and defends the rights of communities that depend on them, and works to stop destructive dams and promote water and energy solutions for a just and sustainable world.

American Rivers: *http://www.americanrivers.org*
A conservation organization standing up for healthy rivers so communities can thrive. It works to protect and restore rivers and maintain clean water that can sustain people, wildlife, and nature.

Blue Planet Project: *http://www.blueplanetproject.net*
A global civil society organization working to secure water governance as a public trust and to guarantee that access to clean water is a basic human right.

World Economic Forum – Water: *http://www.weforum.org/issues/water*
Investigates the role of private–public partnerships in addressing water issues.

Food

WiserEarth: *http://www.wiser.org*
WiserEarth lists 8,725 organizations working on food and agriculture issues, including non-profit, for-profit, governmental, non-governmental, research institutes, foundations, and student groups.

UN Food and Agriculture Organization: *http://www.fao.org/*
Achieving food security for all is at the heart of FAO's efforts; its goal is to make sure people have regular access to enough high-quality food to lead active, healthy lives. FAO's mandate is to raise levels of nutrition, improve agricultural productivity, better the lives of rural populations, and contribute to the growth of the world economy.

Worldwatch Institute – Nourishing the Planet: *http://blogs.worldwatch.org/nourishingtheplanet/*
The Nourishing the Planet project assesses the state of agricultural innovations – from cropping methods to irrigation technology to agricultural policy – with an emphasis on sustainability, diversity, and ecosystem health, as well as productivity. The project aims to both inform global efforts to eradicate hunger and raise the profile of these efforts. The project considers the institutional infrastructure needed by each of the approaches analyzed and suggest what sort of companion investments are likely to determine success – from local seed banks to processing facilities, from pro-poor value chains to marketing bureaus.

The Global Crop Diversity Trust: *http://www.croptrust.org*
A unique public–private partnership raising funds from individual, corporate, and government donors to establish an endowment fund that will provide complete and continuous funding for key crop collections, in eternity. Important collections of crop diversity face urgent and chronic funding shortages. These shortages can lead to loss of diversity, the very building blocks on which adaptive and productive agriculture depends.

Svalbard Global Seed Vault: *http://www.croptrust.org/content/svalbard-global-seed-vault*

Deep inside a snow covered mountain on a remote island in the Svalbard archipelago, halfway between mainland Norway and the North Pole, lies the Svalbard Global Seed Vault. It is a fail-safe, state-of-the-art seed storage facility, built to stand the test of time – and to survive natural or human-made disasters, particularly a changing climate. The Vault holds more than 500,000 samples originating from almost every country in the world.

Energy and Climate

WiserEarth: *http://www.wiser.org*
The World Index of Social and Environmental Responsibility lists 6795 organizations working on energy solutions, and 3,478 organizations working on climate issues worldwide.

International Energy Agency: *http://www.iea.org*
The International Energy Agency (IEA) serves the Organization for Economic Cooperation and Development as an autonomous organization that works to ensure reliable, affordable, and clean energy for its twenty-eight member countries and beyond.

World Energy Outlook: *http://www.worldenergyoutlook.org*
This is the annual report of the IEA that forecasts future energy production and consumption.

The Energy Administration Agency: *http://www.eia.gov*
The U.S. Energy Information Administration (EIA) collects, analyses, and disseminates independent and impartial energy information to promote sound policymaking, efficient markets, and public understanding of energy and its interaction with the economy and the environment.

The Global Energy Assessment: *http://www.iiasa.ac.at/Research/ENE/ GEA/*
Coordinated by the International Institute for Applied Systems Analysis (IIASA), the Global Energy Assessment involves specialists from a range of disciplines, industry groups, and policy areas in defining a new global energy policy agenda, one that is capable of transforming the way society thinks about, uses, and delivers energy and to facilitate

equitable and sustainable energy services for all, in particular the 2 billion people who currently lack access to clean, modern energy.

Sustainable Energy – Without the Hot Air: *http://www.withouthotair. com/*
A pragmatic, numbers-based assessment on the question of whether renewable energy sources can displace fossil fuels, accompanied by policy recommendations, by UK physicist David J. C. McKay. Highly readable and engaging, a very useful contribution to the conversation. The book can be downloaded free at this site.

CleanTech.org: *http://www.cleantech.org/*
CleanTech.org is a leading portal for energy and environmental technology commercialization. Its aim is to be a virtual incubator for clean technologies and a resource to scientists, inventors, entrepreneurs, and investors interested in new clean technologies.

Center for Climate and Energy Solutions: *http://www.c2es.org/*
The Center for Climate and Energy Solutions (formerly the Pew Center on Global Climate Change) brings together business leaders, policymakers, scientists, and other experts to bring a new approach to a complex and often controversial issue. The approach is based on sound science, straight talk, and a belief that we can work together to protect the climate while sustaining economic growth.

The Climate Reality Project: *http://climaterealityproject.org*
Founded and chaired by Al Gore, the Climate Reality Project has more than 5 million members and supporters worldwide, and is bringing the facts about the climate crisis into the mainstream and engaging the public in conversation about how to solve it. "We help citizens around the world discover the truth and take meaningful steps to bring about change."

CO2Now.org: *http://co2now.org*
CO2Now.org republishes and organizes global climate data and related information from leading science and media sources around the world. The website and its online tools are produced independently by informed, non-scientists to give people of many backgrounds easy

access to the world's most current and reliable numbers, targets, and reports on the planet we share. CO_2Now.org works to advance CO_2 literacy as a stepping stone to decisions and solutions that will bring humanity's main environmental crises to an end: global warming, climate change, and ocean acidification.

Notes

1. New Questions for Business

1 J.M. Burns, *Leadership* (New York: Harper and Row, 1978), 20.
2 See P. Berger and T. Luckmann, *The Social Construction of Reality: A Treatise in the Sociology of Knowledge* (New York: Anchor, 1967).
3 See P. Senge, A. Kleiner, C. Roberts, R. Ross, and B. Smith, *The Fifth Discipline Fieldbook: Strategies and Tools for Building a Learning Organization* (New York: Crown Business, 1994).
4 G. Morgan, *Images of Organization* (Beverly Hills, CA: Sage, 1997).
5 Alfred J. Morrow, *The Practical Theorist: The Life and Work of Kurt Lewin* (New York: Basic Books, 1969), viii.
6 W. Edwards Deming, *The New Economics for Industry, Government, Education* (Cambridge, MA: MIT Press, 1993).
7 See M. Jacobs, "Sustainable Development as a Contested Concept," in A. Dobson, ed., *Fairness and Futurity: Essays on Environmental Sustainability and Social Justice* (Oxford: Oxford University Press, 1999), 21–45.
8 W. Gallie, "Essentially Contested Concepts," *Proceedings of the Aristotelian Society* 56 (1956): 167–98.
9 World Commission on Environment and Development, *Our Common Future* (Oxford: Oxford University Press, 1987).
10 T.N. Gladwin, J.J. Kennelly, and T.-S. Krause, "Shifting Paradigms for Sustainable Development: Implications for Management Theory and Research," *Academy of Management Review* 20 (1995): 874–907. For other similar constructions of paradigms in sustainability, see C.P. Egri and L.T. Pinfield, "Organizations and the Biosphere: Ecologies and Environments," in S. R. Clegg, C. Hardy, and W. Nord, eds., *Handbook of Organizational Studies* (London: Sage, 1996), 459–83; B. Hopwood, M. Mellor, and G. O'Brien,

"Sustainable Development: Mapping Different Approaches," *Sustainable Development* 13 (2005): 38–52.

11 J. Elkington, *Cannibals with Forks: The Triple Bottom Line of Twenty-First Century Business* (Gabriola Island, BC: New Society Publishers, 1998).

12 For an examination of the embedded perspective, or general lack thereof, in the management literature, see J. Marcus, E. Kurucz, and B. Colbert, "Conceptions of the Business–Society–Nature Interface: Implications for Management Scholarship," *Business and Society* 49(3) (2010): 402–38.

13 H. Mintzberg, *Managers Not MBAs: A Hard Look at the Soft Practice of Managing and Management Development* (San Francisco: Berrett-Koehler, 2004).

14 See J. Raelin, "'I Don't Have Time to Think!' versus the Art of Reflective Practice," *Reflections* 4(1) (2002): 66–79, for a discussion of the action bias in organizations, and P.R. Hedberg, "Learning through Reflective Classroom Practice: Applications to Educate the Reflective Manager," *Journal of Management Education* 33(1) (2009): 10–36, for a discussion of such bias in business school education.

15 D. Schon, *The Reflective Practitioner: How Professionals Think in Action* (New York: Basic Books, 1983).

16 A. Cunliffe, "On Becoming a Critically Reflexive Practitioner," *Journal of Management Education* 28(4) (2004): 408.

17 M.E. Porter and M.R. Kramer, "Creating Shared Value: How to Reinvent Capitalism – and Unleash a Wave of Innovation and Growth," *Harvard Business Review*, January–February 2011, 64.

2. Envisioning a New Way of Doing Business: Thinking Skills for Sustainable Organizations

1 See S. Hart, *Capitalism at the Crossroads: Next Generation Strategies for a Post-Crisis World*, 3rd ed. (Upper Saddle River, NJ: Wharton School Publishing, 2010); and R. Welford, *Environmental Strategy and Sustainable Development* (New York: Routledge, 1995).

2 See D. Wheeler, B.A. Colbert, and R.E. Freeman "Focusing on Value: Reconciling Corporate Social Responsibility, Sustainability and a Stakeholder Approach in a Network World," *Journal of General Management* 28(3) (2003): 1–28.

3 E.C. Kurucz, B.A. Colbert, and D. Wheeler, "The Business Case for Corporate Social Responsibility," in A. Crane, A. McWilliams, D. Matten, J. Moon, and D. Seigel, eds., *The Oxford Handbook on Corporate Social Responsibility* (Oxford: Oxford University Press, 2208), 83–112.

4 See A.L. Cunliffe, "The Philosopher Leader: On Relationalism, Ethics and Reflexivity – a Critical Perspective to Teaching Leadership," *Management Learning* 40(1) (2009): 87–101, for an excellent discussion on the distinction

between critical reflexivity and self-reflexivity and the importance of the philosopher leader engaging in critical management studies.

5 See Jacob Gordon, "The TH Interview: Yvon Chouinard, Founder of Patagonia (Part One)," *treehugger* (7 February 2008), retrieved 16 February 2012 from http://www.treehugger.com/treehugger-radio/the-th-interview-yvon-chouinard-founder-of-patagonia-part-one.html.

6 Bob Shapiro, "Greenpeace Business Conference 1999 with Robert Shapiro and Peter Melchott," *Industry Mergers and Integration* (1999), retrieved from 10 March 2012 http://www.biotech-info.net/business_conf.html.

7 Adapted from R. Anderson, *Mid-Course Correction: Toward a Sustainable Enterprise: The Interface Model* (White River Junction, VT: Chelsea Green Publishing, 1999).

8 R. Ackoff, "The Future of Operational Research Is Past," *The Journal of the Operational Research Society* 30(2) (1979): 93–104.

9 M. Schneider and M. Somers, "Organizations as Complex Adaptive Systems: Implications of Complexity Theory for Leadership Research," *The Leadership Quarterly* 17 (2006): 351–65.

10 B.A. Colbert, "The Complex Resource-Based View: Implications for Theory and Practice in Strategic Human Resource Management," *Academy of Management Review* 29(3) (2004), 341–58; S. Maguire, B. McKelvey, L. Mirabeau, and N. Oztas, "Complexity Science and Organization Studies," in S. Clegg, C. Hardy, T. Lawrence, and W.R. Nord, eds., *The Sage Handbook of Organization Studies*, 2nd ed. (Thousand Oaks, CA: Sage, 2006), 400–17.

11 R. Stacey, *Strategic Management and Organizational Dynamics: The Challenge of Complexity*, 5th ed. (Essex, UK: Pearson Education, 2007).

12 R. Martin, *The Opposable Mind: Winning through Integrative Thinking* (Boston: Harvard Business Press, 2007).

13 K. Cameron, "Effectiveness as Paradox: Consensus and Conflict in Conceptions of Organizational Effectiveness," *Management Science* 32 (1986): 539–53.

14 H. Rittel and M. Webber, "Dilemmas in a General Theory of Planning," *Policy Sciences* 4 (1973): 155–69; N. Roberts, and J. Camillus, "Strategy as a Wicked Problem," *Harvard Business Review*, May 2008, 99–106.

15 R.E. Freeman, J.S. Harrison, A.C. Wicks, B.L. Parmar, and S. de Colle, *Stakeholder Theory: The State of the Art* (Cambridge: Cambridge University Press, 2010).

16 Insurance information about the UK retrieved 14 September 2011 from http://www.sustainabilityatwork.org.uk/casestudies/view/44.

17 R.E. Freeman, *Strategic Management: A Stakeholder Approach* (New York: Cambridge University Press, 2010).

18 R.K. Mitchell, B.R. Agle, and D.J. Wood, "Toward a Theory of Stakeholder Identification and Salience: Defining the Principles of Who and What Really Counts," *Academy of Management Review* 22 (1997): 853–86.

19 See "Definition of IT," *Rotman: A New Way to Think*, http://www.rotman. utoronto.ca/integrativethinking/details.aspx?ContentID=371.

20 J. Tidd, J. Bessant, and K. Pavitt, *Managing Innovation: Integrating Technological, Market and Organizational Change*, 3rd ed. (West Sussex, UK: John Wiley, 2005).

21 D. Wheeler and M. Sillanpaa, *The Stakeholder Corporation: A Blueprint for Maximizing Stakeholder Value* (London: Pitman, 1997).

22 S. Hart and S. Sharma, "Engaging Fringe Stakeholders for Competitive Imagination," *Academy of Management Executive* 18(1) (2004): 7–18.

23 R.E. Freeman, *Strategic Management: A Stakeholder Approach* (New York: Cambridge University Press, 2010).

24 For more on HoneyCare Africa, see http://www.honeycareafrica.com/.

25 For more on this, see B.A. Colbert, E.C. Kurucz, and D. Wheeler, "Building the Sustainable Organization through Adaptive, Creative Coherence in the HR System," in R. Burke and C. Cooper, eds., *Building More Effective Organizations: HR Management and Performance in Practice* (Cambridge: Cambridge University Press, 2007), 310–33.

26 J. Grant, *The Green Marketing Manifesto* (West Essex, UK: John Wiley, 2007).

27 K. Andrews, *The Concept of Corporate Strategy* (Homewood, NY: Irwin, 1971).

28 M. Porter, *Competitive Strategy* (New York: Free Press, 1980).

29 M. Porter and M. Kramer, "Creating Shared Value," *Harvard Business Review*, January–February 2011, 63–77.

30 G. Johnson and K. Scholes, *Exploring Corporate Strategy* (London: Prentice Hall Europe, 1997).

31 S. Hart and M. Milstein, "Creating Sustainable Value," *Academy of Management Executive* 17(2) (2003): 56–67.

32 See J. Marcus, E.C. Kurucz, and B.A. Colbert, "Conceptions of the Business-Society-Nature Interface: Implications for Management Scholarship," *Business & Society* 49(3) (2010): 402–38.

33 J. Barney, *Gaining and Sustaining Competitive Advantage* (Reading, MA: Addison-Wesley, 1997).

34 C.M. Christensen, *The Innovators Dilemma: The Revolutionary Book that Will Change the Way You Do Business* (Boston: Harvard Business School Press, 1997).

35 R. Kaplan and D. Norton, *Strategy Maps: Converting Intangible Assets into Tangible Outcomes* (Boston: Harvard Business School Press, 2004).

36 See Alan Shapiro commenting on this in C. Holliday, S. Schmidheiny, and P. Watts, *Walking the Talk: The Business Case for Sustainable Development* (Sheffield, UK: Greenleaf, 2002).

37 See J. Brown and D. Isaacs. *The World Cafe: Shaping Our Future through Conversations that Matter* (San Francisco: Berrett-Kohler, 2005).

38 A. Webber, "What's So New about the New Economy?" *Harvard Business Review*, January–February 1993, 24–42.

39 G. Hamel and R. Lieber, "Killer Strategies that Make Shareholders Rich," *Fortune*, 23 June 1997, 70.

40 B. Banathy, *Designing Social Systems in a Changing World* (New York: Plenum Press, 1996).

41 J.M. Liedtka and J.W. Rosenblum, "Shaping Conversations: Making Strategy, Managing Change," *California Management Review* 39(1) (1996): 141–57; and J.M. Liedtka, "Strategy Formulation: The Roles of Conversation and Design," in M.A. Hitt and E. Freeman, eds., *The Blackwell Handbook of Strategic Management* (New York: Blackwell Publishers, 2001), 70–93.

42 J.M. Liedtka, "Strategy Formulation: The Roles of Conversation and Design," in M.A. Hitt and E. Freeman, eds., *The Blackwell Handbook of Strategic Management* (New York: Blackwell Publishers, 2001), 85.

43 K. van der Heijden, *The Art of Strategic Conversation* (New York: Wiley, 1996).

44 For more on this, see J. Brown and D. Isaacs, *The World Cafe: Shaping Our Future through Conversations that Matter* (San Francisco: Berrett-Kohler, 2005).

45 F. Edmonds, "Hewlett Packard: Sustainability as a Competitive Advantage," *Toronto Speaker Series* (10 February 2011), retrieved 14 March 2012 from http://ecoopportunity.net/2011/02/hp-sustainability-as-a-competitive-advantage-february-10-2011/.

46 P. Smith, "Taking Sustainable Technology beyond the Workplace," Sustainable Development in Government (5 February 2011), retrieved 11 February 2012 from http://sd.defra.gov.uk/2011/02/taking-sustainable-technology-beyond-the-workplace/.

47 Cisco, *The Sustainable Business Practice Study* (London: Cisco UK & Ireland, 2008), retrieved 15 February 2012 from http://www.cisco.com/cisco/web/UK/Cisco-SBPS.pdf.

48 C.J. Palus and W.H. Drath, "Putting Something in the Middle: An Approach to Dialogue," *Reflections* 3(2) (2001): 28–39.

49 Kerry Molinaro quoted in "IKEA Launches 2009 Global Sustainability Report," *IKEA* (6 May 2010), retrieved 12 December 2011 from http://www.ikea.com/ca/en/about_ikea/newsitem/2010_sustainbility_report.

50 I. Cheshire, "Imagining a New Sustainable Capitalism," *The Guardian Professional Network* (24 March 2011), retrieved 3 February 2012 from http://www.guardian.co.uk/sustainable-business/blog/kingfisher-ceo-ian-cheshire-sustainable-capitalism.

51 For more on Vancity, see https://www.vancity.com/AboutUs/.

52 J. Liedtka and T. Ogilvie, *Designing for Growth: A Design Thinking Toolkit for Managers* (New York: Columbia University Press, 2011).

53 J. Liedtka and H. Mintzberg, "Time for Design," *Design Management Review* 17(2) (2006): 10.

54 J. Liedka, "Business Strategy and Design: Can This Marriage Be Saved?" *The Design Management Review* 21(2) (2010): 11.

55 For more on design driven by constraints and desirability, feasibility, and viability, see T. Brown, *Change by Design: How Design Thinking Transforms Organizations and Inspires Innovation* (New York: HarperCollins, 2009).

56 For more on Frito Lay's compostable Sun Chips bags, see http://www .greenbiz.com/news/2011/02/24/compostable-sun-chips-bags-second-quieter-chance#ixzz1GDUnfkWB.

57 For more on the Aquaduct Bike, see http://www.ideo.com/work/aquaduct/.

58 For more on Playpumps, see http://www.playpumps.co.za/.

59 J. Benyus, *Biomimicry: Innovation Inspired by Nature* (New York: HarperCollins, 1997), 2–3.

60 For more on Calera Cement, see www.calera.com.

61 S. Hart and M. Milstein, "Global Sustainability and the Creative Destruction of Industries," *MIT Sloan Management Review* 41(1) (1999): 23–33.

62 See "Human-Centered Design Toolkit," *IDEO* (2012) at http://www.ideo. com/work/human-centered-design-toolkit/.

63 For more on IBM's Smarter Planet, see http://www.ibm.com/ smarterplanet/ca/en/.

64 For more on Better Place, see http://www.betterplace.com/.

65 L. Dyer, *Critical Thinking for Business Students*, 2nd ed. (Concord, ON: Captus Press, 2011).

66 R. Paul and L. Elder, *The Miniature Guide to Critical Thinking: Concepts and Tools* (Tomales, CA: The Foundation for Critical Thinking, 2001).

67 J.M. Liedtka, "Strategy Formulation: The Roles of Conversation and Design," in M.A. Hitt and E. Freeman, eds., *The Blackwell Handbook of Strategic Management* (New York: Blackwell Publishers, 2001), 78.

68 For more on ASI, see http://www.sarep.ucdavis.edu/sarep/about/def.

69 For more information, see the Center for Urban Education about Sustainable Agriculture, http://www.cuesa.org/page/sustainability.

3. Learning Our Way Forward: Transforming Organizations and Society

1 "A Letter from Co-Founder Jeffrey Hollender: In Search of Revolutionary Responsibility," *Seventh Generation, Corporate Consciousness Report 2.0*

(2009), retrieved 14 September 2011 from http://www.7genreport.com/intro-duction/index.php.

2 R. Cyert and J. March, *A Behavioural Theory of the Firm* (Oxford: Blackwell Press, 1963).

3 For a good discussion on the use of organizational learning in manage-ment theory, see C. Fiol and M. Lyles, "Organizational Learning," *Academy of Management Review* 10 (1985): 803–13.

4 For an overview of how learning has been engaged in management theory and practice, see M. Easterby-Smith and M.A. Lyles, eds., *The Blackwell Handbook of Organizational Learning and Knowledge Management* (Oxford: Blackwell Press, 2003).

5 For more on single- and double-loop learning, see C. Argyris and D.A. Schön, *Theory in Practice: Increasing Professional Effectiveness* (San Francisco: Jossey-Bass, 1974); and C. Argyris and D.A. Schön, *Organizational Learning II: Theory, Method and Practice* (Reading, MA: Addison-Wesley, 1996).

6 P. Tosey, M. Visser, and P. Saunders, "The Origins and Conceptual-izations of 'Triple Loop' Learning: A Critical Review," *Management Learning* (2011), published online before print, 2 December 2011, doi: 10.1177/1350507611426239.

7 P.R. Hedberg, "Learning through Reflective Classroom Practice: Applica-tions to Educate the Reflective Manager," *Journal of Management Education* 33(1) (2007): 10–36.; M. Van Manen, "On the Epistemology of Reflective Practice," *Teachers and Teaching: Theory and Practice* 1(1) (1995): 33–50; G. Dehler, "Prospects and Possibilities of Critical Management Education: Critical Beings and a Pedagogy of Critical Action," *Management Learning* 40(1) (2009): 31–49.

8 Strong sustainability often includes simultaneous consideration of deep ecology principles and social justice concerns. For an agricultural ex-ample touching on both, see Olivier de Schutter, "Report Submitted by the Special Rapporteur on the Right to Food," United Nations General Assembly Human Rights Council, Doc. A/HRC/16/49 (20 December 2010), available online at http://www.srfood.org/images/stories/pdf/officialreports/20110308_a-hrc-16-49_agroecology_en.pdf.

9 P.A. Victor, J.E. Hanna, and A. Kubursi, "How Strong Is Weak Sustain-ability?" In S. Faucheux, M. O'Connor, and J. van der Straaten, eds., *Sus-tainable Development: Concepts, Rationalities and Strategies* (London: Kluwer Academic Publishers, 1998), 195–210.

10 S. Sterling, "Higher Education, Sustainability and the Role of Systemic Learning," in P.B. Corcoran and A.E. Wals, eds., *Higher Education and the Challenge of Sustainability: Problematics, Promise and Practice* (Boston: Kluwer Academic Publishers, 2004), 49–70.

11 For more on Seventh Generation, see http://www.seventhgeneration.com/seventh-generation-mission/report/2010.

12 "Our Company," *Seventh Generation Corporate Consciousness Report 2.0*, retrieved 14 September 2011 from http://www.7genreport.com/introduction/ourcompany.php.

13 Julie Scelfo, "Looking Beyond the E.P.A.'s Seal of Approval," *The New York Times*, 15 April 2009, retrieved 22 August 2011 from http://www.nytimes.com/2009/04/16/garden/16greenhome.html?_r=2&ref=garden.

14 "A Letter from Co-Founder Jeffrey Hollender: In Search of Revolutionary Responsibility," *Seventh Generation Corporate Consciousness Report 2.0* (2009), retrieved 14 September 2011 from http://www.7genreport.com/introduction/index.php.

15 G. Bateson, *Steps to an Ecology of Mind: Collected Essays in Anthropology, Psychiatry, Evolution and Epistemology* (London: Paladin, Granada, 1973).

16 "Higher Education, Sustainability and the Role of Systemic Learning," in P.B. Corcoran and A.E. Wals, eds., *Higher Education and the Challenge of Sustainability: Problematics, Promise and Practice* (Boston: Kluwer Academic Publishers, 2004), 49–70.

17 John Grant refers to this as "green" in *The Green Marketing Manifesto* (West Essex, UK: John Wiley, 2007).

18 For more on Frito Lay Product's sustainability initiatives, see http://www.fritolay.com/our-planet.html.

19 For more on the 3P's initiative, see http://solutions.3m.com/wps/portal/3M/en_US/3M-Sustainability/Global/Environment/3P/.

20 For more on gDiapers, see http://www.gdiapers.com/.

21 John Grant refers to this as "greener" in *The Green Marketing Manifesto* (West Essex, UK: John Wiley, 2007).

22 For more on CarSharing, see www.carsharing.org.

23 S. Waddell, *Societal Learning and Change* (Sheffield, UK: Greenleaf Publishing, 2005).

24 John Grant refers to this as "greenest" in *The Green Marketing Manifesto* (West Essex, UK: John Wiley, 2007).

25 For more on Kiva, see http://www.kiva.org/.

26 A. Carlman, "Development 2.0? The Case of Kiva.org and Online Social Lending for Development" (M.Phil. thesis, Stellenbosch University, 2010), retrieved 14 August 2011 from http://irl.sun.ac.za/handle/10019.1/4226.

27 For more on Development 2.0, see ibid., and M. Thompson, "ICT and Development Studies: Towards Development 2.0," *Journal of International Development* 20 (2008): 821–35.

28 For more on E+CO, see http://eandco.net/about.

29 For more on this, see O. Branzei and K. McKague, *A Model of Clean Energy Entrepreneurship in Africa: E+CO's Path to Scale* (London, ON: Richard Ivey School of Business at the University of Western Ontario, 2007).

30 For more on the SLEN model, see D. Wheeler, K. McKague, J. Thompson, R. Davies, J. Medalye, and M. Prada, "Creating Sustainable Local Enterprise Networks," *MIT Sloan Management Review* 47(1) (2005): 33–40.

31 See L. Smircich and G. Morgan, "Leadership: The Management of Meaning," *Journal of Applied Behavioural Science* 18(3) (1982): 257–73, for a discussion of management as a process of meaning-making.

32 See J. Kania and M. Kramer, "Collective Impact," *Stanford Social Innovation Review* (Winter 2011): 36–41, retrieved 15 August 2011 from http://www.ssireview.org/articles/entry/collective_impact. For a description of Mars' initiatives around Cocoa Sustainability, see http://cocoasustainability.resolvedigital.com/.

33 See Ronald Wright, "A Short History of Progress," The 2004 CBC Massey Lectures, at http://www.cbc.ca/ideas/massey-archives/2004/11/07/massey-lectures-2004-a-short-history-of-progress/. The "Easter Island" story begins in Part 3 at 7:42.

34 There are competing interpretations of what historically transpired on Easter Island. Ronald Wright, in *A Short History of Progress* (Toronto: House of Anansi Press, 2004), interprets the history as a cautionary tale of environmental destruction, as does Jared Diamond in *Collapse: How Societies Choose to Fail or Succeed* (New York: Penguin Group, 2005). Excellent alternative explanations describing the effects of rats on the island, slave traders, and exploitation by imperialist explorers are presented in Terry Hunt and Carl Lipo, *The Statues That Walked* (New York: Free Press, 2011), and Beverley Haun, *Inventing 'Easter Island'* (Toronto: University of Toronto Press, 2005). We draw on Wright's allegory here as an opportunity to delve into single-, double-, and triple-loop learning. An alternative explanation involving exploitation of the island's people and resources by forces of global commerce and trade would make an equally good learning scenario.

4. Complex Global Issues as the Context for Value Creation

1 All of these figures are drawn from UN Population data that can be found at http://www.un.org/esa/population/unpop.htm.

2 For an overview see R. Lee, "The Demographic Transition: Three Centuries of Fundamental Change," *The Journal of Economic Perspectives* 17(1) (2003): 167–90.

3 See D. Kirk, "Demographic Transition Theory," *Population Studies* 50(3) (1996): 361–87.

4 See M. Myrskyla, H-P Kohler, and F. Billari, "Advances in Development Reverse Fertility Declines," *Nature* 460 (2009): 741–3.

5 See UNPD, *World Population to 2300* (2004), retrieved 11 October 2011 from http://www.un.org/esa/population/publications/publications.htm.

6 UNPD, *UN Development Report 2006*, retrieved 12 October 2012 from http://hdr.undp.org/en/media/HDR06-complete.pdf. For more information see http://www.unesco.org/new/en/natural-sciences/environment/water/wwap/facts-and-figures/basic_needs.shtml.

7 Ibid.

8 See "Billions Daily Affected by Water Crisis," retrieved from 12 July 2012 from http://water.org/water-crisis/one-billion-affected.

9 See http://www.waterkeeper.org.

10 See *Yes! Magazine – The Water Solutions Issue*, Summer 2010, retrieved 14 October 2011 from http://www.yesmagazine.org/issues/water-solutions/water-will-there-be-enough. Sandra Postel is director of the Global Water Policy Project, the first freshwater fellow of the National Geographic Society, and the author of *Last Oasis: Facing Water Scarcity* (New York: W.W. Norton, 1997).

11 See http://www.waterfootprint.org for in-depth studies and statistics on water use.

12 See EPA WaterSense, http://www.epa.gov/watersense/pubs/indoor.html.

13 See 2030 Water Resources Group, *Charting Our Water Future: Economic Frameworks to Inform Decision-Making* (2009), retrieved 14 October 2011 from http://www.2030waterresourcesgroup.com/water_full/Charting_Our_Water_Future_Final.pdf.

14 Food and Agriculture Organization of the United Nations, *The State of Food Insecurity in the World 2010* (Rome: FAOUN, 2010), retrieved 22 October 2011 from http://www.fao.org/publications/sofi/en/.

15 See FAO Food Price Index, http://www.fao.org/worldfoodsituation/wfs-home/foodpricesindex/en/.

16 For an extended examination of global feast and famine, see R. Patel, *Stuffed and Starved: The Hidden Battle for the Global Food System* (Hoboken, NJ: Melville House Publishing, 2008).

17 For multiple critiques of the Western food industry, see T. Pawlick, *The End of Food: How the Food Industry Is Destroying Our Food Supply and What You Can Do About It* (Vancouver: Greystone Books, 2006); M. Pollan, *The Omnivore's Dilemma: A Natural History of Four Meals* (New York: Penguin Press, 2006); M. Pollan, *In Defense of Food: The Myth of Nutrition and the Pleasures of Eating* (New York: Penguin Press, 2009); and P. Roberts, *The End of Food* (New York: Mariner Books, 2009).

18 The Royal Society, *Reaping the Benefits: Science and the Sustainable*

Intensification of Global Agriculture (21 October 2009), retrieved 23 October 2011 from http://royalsociety.org/policy/publications/2009/reaping-benefits/.

19 J. Cribb, *The Coming Famine: The Global Food Crisis and What We Can Do to Avoid It* (Berkeley: University of California Press, 2010).

20 Ibid., 9.

21 See Patrick Déry and Bart Anderson, "Peak Phosphorous," *Energy Bulletin* (13 August 2007), in which they state: "Even if we find a real substitute for fossil fuels, it will be impossible to maintain population growth because phosphate deposits are probably in decline. It will be impossible to maintain an agriculture without recycling nutrients." Retrieved 24 October 2011 from http://www.energybulletin.net/node/33164.

22 Figures are drawn from U.S. Energy Information Administration, *International Energy Outlook 2011* (19 September 2011), the annual forecast provided by the Energy Information Agency of the U.S. Department of Energy, retrieved 25 October 2011 from http://www.eia.gov/forecasts/ieo/.

23 M. King Hubbert, *Nuclear Energy and the Fossil Fuel*, Document No. 56-007 (Washington, DC: American Petroleum Institute, 1956), retrieved 11 October 2011 from http://www.onepetro.org/mslib/servlet/onepetropreview?id=API-56-007.

24 See the Association for the Study of Peak Oil and Gas (ASPO at http://www.peakoil.net), founded by petroleum geologist Dr. Colin Campbell; see also http://www.theoildrum.com.

25 See International Energy Agency, *World Energy Outlook 2010* (Paris: IEA, 2010), http://www.iea.org/weo/2010.asp.

26 See Terry Macalister, "Key Oil Figures Were Distorted by US Pressure, Says Whistleblower," *The Guardian*, 9 November 2009, retrieved 2 November 2011 from http://www.guardian.co.uk/environment/2009/nov/09/peak-oil-international-energy-agency.

27 J.D. Hughes, "The Energy Issue," in T. Homer-Dixon, ed., *Carbon Shift: How the Twin Crises of Oil Depletion and Climate Change Will Define the Future* (Toronto: Random House, 2009), 60–1.

28 To substantiate the arguments regarding changing climate conditions and the probability that humans are a major force, we rely on the Intergovernmental Panel on Climate Change 4th Assessment Report synthesis, 2007, retrieved 11 November 2011 from http://www.ipcc.ch/pdf/assessment-report/ar4/syr/ar4_syr.pdf, and on the Stern Review, 2006, for an assessment of potential impacts, retrieved 11 November 2011 from http://webarchive.nationalarchives.gov.uk/+/http:/www.hm-treasury.gov.uk/sternreview_index.htm. For a 2000 year picture of global temperature fluctuations, see M.E. Mann et al., "Proxy-based Reconstructions of Hemispheric and Global Surface Temperature Variations over the Past Two Millennia,"

PNAS 105(36) (2008): 13252–7. For an overview of the organized "climate denial industry," see J. Hoggan and R. Littlemore, *Climate Cover-Up: The Crusade to Deny Global Warming* (Vancouver: Greystone Books, 2009); and M. Mann, *The Hockey Stick and the Climate Wars: Dispatches from the Front Lines* (New York: Columbia University Press, 2012).

29 The IPCC 4th Assessment was issued in 2007, for which the group was awarded the Nobel Prize along with Al Gore.

30 Al Gore provides an example of this in "New Thinking on the Climate Crisis," *TED Talks* (March 2008), available at http://www.ted.com/talks/ al_gore_s_new_thinking_on_the_climate_crisis.html. The IPCC had a statistically driven statement of 99 per cent confidence ("virtually certain" in IPCC parlance) of anthropogenic climate change; political pressure from China softened that to "at least 90 per cent" ("very likely" was the term therefore used in the reports).

31 See Intergovernmental Panel on Climate Change, *Summary for Policy Makers* (Geneva: IPCC, 2007), 10, retrieved 17 November 2011 from http://www .ipcc.ch/publications_and_data/publications_and_data_reports.shtml#1.

32 See Bill McKibben's website www.350.org for more on the significance of this number.

33 See The Royal Society, *Climate Change: A Summary of the Science* (2010) for a concise overview of climate science: where there is broad consensus, and where there is greater uncertainty; available at http://royalsociety.org/ policy/publications/2010/climate-change-summary-science/.

34 Kurt Campbell et al., *The Age of Consequences: The Foreign Policy and National Security Implications of Global Climate Change* (Washington, DC: CSIS/ CNAS, 2007), retrieved 12 November 2011 from http://csis.org/files/media/ csis/pubs/071105_ageofconsequences.pdf.

35 See Climate Interactive, "The Climate Scoreboard," retrieved 8 May 2012 from http://climateinteractive.org/scoreboard.

36 For some of the probable and potential impacts of diminishing conventional oil, see J. Rubin, *Why Your World Is about to Get a Whole Lot Smaller* (Toronto: Random House, 2009); P. Roberts, *The End of Oil* (New York: Mariner Books, 2004); R. Heinberg, *The Party's Over: Oil, War and the Fate of Industrial Societies* (Gabriola Island, BC: New Society Publishers, 2003); D. Goodstein, *Out of Gas: The End of the Age of Oil* (New York: Norton, 2004).

37 See D. Keith, "Dangerous Abundance," and M. Jaccard, "Peak Oil and Market Feedbacks," in T. Homer-Dixon, ed., *Carbon Shift: How the Twin Crises of Oil Depletion and Climate Change Will Define the Future* (Toronto: Random House, 2009), 27–57, and 97–131.

38 For this line of argument, see J.D. Hughes, "The Energy Issue," in T. Homer-Dixon, ed., *Carbon Shift: How the Twin Crises of Oil Depletion and Climate Change Will Define the Future* (Toronto: Random House, 2009), 58–95.

39 David Keith makes this argument in "Dangerous Abundance," in T. Homer-Dixon, ed., *Carbon Shift: How the Twin Crises of Oil Depletion and Climate Change Will Define the Future* (Toronto: Random House, 2009), 27–57.

40 See G. Monbiot, *Heat: How to Stop the Planet from Burning* (Toronto: Doubleday Canada, 2006); E. Kolbert, *Field Notes from a Catastrophe: Man, Nature, and Climate Change* (New York: Bloomsbury, 2006). For an economic assessment of climate impacts, see N. Stern, *The Global Deal: Climate Change and the Creation of a New Era of Progress and Prosperity* (Philadelphia: Perseus Books, 2009); for the potential for global conflict driven by climate change, see G. Dyer, *Climate Wars* (Toronto: Random House Canada, 2008).

41 C. Stager, *Deep Future: The Next 100,000 Years of Life on Earth* (Toronto: Harper Collins, 2011), 16–17.

5. Managing for Stakeholders in a Complex World

1 See S. de Luque, M.F. Washburn, D.A. Waldman, and R.J. House, "Unrequited Profits: The Relationship of Economic and Stakeholder Values to Leadership and Performance," *Administrative Science Quarterly* 53 (2008): 626–54.

2 For a full examination of the key issues in stakeholder theory, see R.E. Freeman, J.S. Harrison, A.C. Wicks, B.L. Parmar, and S. de Colle, *Stakeholder Theory: The State of the Art* (Cambridge: Cambridge University Press, 2010).

3 For an overview of the evolution of systems theory see R. Stacey, *Strategic Management and Organizational Dynamics: The Challenge of Complexity*, 4th ed. (Essex, UK: Pearson Education, 2003).

4 See M. Waldrop, *Complexity: The Emerging Science at the Edge of Order and Chaos* (London: Viking, 1992), for a fine overview of the development of complexity thinking.

5 To see this phenomenon of emergence, watch a video of "Starlings on Otmoor" at http://www.youtube.com/watch?v=uP_UpyBWDhg.

6 J.H. Holland, *Emergence: From Chaos to Order* (Cambridge: Perseus, 1998).

7 See I. Prigogene and I. Stengers, *Order Out of Chaos: Man's New Dialogue with Nature* (New York: Bantam Books, 1984).

8 See S.A. Kauffman, *Origins of Order: Self-Organization and Selection in Evolution* (Oxford: Oxford University Press, 1992).

9 R. Stacey, *Strategic Management and Organizational Dynamics: The Challenge of Complexity*, 4th ed. (Essex, UK: Pearson Education, 2003); D. Griffin, P. Shaw, and R. Stacey, "Speaking of Complexity in Management Theory and Practice,. *Organization* 5(3) (1998): 315–34; J. Fonseca, *Complexity and Innovation in Organizations* (London: Routledge, 2002).

10 R.E. Freeman, "Divergent Stakeholder Theory," *Academy of Management Review* 24(2) (1999): 233–6.
11 B.L. Parmar, R.E. Freeman, J.S. Harrison, A. Wicks, L. Purnell, and S. de Colle, "Stakeholder Theory: The State of the Art," *The Academy of Management Annals* 4(1) (2010): 403–45.
12 This model is adapted from our earlier work; see E.C. Kurucz, B.A. Colbert, and D. Wheeler, "The Business Case for Corporate Social Responsibility," in A. Crane, A. McWilliams, D. Matten, J. Moon, and D. Seigel, eds., *The Oxford Handbook on Corporate Social Responsibility* (Oxford: Oxford University Press, 2008), 83–112.
13 In earlier work we termed these *value-based networks*; see D. Wheeler, B.A. Colbert, and R.E. Freeman, "Focusing on Value: Reconciling Corporate Social Responsibility, Sustainability and a Stakeholder Approach in a Network World," *Journal of General Management* 28(3) (2003): 1–28.
14 R.K. Mitchell, B.R. Agle, and D.J. Wood, "Toward a Theory of Stakeholder Identification and Salience: Defining the Principle of Who and What Really Counts," *Academy of Management Review* 22(4) (1997): 853–86.
15 S.L. Hart and S. Sharma, "Engaging Fringe Stakeholders for Competitive Imagination," *Academy of Management Executive* 18(1) (2004): 7–18.

6. Sustainability Conversations: Conceptions of Practicing Managers

 1 We adopt this definition from R. Talisse, *On Rawls: A Liberal Theory of Justice and Justification* (Belmont, CA: Wadsworth, 2001).
 2 KPMG, *KPMG International Survey of Corporate Responsibility Reporting 2008* (October 2008), retrieved 11 August 2011 from http://www.kpmg.com/lu/en/issuesandinsights/articlespublications/pages/kpmginternationalsurveyon-corporateresponsibilityreporting2008.aspx.
 3 See United Nations Global Compact, http://www.unglobalcompact.org/index.html; Global100, http://www.global100.org/about-us/who-we-are.html; *MIT Sloan Management Review,* http://sloanreview.mit.edu/sustainability; McKinsey & Company, *McKinsey Quarterly,* http://www.mckinseyquarterly.com/special_topics.aspx?stid=75; World Business Council on Sustainable Development, http://www.wbcsd.org; and Walmart's Share-Green portal, http://sharegreen.ca.
 4 D. Wheeler, A. Zohar, and S. Hart, "Educating Senior Executives in a Novel Strategic Paradigm: Early Experiences of the Sustainable Enterprise Academy," *Business Strategy and the Environment* 14(4) (2005): 172–85.
 5 R.D. Benford and D.A. Snow, "Framing Processes and Social Movements: An Overview and Assessment," *Annual Review of Sociology* 26 (2000): 611–39.

6 D. Bohm, *On Dialogue* (New York: Routledge, 1996).
7 It is important to note here that a "triple-bottom line" outcome for a business organization will be more likely to be framed in financial terms, for example, shareholder value created or profitability, whereas in societal and governmental terms more emphasis may be placed on economic outcomes, for example, jobs created, expenditures in local supply chains and economies, and so on. These are not synonymous terms and indeed may be opposing concepts, for example, during periods of downsizing.
8 S. Fromartz, "5 companies, 5 strategies, 5 transformation," *MIT Sloan Management Review* 51(1) (2009): 40–5.
9 See http://nikeinc.com/news/nike-issues-fy04-corporate-responsibility-report.
10 For an in-depth description of such a situation at the New York Port Authority, see J.E. Dutton and J.J. Dukerich, "Keeping an Eye on the Mirror: Image and Identity in Organizational Adaptation," *Academy of Management Journal* 34 (1991): 517–54.
11 See www.betterplace.com.
12 D. Bohm, *On Dialogue* (New York: Routledge, 1996).
13 For an examination of the role of strategic conversation in social systems and organizations, see B.H. Banathy, *Designing Social Systems in a Changing World* (New York: Plenum Press, 1996); and J.M. Liedtka, "Strategy Formulation: The Roles of Conversation and Design," in M.A. Hitt, R.E. Freeman, and J.S. Harrison, eds., *Handbook of Strategic Management* (Oxford: Blackwell, 2001), 70–93.

7. Wicked Problems and Complex Processes: The Social Dynamics of Sustainability

1 See D. Curran, "Wicked," *Alternatives Magazine*, August 2009, 8–11.
2 For more discussion on the characteristics of wicked problems, see H. Rittel and M. Webber, "Dilemmas in a General Theory of Planning," *Policy Sciences* 4 (1973): 155–69; N. Roberts, "Wicked Problems and Network Approaches to Resolution," *International Public Management Review* 1(1) (2000): 1–19; J. Camillus, "Strategy as a Wicked Problem," *Harvard Business Review*, May 2008, 99–106; E. Van Bueren, E. Klijn, and J. Koppenjan, "Dealing with Wicked Problems in Networks: Analyzing an Environmental Debate from a Network Perspective," *Journal of Public Administration Research and Theory* 13(2) (2003): 193–212; J. Conklin, "Building Shared Understanding of Wicked Problems," *Rotman Magazine*, Winter 2009, 15–20.

3 For more on single-, double-, and triple-loop learning, see M. Keen, V.A. Brown, and R. Dyball, *Social Learning and Environmental Management* (London: Earthscan, 2005).

4 V.A. Brown, J.A. Harris, and J.Y. Russell, *Tackling Wicked Problems: Through the Transdisciplinary Imagination* (London: Earthscan, 2010).

5 S.L. Hart, Capitalism at the Crossroads: Next Generation Business Strategies for a Post-crisis World (Upper Saddle River, NJ: Wharton, 2010); M. *Berns, A. Townend, Z. Khayat, B. Balagopal, M. Reeves, M.S. Hopkins, and N. Kruschwitz*, "Sustainability and Competitive Advantage," MIT Sloan Management Review 51(1) (2009): 18–26.

6 D. Wheeler, J. Medalye, and M. Adams, "Creating Sustainable Value through Entrepreneurial and Stakeholder Inclusive Responses to Climate Change: An Historical-Institutional Perspective," *notizie di POLITEIA* 26(98) (2010): 11–30.

7 For more on the business case, see E. Kurucz, B.A. Colbert, and D. Wheeler, "The Business Case for Corporate Social Responsibility," in A. Crane, A. McWilliams, D. Matten, J. Moon, and D. Seigel, eds., *The Oxford Handbook on Corporate Social Responsibility* (Oxford: Oxford University Press, 2008), 83–112.

8 For a fuller description, see S.L. Hart, *Capitalism at the Crossroads: Next Generation Business Strategies for a Post-crisis World* (Upper Saddle River, NJ: Wharton, 2010).

9 See B. Hopwood, M. Mellor, and G. O'Brien, "Sustainable Development: Mapping Different Approaches," *Sustainable Development* 13 (2005): 38–52, for a discussion of sustainability initiatives that support the status quo and those that are focused more on transformation.

10 See T.N. Gladwin, J.J. Kennelly, and T-S. Krause, "Shifting Paradigms for Sustainable Development: Implications for Management Theory and Research," *Academy of Management Review* 20 (1995): 874–907; M. Redclift, *Wasted: Counting the Costs of Global Consumption* (London: Earthscan, 1996); D. Springett, "Business Conceptions of Sustainable Development: A Perspective from Critical Theory," *Business Strategy and the Environment* 12 (2003): 71–86.

11 For more detail on the Tata case, see O. Branzei, *Tata: Leadership with Trust*, Ivey Case #9B10M025 (London, ON: Ivey Publishing, 2010).

12 J. Brown and D. Isaacs, *World Cafe: Shaping Our World through Conversations that Matter* (San Francisco: Berett-Koehler, 2005).

13 See P. Shaw, *Changing the Conversation: Organizational Change from a Complexity Perspective* (London: Routledge, 2002); R. Stacey, *Complex Responsive Processes in Organizations: Learning and Knowledge Creation* (London: Routledge, 2001).

14 R. Stacey, *Strategic Management and Organizational Dynamics: The Challenge of Complexity*, 4th ed. (Essex, UK: Pearson Education, 2003), 351.
15 See I. Prigogene and I. Stengers, *Order Out of Chaos: Man's New Dialogue with Nature* (New York: Bantam Books, 1984); S.A. Kauffman, *At Home in the Universe* (New York: Oxford University Press, 1995).
16 R. Stacey, *Strategic Management and Organizational Dynamics: The Challenge of Complexity*, 4th ed. (Essex, UK: Pearson Education, 2003), 377.
17 See E. Schein, *Process Consultation Revisited* (Reading, MA: Addison-Wesley, 1998).
18 D. Goleman, *Emotional Intelligence*, 2nd ed. (New York: Random House, 2005).
19 L. Dyer, *Critical Thinking for Business Students* (Concord, ON: Captus Press, 2006).
20 J.A. Raelin, "'I Don't Have Time to Think!' versus the Art of Reflective Practice," *Reflections* 4(1) (2002): 66–79.
21 J. Kabat-Zinn, *Wherever You Go There You Are* (New York: Hyperion, 1994).
22 See M. Scully and W.E. Creed, "Subverting Our Stories of Subversion," in G. Davis, D. McAdam, W.R. Scott, and M.N. Zald, eds., *Social Movements and Organization Theory* (New York: Cambridge University Press, 2005), 310–32.
23 See D.A. Snow, S.A. Soule, and H. Kriesi, *The Blackwell Companion to Social Movements*, 2nd ed. (Oxford: Blackwell, 2007).
24 B.A. Colbert and E.C. Kurucz, "Three Conceptions of Triple-Bottom Line Sustainability and the Role for HRM," *Human Resource Planning* 30(1) (2007): 21–9.
25 R.E. Freeman, J.S. Harrison, and A.C. Wicks, *Managing for Stakeholders: Survival, Reputation, Success* (New Haven, CT: Yale University Press, 2007).

8. From Stakeholder Management to Social Integration: Building Collaboratively Competitive Organizations

1 L.W. Milbraith, *Envisioning a Sustainable Society: Learning Our Way Out* (Albany, NY: State University of New York Press, 1989).
2 C. Holliday, S. Schmidheiny, and P. Watts, *Walking the Talk: The Business Case for Sustainable Development* (Sheffield, UK: Greenleaf, 2002).
3 See E.C. Kurucz, B.A. Colbert, and D.C. Wheeler, "The Business Case for Corporate Social Responsibility," in A. Crane, A. McWilliams, D. Matten, J. Moon, and D. Seigel, eds., *The Oxford Handbook on Corporate Social Responsibility* (Oxford: Oxford University Press, 2008), 83–112, for an in-depth discussion of this.

4 M. Keen, V. Brown, and R. Dyball, *Social Learning in Environmental Management* (London: EarthScan, 2005).
5 R. DeFillippi and S. Ornstein, "Psychological Perspectives Underlying Theories of Organizational Learning," in M. Easterby-Smith and M.A. Lyles, eds., *The Blackwell Handbook of Organizational Learning and Knowledge Management* (Oxford: Blackwell Press, 2003), 19–37, draw on Bandura's 1977 seminal work "Social Learning Theory" in order to establish these parameters.
6 E. Wenger, *Communities of Practice: Learning, Meaning and Identity* (New York: Oxford University Press, 1998).
7 J.S. Brown and P. Duguid, "Organizational Learning and Communities of Practice: Toward a Unified View of Working, Learning and Innovation," *Organization Science* 2(1) (1991): 40–57.
8 See E. Wenger, R. McDermott, and W.M. Snyder, *Cultivating Communities of Practice* (Boston: Harvard Business Press, 2002).
9 See C. Monaghan, "Communities of Practice: A Learning Strategy for Management Education," *Journal of Management Education* 35(3) (2011): 428–53.
10 See M. Easterby-Smith, M. Crossan, and D. Nicolini, "Organizational Learning: Debates Past, Present and Future," *Journal of Management Studies* 37(6) (2000): 783–96.
11 See D. Coughlan, "Organizational Learning as a Dynamic Inter-level Process," in M.A. Rahim, R.T. Golembiewski, and L.E. Pate, *Current Topics in Management*, vol. 2 (Greenwich, CT: JAI Press, 1997), 27–44.
12 See "Loblaw Sustainable Seafood Commitment" available at http://loblaw.ca/Theme/Loblaw/files/LoblawSeafood_2012_EN.pdf.
13 D. Armitage, M. Marschke, and R. Plummer, "Adaptive Co-management and the Paradox of Learning," *Global Environmental Change* 18(1) (2008): 86–98.
14 See P. DiMaggio and W. Powell, "The Iron Cage Revisited: Institutional Isomorphism and Collective Rationality in Organizational Fields," *American Sociological Review* 48 (1983): 147–60, for a discussion of the concepts of inertia and legitimacy.
15 C.M. Christensen, *The Innovator's Dilemma: When New Technologies Cause Great Firms to Fail* (New York: HarperBusiness, 1997).
16 See graph "Top Ten Brands in 2011" on "Best Global Brands," *Interbrand*, retrieved 20 February 2012 http://www.interbrand.com/en/best-global-brands/Best-Global-Brands-2011.aspx.
17 See "Coke Appoints First Sustainability Officer," *Reuters* (24 May 2011), retrieved 20 February 2012 from http://www.reuters.com/article/2011/05/24/idUS399957228020110524.
18 See S. Hart and M. Milstein, "Global Sustainability and the Creative Destruction of Industries," *Sloan Management Review* 4(1) (1999): 23–33, for an

excellent discussion on the challenges and opportunities of creative destruction and sustainability.

19 R.L. Martin, *Fixing the Game: Bubbles, Crashes and What Capitalism Can Learn from the NFL* (Boston: Harvard Business Review Press, 2011).

20 J. van Kleef and N.J. Roome, "Developing Capabilities and Competence for Sustainable Business Management as Innovation: A Research Agenda," *Journal of Cleaner Production* 15 (2007): 38–51.

21 For more on social intrapreneurship, see Allianz, IDEO, Skoll Foundation, and SustinAbility, *The Social Intrapreneur: A Field Guide for Corporate Change-makers* (2008), retrieved 20 February 2012 from http://www.echoinggreen.org/sites/default/files/The_Social_Intrapreneurs.pdf.

22 For more on social entrepreneurship, see J. Elkington and P. Hartigan, *The Power of Unreasonable People: How Social Entrepreneurs Create Markets that Change the World* (Boston: Harvard Business Press, 2008).

23 See W.G. Bennis and J. O'Toole, "How Business Schools Lost Their Way," *Harvard Business Review*, May 2005, 96–104.

24 See *SHE: sustainable health enterprises* at http://www.sheinnovates.com/our-ventures.html, and Alice Rawsthorn, "Debating Sustainability," *The New York Times*, 31 January 2010, 2, retrieved 11 August 2011 from http://www.nytimes.com/2010/02/01/arts/01iht-design1.html?pagewanted=1&_r=1.

25 G. Hardin, "The Tragedy of the Commons," *Science* 162 (1968): 1243–48.

26 First introduced by economist Alfred Kahn in 1966 in an essay of the same name. P. Bliss and J. McCullough, "The Tyranny of Small Decisions, Temporal Conflict and the Necessity for Politicization of the Marketplace," *Business & Society* 19 (1980): 48–57, and W. Odum, "Environmental Degradation and the Tyranny of Small Decisions," *Bioscience* 32(9) (1982): 728–29, both describe how the tyranny of small decisions relates to social and environmental destruction.

27 R. Myers, J.Hutchings, and N. Barrowman, "Why Do Fish Stocks Collapse? The Example of Cod in Atlantic Canada," *Ecological Applications* 7(1) (1997): 91–106.

28 Ibid.

29 L.D. Brown, and J. Fox, "Accountability within Transnational Coalitions," in L.D. Brown and J. Fox, eds., *The Struggle for Accountability: The World Bank, NGOs and Grassroots Movements* (Cambridge, MA: MIT Press, 1998).

30 S. Waddell, Societal Learning and Change (Sheffield, UK: Greenleaf Publishing, 2005).

31 J. Diamond, *Collapse: How Societies Choose to Fail or Succeed* (New York: Penguin, 2011).

32 S. LeBlanc, *Constant Battles: The Myth of the Peaceful Noble Savage* (New York: St. Martin's Press, 2003).

33 UNEP Ozone Secretariat, "Key Achievements of the Montreal Protocol to Date," retrieved 1 June 2012 from http://www.ozone.unep.org/Publications/MP_Key_Achievements-E.pdf.

34 "CFC Substitutes: Good for the Ozone Layer, Bad for Climate?" *Science Daily* (24 February 2012), retrieved 3 June 2012 from http://www.sciencedaily.com/releases/2012/02/120224110737.htm.

35 Sherwood Rowland, "CFCs, Ozone Depletion and the Public Role of Scientists," *Real Climate* (13 March 2012), retrieved 8 May 2012 from http://www.realclimate.org/index.php/archives/2012/03/sherwood-roland-cfcs-ozone-depletion-and-the-public-role-of-scientists/.

36 S. Waddell, *Societal Learning and Change* (Sheffield, UK: Greenleaf Publishing, 2005).

37 For more on the Canadian Boreal Forest Agreement, see *The Canadian Boreal Forest Agreement*, retrieved 8 May 2012 from http://canadianborealforestagreement.com/.

38 Forest Products Association of Canada, "Setting a New Standard for Conservation" (May 2010), retrieved 28 June 2010 from http://www.fpac.ca/index.php/en/cbfa/.

39 Ibid.

40 Ibid.

41 For more on SABCOHA, see http://www.sabcoha.org/, and see "Helping Business to Tackle AIDS," *SouthAfrica.info*, retrieved 24 April 2012 from http://www.southafrica.info/business/economy/development/sabcoha.htm.

42 See "Helping Business to Tackle AIDS," *SouthAfrica.info*, retrieved 24 April 2012 from http://www.southafrica.info/business/economy/development/sabcoha.htm.

43 Ibid.

44 D.N. Michael, "Neither Hierarchy nor Anarchy: Notes on Norms for Governance in a Systemic World," in W. Truitt Anderson, ed., *Rethinking Liberalism* (New York: Avon Books, 1983).

45 For more on adaptive co-management, see D. Armitage, F. Berkes, and N. Doubleday, eds., *Adaptive Co-Management: Collaboration, Learning and Multi-Level Governance* (Vancouver: UBC Press, 2007).

46 C. Pahl-Wostl and M. Hare, "Processes of Social Learning in Integrated Resources Management," *Journal of Community & Applied Social Psychology* 14(3) (2004): 193–206.

47 C. Folke, T. Hahn, P. Olsson, and J. Norberg, "Adaptive Governance of Social-ecological Systems," *Annual Review of Environment and Resources* 30(8) (2005): 441–73.

48 S. Hart and M. Milstein, "Creating Sustainable Value," *Academy of Management Executive* 15(2) (2003): 56–67.

49 For more on Selco Solar India, see http://www.selco-india.com/.

50 J. Liedka and H. Mintzberg, "Time for Design," *Design Management Review* 17(2) (2006): 10–18.

51 D. Wheeler, K. McKague, J. Thomson, R. Davies, J. Medalye, and M. Prada, "Creating Sustainable Local Enterprise Networks," *MIT Sloan Management Review* 47(1) (2005): 33–40.

52 See J. Brugmann and C.K. Prahalad, "Cocreating Business's New Social Compact," *Harvard Business Review*, February 2007, 80–90; and E. Simanis and S. Hart, *The Base of the Pyramid Protocol: Toward Next Generation BoP Strategy*, 2nd ed. (Ithaca, NY: Cornell University, Johnson School of Management, 2008), retrieved 12 July 2011 from http://www.bop-protocol.org/docs/BoPProtocol2ndEdition2008.pdf.

53 See J. Alves, M.J. Marques, I. Saur, and M. Marques, "Creativity and Innovation through Multidisciplinary and Multisectoral Cooperation," *Creativity and Innovation Management* 16(1) (2009): 27–34.

54 B Lab, *B Corporation 2011 Annual Report, If Not Now, When?* retrieved 29 May 2011 from http://www.bcorporation.net/B-Media/2011-Annual-Report.

55 Information on Benefit Corporations retrieved 7 November 2012 from http://www.benefitcorp.net; information on Certified B Corporations retrieved 7 November 2012 from http://222.bcorporation.net.

56 L.W. Milbraith, *Envisioning a Sustainable Society: Learning Our Way Out* (Albany, NY: State University of New York Press, 1989).

57 See J. van Kleef and N. Roome, "Developing Capabilities and Competence for Sustainable Business Management as Innovation: A Research Agenda," *Journal of Cleaner Production* 15 (2007): 38–51.

58 Jonathan Barderlline, "Walmart, Patagonia Strengthen Pact to Measure Apparel Impact" (1 March 2011), *Greenbiz.com*, retrieved 3 November 2011 from http://www.greenbiz.com/news/2011/03/01/walmart-patagonia-strengthen-pact-measure-apparel-impact#ixzz1GDUXSgVM.

59 Ibid.

60 R. Plummer and J.E. FitzGibbon, "Connecting Adaptive Co-management, Social Learning and Social Capital through Theory and Practice," in D. Armitage, F. Berkes, and N. Doubleday, eds., *Adaptive Co-Management: Collaboration, Learning and Multi-Level Governance* (Vancouver: UBC Press, 2007), 38–61.

61 B. Crosby and J. Brison, "Integrative Leadership and the Creation and Maintenance of Cross-sector Collaborations," *The Leadership Quarterly* 21(2) (2010): 211–30.

62 S. Waddell, *Societal Learning and Change* (Sheffield, UK: Greenleaf Publishing, 2005).

63 "Document," BetterManagement.com, retrieved16 July 2011 from http://
www.bettermanagement.com/library/library.aspx?LibraryID=14220.

64 R. Barrington, "The Pharmaceutical Sector: What Is a Sustainable Pharma
Company?" *Article 13*, retrieved 8 February 2012 from http://www.article13.
com/A13_ContentList.asp?strAction=GetPublication&PNID=1260.

9. Reconstructing Value: Leadership in Reinventing Notions of Success

1 J. Rifkin, *The Empathic Civilization: The Race to Global Consciousness in a
World in Crisis* (New York: Penguin, 2009).

2 See DuPont, "Company at a Glance," accessed 28 January 2012 from http://
www2.dupont.com/Our_Company/en_CA/glance/index.html.

3 For the discussion in this section, we draw on R. Talisse, *On Rawls: A Liberal Theory of Justice and Justification* (Belmont, CA: Wadsworth, 2001).

4 For a description of how modern human rights evolved, see L. Hunt, *Inventing Human Rights: A History* (New York: Norton, 2007).

5 R. Talisse, *On Rawls: A Liberal Theory of Justice and Justification* (Belmont,
CA: Wadsworth, 2001), 18.

6 See E. Hess, *Smart Growth: Building an Enduring Business by Managing the
Risks of Growth* (New York: Columbia University Press, 2010), for a critique
of the orthodoxy of steady upward earnings growth.

7 See J. Stiglitz, A. Sen, and J-P Fitoussi, *Mis-measuring Our Lives: Why GDP
Doesn't Add Up* (New York: The New Press, 2010). Access the full report at
www.stiglitz-sen-fitoussi.fr. For further critique of GDP as a measure of social progress and problems associated with the economic growth imperative, see T. Jackson *Prosperity without Growth: Economics for a Finite Planet*
(London: Earthscan: London, 2009).

8 OECD, *Better Life Initiative: Compendium of Well-being Indicators* (Paris:
OECD, 2011), retrieved 25 February 2012 from http://www.oecd.org/
std/47917288.pdf.

9 See the Canadian Index of Wellbeing at http://ciw.ca/en/ . The CIW has
published two reports to date: *How Are Canadians Really Doing? The First
Report of the Canadian Index of Wellbeing* (Waterloo, ON: CIW, 2009), and
*How Are Canadians Really Doing: Highlights: The Canadian Index of Wellbeing
1.0* (Waterloo, ON: CIW, 2011), both available on its website.

10 Canadian Index of Wellbeing, "What Is Wellbeing?" retrieved 21 October
2011 from http://ciw.ca/en/WellbeingInCanada/WhatIsWellbeing.html.

11 For a full description of decoupling, see United Nations Environment
Programme (UNEP), *Decoupling Natural Resource Use and Environmental
Impacts from Economic Growth: A Report of the Working Group on Decoupling to
the International Resource Panel*, M. Fischer-Kowalski et al. (Nairobi, Kenya:

UNEP, 2011). The report can be found at http://www.unep.org/resource panel/decoupling/files/pdf/Decoupling_Report_English.pdf.

12 For more detail, see F. Krausmann, S. Gingrich, N. Eisenmenger, K.H. Erb, H. Haberl, and M. Fischer-Kowalski, "Growth in Global Materials Use, GDP and Population during the Twentieth Century," *Ecological Economics* 68(10) (2009): 2696–705.

13 United Nations Environment Programme (UNEP), *Decoupling Natural Resource Use and Environmental Impacts from Economic Growth: A Report of the Working Group on Decoupling to the International Resource Panel*, M. Fischer-Kowalski et al. (Nairobi, Kenya: UNEP, 2011).

14 T. Jackson, *Prosperity without Growth: Economics for a Finite Planet* (London: Earthscan, 2009), 67.

15 See J. Rawls, *A Theory of Justice* (Cambridge, MA: Harvard University Press, 1971), 302. While Rawls' principles are simple, their justification and explanation are long and complex. There is a substantial industry of political philosophy texts responding to Rawls' theory of justice as fairness, both in support and in opposition.

16 United Nations Environment Programme (UNEP), *Decoupling Natural Resource Use and Environmental Impacts from Economic Growth: A Report of the Working Group on Decoupling to the International Resource Panel*, M. Fischer-Kowalski et al. (Nairobi, Kenya: UNEP, 2011), 32.

17 DuPont News Release, "DuPont Forms Advisory Committee on Agricultural Innovation & Productivity for the 21st Century" (11 February 2010), retrieved 1 May 2012 from http://investors.dupont.com/phoenix. zhtml?c=73320&p=irol-newsArticle&ID=1387240&highlight=.

18 B. Flyvbjerg, *Making Social Science Matter: Why Social Inquiry Fails and How It Can Succeed Again* (New York: Cambridge University Press, 2011).

Index